# CALIFORNIA WORKERS RIGHTS

# CALIFORNIA WORKERS RIGHTS

## A Manual of Job Rights, Protections and Remedies

by

### Joan Marie Braconi
### and
### Alan Nicholas Kopke

Center for Labor Research and Education
Institute of Industrial Relations
University of California, Berkeley

The viewpoints expressed in this book are those of the authors, and not necessarily those of the Labor Center, the Institute of Industrial Relations, or the University of California.

SECOND PRINTING

Manufactured in the United States of America

Library of Congress Cataloging-in-Publication Data

Braconi, Joan Marie, 1944-
  California workers rights

  Includes index.
  1. Labor laws and legislation--California.
2. Labor laws and legislation--United States.
I. Kopke, Alan Nicholas, 1942-      II. University
of California, Berkeley.  Center for Labor Research
and Education.  III. Title.
KFC556.B7 1986            344.794'01   86-11788
ISBN: 0-937817-00-7   347.94041

**JOAN BRACONI** is a Program Coordinator at the Center for Labor Research and Education. A member of the AFT, she trains union representatives in organizing, grievance handling, collective bargaining, and other subjects. She is a former Field Representative and Organizer for SEIU.


**ALAN NICHOLAS KOPKE** practices labor law in Berkeley, California. He is a former member of IAM and SEIU. A graduate of Hastings College of the Law, he represents unions and individual workers. He also teaches and writes on labor law.


**THE CENTER FOR LABOR RESEARCH AND EDUCATION** is a component of the Institute of Industrial Relations, University of California, Berkeley, California 94720 (415/642-0323). The labor movement is confronted with complex issues demanding creative responses and increased skills from both labor leaders and rank and file unionists. Over two decades ago California labor leaders, recognizing the role education might play in confronting these issues, urged the formation of the Center for Labor Research and Education at the University of California at Berkeley. The Berkeley Center offers a variety of labor education programs matched to the needs and structure of local unions, Internationals, central labor bodies, and district or trade councils. The Center provides training, publications, and consultations for the labor movement, and holds conferences on important issues.

# A NOTE TO USERS OF THIS MANUAL

Inevitably there will be typographical and other errors in this book. We invite readers to send us notice of all errors and omissions they discover, so that future editions can be corrected.

Readers will learn of new laws, regulations, interpretations, policies, and decisions. We invite you to send us this information so that future editions can be fully up-to-date.

We have omitted topics which seem overly specialized or otherwise out of place in this manual. Similarly, we have omitted certain technicalities of the wage and hour rules, lest the book become overlong. If we have left out topics which are of wide interest or which are needed to avoid misleading statements, please let us know.

Please address your communications to:

Joan Braconi
Center for Labor Research and
Education
Instititute of Industrial Relations
University of California
Berkeley, California 94720

## TABLE OF CONTENTS

# FOREWORD

There has long been a need for a readable compilation of those protections which guard the workers of California under state and federal law.

This book meets that need and, further, includes the enforcement agencies to which workers may turn for assistance.

In almost every instance, these laws have their origin in the reform agitation of California unions. This was so whether the issue was the Workers Compensation law of 1914 or the Agricultural Labor Relations Act of 1975.

Labor unions will find **California Workers Rights** a valuable guide in understanding and implementing those laws upon which worker rights depend.

John F. Henning
Executive Secretary-Treasurer
California Labor Federation, AFL-CIO

# ACKNOWLEDGMENTS

Special thanks for their input and assistance to: Sue Cobble, Cathy Davis, Ruth Edelstein, Ann Miley, Kathy Mooney, and Tom Rankin.

# CALIFORNIA WORKERS RIGHTS

## PREFACE

This book is based on the most up-to-date information available, including new laws and court rulings up to the time of publication. The authors have carefully researched each right and protection cited. But the rights described are continually evolving: the Legislature and Congress pass new laws and amend old ones; federal and state courts issue interpretations; administrative agencies issue and amend regulations, develop and modify enforcement policies; and long-ignored or forgotten rights are revived by union or worker action. We recommend that you determine the up-to-the minute legal situation before taking legal action: consult with a lawyer, a union, or an enforcement agency (or all three). Also, be sure to read Chapter 1, INTRODUCTION, about how to enforce the rights described in later chapters.

We have given our best understanding and interpretation of your rights. Legal issues, however, are always open to differences in interpretation. In some cases, laws listed in specific sections of this book will not seem to spell out the rights we describe. In these sections we are summarizing the interpretations given by the courts and/or enforcement agencies. If you have any questions, consult your union or attorney.

## CHAPTER 1

## INTRODUCTION

**HOW TO USE THIS BOOK**

The body of law pertaining to employers, workers, and the workplace in California is immense. This book focuses on selected areas: hiring rights, wages and benefits, blacklisting, records (including personnel files, police and government records, and medical files), health and safety, whistleblowing, workers' compensation, and organizing. To locate the section that addresses your concerns, consult the TABLE OF CONTENTS. Listed there you will find the rights examined in each chapter.

Once you locate the relevant chapter and section, you will find a description of your rights, the laws that protect your rights, and the agencies responsible for enforcing your rights. Where an administrative regulation or enforcement policy is essential for understanding your rights, the regulation or policy memo is also listed. Important exceptions are listed. Sometimes the protections are extended only to certain workers. In other cases, there may be important limits on how or when a worker may demand the protections.

You can take the information in each section to a law library and examine (and copy) the statutes and regulations listed. Every county maintains a public law library (usually in the courthouse). Almost all law schools also maintain large law libraries. Since these are usually government depositories, they must allow the general public to use the materials. Ask the law librarian where to find the law you are interested in. If you need to see an administrative policy memo, you should contact the issuing agency. If you give the memo number and pay a small fee, you have the right to a copy.

You will find many references to Industrial Welfare Commission (I.W.C.) Orders. The I.W.C. has issued 15 Orders, covering almost all categories of workers in California. (See I.W.C. Exceptions in the GLOSSARY for those not covered.) To obtain a free copy of the Order applying to your job, call the Industrial

Welfare Commission. (See the APPENDIX for phone numbers and addresses.)

This book also includes a GLOSSARY and an APPENDIX. Most of the terminology used in the book requires no special knowledge or legal vocabulary. Those terms that are unusual or that have special meanings are marked with an asterisk (*); full descriptions appear in the GLOSSARY. The APPENDIX provides the names, addresses and phone numbers of state and federal enforcement agencies as well as the names, addresses and phone numbers of central labor councils and regional labor organizations.

## CONFRONTING YOUR EMPLOYER - - DON'T DO IT WITHOUT HELP

It is usually best, especially where you are not covered by a collective bargaining agreement, to avoid a one-to-one confrontation with your employer. If your employer makes an honest mistake in the computation of your hours or rate of pay, it is probably appropriate to speak to (or write a memo to) the payroll or personnel office and work out the mistake informally. If however you believe that the rights violation is purposeful, it is probably best to let a third party confront the employer: a union steward, a labor commissioner, or other enforcement officer.

If you decide to take action against your employer, you give yourself additional protection by making that action a concerted activity. This means several employees, together, take an action, file a complaint, withhold their labor, or take some other step to protect their wages, hours, or working conditions.

If most of your fellow employees believe they need to take some action to protect or improve working conditions, it would be wise to contact a union. A union can help in several ways. It can deal directly and effectively with the enforcement agency on your behalf. An experienced union representative can help gather all of the relevant facts to present to the agency. When the union is involved, the agency is more likely to conduct a timely and thorough investigation of the charge(s).

The most important way a union can help is through a collective bargaining agreement. Your employer is legally obligated to abide by the provisions of a union agreement. Unions can negotiate rights and protections which are more favorable than those provided by law. The collective bargaining agreement will contain its own enforcement mechanism, the grievance procedure. This will be faster and less costly than court proceedings. For information on your right to join and be represented by a union, see Chapter 7, BASIC ORGANIZING RIGHTS AND PROTECTIONS. Refer to the APPENDIX for a listing of labor councils. The council in your area will refer you to the union best suited to represent your classification of work or industry.

## PREPARING TO ENFORCE YOUR RIGHTS

In order to enforce your rights and prove a claim against your employer, you will need documented evidence. It may be difficult to put together the evidence you need after your rights have been violated.

It is important that you keep work records. From the time you make an application for employment, you should keep all records and documents relating to that job. Keep a calendar indicating hours actually worked. Keep all pay stubs. Keep all documents and memos regarding benefits such as health and welfare, pension, vacation policy, sick leave bonuses, severance pay, and all insurance coverages. Keep all documents regarding work rules. Keep a daily log, particularly if you are involved in a union organizing campaign or if you have been visibly enforcing your rights. Indicate in the log any conversation between you and your supervisor or employer, particularly anything that you might view as "threatening." Keep copies of the receipts and vouchers for work-related expenses. Keep credit card records. Store all of your logs and documents and records at home; do not leave them at work.

## USING SMALL CLAIMS COURT

In many sections we list "civil action" as an enforcement mechanism.

Filing a law suit to enforce your rights nearly always requires a lawyer. However, if you are seeking a relatively small sum of money, then you might consider going to small claims court. Neither side can be represented by lawyers in small claims.

Your local small claims court should have a legal adviser who will assist you in filing your case. Be sure to have copies of the laws and regulations relevant to your claims, since the small claims judge will probably have little experience with employment disputes. You can also check any of several widely available books for tips on how to win in small claims.

## USING AN ATTORNEY

This book is designed to help you enforce your rights without having to retain an attorney, but in some instances you will need an attorney's assistance. If you have a union representative, s/he may be able to provide you with all the help you need. If not, ask him/her to refer you to an attorney.

If you seek a lawyer on your own, be sure to look for one with knowledge in the field of labor and employment law. This is a very specialized field and it is important to find someone with some expertise in your problem area. Don't be shy about asking two or three lawyers for an opinion. Check with enforcement agencies and compare what you hear and learn from various sources.

If you hire a lawyer, but then think that you are not being properly represented, take action. Discuss your complaint with your attorney. Call other lawyers. You have the right to change lawyers at any time; make sure you get good service.

## USING AN ENFORCEMENT AGENCY

Gather together all the documents, facts, and witnesses you can before you contact the enforcement agency that handles your problem. Have the names and home phone numbers and addresses of your witnesses. Get written statements from them if possible. Try to find out how other employees have been treated in similar situations. If you have a union, or if a union has investigated your workplace, work with the union; joint effort is most likely to get effective action from the enforcement agency.

Contact the enforcement agency as soon as possible. Don't be put off, however, if someone tells you that the "time limits" have run out or that the "statute of limitations" has expired on your complaint. Lawyers spend years studying all the exceptions to time limits and statutes of limitations. Consult with your union or attorney as well as the agency; when all of the facts are known, late filing of the complaint is very often successful.

Be persistent when dealing with enforcement agencies. If an intake worker (or other agency employee) says you don't have a case, don't be discouraged. Workers at these agencies, especially intake workers, may not know all of the important legal principles affecting your case. File a complaint anyway, and push to have it investigated. Check what the worker says against what you read, learn through your union, and hear from lawyers.

It is important to keep in mind that when investigating your case, the enforcement agency will contact your employer. You must anticipate that your employer will have a reason or excuse that sounds convincing. You must be prepared to promptly counter your employer's explanation. For example, suppose that you are denied a promotion for an illegal reason. When the enforcement agency inquires, the employer explains that you were tardy six times in the last year. You need to be ready with evidence showing that other employees who were late more than six times got the promotion that you were denied. Then your employer's "explanation" will be revealed as false, and the agency will be able to protect your rights. If you don't have a union to collect this sort of information, you and your friends at work will have to do the job yourselves.

See the APPENDIX for listings of the principal enforcement agencies, with their addresses and phone numbers.

## USING THE DISTRICT ATTORNEY OR ATTORNEY GENERAL

We list "district attorney" or "state attorney general" as an enforcement mechanism in many sections. In almost every case, this means that an employer who violates the law discussed is guilty of a criminal offense.

Only a public prosecutor can initiate criminal charges. Usually this will be the district attorney in your county (or city and county). Sometimes a city attorney, or the State Attorney General, or the United States Attorney for your area, will bring criminal charges.

It is difficult to get prosecutors to enforce most labor laws. Sometimes merely bringing a criminal violation to the attention of the authorities will be enough to stimulate its correction by the employer. If more is needed, it will usually be necessary for you to work together with your union, a labor council, and perhaps some local politicians or news media people, to trigger action by the prosecutors.

In almost every case, it is best to discuss your situation with a lawyer before making a criminal complaint. It is especially important not to publicize your criminal charges, and not to threaten criminal action, until you have explored the ramifications.

## USING YOUR UNION GRIEVANCE PROCEDURE

We do not list a union grievance procedure as an enforcement mechanism because it is only available to those workers covered by a collective bargaining agreement (a union contract). If you are so covered, the grievance procedure will often be your best choice. Most contracts allow the union (or a worker) to grieve violations of the law (as well as other violations of the contract). The union agreement will be most useful if it spells out that any violation of federal or state law is subject to the grievance and arbitration procedures. For example, the contract may provide:

*"The employer agrees to abide by all federal and state laws and regulations and all local ordinances."*

It would be difficult for an employer to argue against including this provision in a contract, and utilizing the contractual procedures will save everyone time and money.


## FILING A COMPLAINT WITH THE LABOR COMMISSIONER

The labor commissioner has the authority to enforce the labor laws of the State of California. The labor commissioner has the authority to investigate employee complaints and hold hearings on wage claims and related issues. In addition, some deputy labor commissioners are designated as "peace officers" and have the authority to arrest violators of the state labor laws. Many of the rights and protections outlined in this book are enforced by the labor commissioner through administrative hearings and, in some cases, subsequent court actions. Among the claims that the labor commissioner can hear are:

- wage claims
- mechanics liens
- misrepresentation of conditions of employment
- unreturned bond money
- unreturned worker tools
- vacation pay and severance pay claims
- lost wages resulting from certain unlawful discharges
- other wage and benefits claims.

For most wage or hour complaints, it is best to file a federal complaint as well as a labor commissioner complaint. (1) You can have two investigators working on your claim(s), instead of one. (2) Federal and state enforcement policies often differ. (3) The federal agency may be less susceptible to political pressures. (4) Federal laws and regulations provide a great many protections which may not be available under state law.

EXCEPTIONS: Where there is a collective bargaining agreement with a binding arbitration clause, the labor commissioner will not hear wage claims which involve the interpretation or application of the agreement (unless both the union and management agree to present the issue to the labor commissioner). But even in cases where a wage complaint is handled through arbitration, the labor comissioner can initiate criminal prosecution if the employer has committed a crime.

As a matter of administrative policy, the labor commissioner will usually not handle complaints against government employers (except for health and safety complaints--see Chapter 5, WORKING CONDITIONS: SAFETY, HEALTH AND SANITATION).

The federal U.S. Department of Labor, Wage and Hour Division, will handle complaints even where there is a union contract or where the employer is a government agency.

## PROTECTING YOUR LEGAL RIGHTS WHERE THERE IS A CONTRACTUAL AGREEMENT TO ARBITRATE

Even though you are covered by an arbitration agreement, you can go to court or to an agency to enforce almost all the rights described in this book (apart from wage claims). If you have a union, be sure to discuss your problem with the union officers. To preserve your rights, make sure you do not sign any "waiver" or "release" or "settlement" that your employer presents to you at an "exit interview" (or at any other time when you are without legal advice). (Your employer cannot legally refuse to pay your unpaid wages, or pension contribution, or vacation or severance pay because you refuse to sign a release.)

**Wage and hour claims are controlled by special rules:**

**Union Contracts** -- In general, the labor commissioner will not enforce your wage claims if you are covered by a union contract with binding arbitration. Instead, you have to go through your union and use the grievance procedure. But there are exceptions:

(1) The labor commissioner will enforce your rights under an Industrial Welfare Commission (IWC) Order. (See Chapter 4, WAGES, BENEFITS AND HOURS OF WORK.)

(2) The labor commissioner will enforce any wage or other claim concerning loss of pay due to unsafe working conditions. (See Chapter 5, WORKING CONDITIONS: SAFETY, HEALTH AND SANITATION.) If you have lost wages or lost your job because of unsafe conditions, you can go to the labor commissioner (and to the U.S. Dept. of Labor), even though you have arbitration rights.

(3) The labor commissioner will enforce any of your non-wage claims (even though you have arbitration rights), just so long as they are based on a law (and not just on your union contract).

(4) The labor commissioner will enforce your wage claims even though you have a union contract, if there is no arbitration procedure in the contract, or if wages are specifically excluded from the arbitration process, or if the employer and union have both agreed to labor commissioner enforcement.

(5) The labor commissioner will enforce your wage claims, even though you have arbitration rights, if your employer is going out of business, or has gone bankrupt, or is threatening bankruptcy, or has bounced payroll checks.

(6) The labor commissioner will enforce your wage claims, even though you also have arbitration rights, if you earned the money on any "public works" (that is, jobs paid for by state or local government money).

LAW: Labor Code section 229; Labor Standards Enforcement Division Memos 76-6 and 79-3.

ENFORCEMENT: Labor commissioner.

Individual and/or Non-Union Agreements to Arbitrate -- You can go to the labor commissioner, or go to court, to collect wages due you, even if you have signed an agreement to arbitrate any disputes with your employer. This applies to any private, or individual, or non-union group agreement to arbitrate. You have the choice to arbitrate, or sue in court, or use the labor commissioner. The choice is up to you, even though you have signed a promise to arbitrate.

LAW: Labor Code section 229.

ENFORCEMENT: Labor commissioner; civil action.

Federal Wage Protections and Arbitration Agreements -- You always have the right to have your federal wage and hour claims enforced, even when an arbitration agreement exists. You can go directly to court, or you can ask the Wage and Hour Division of the U.S. Dept. of Labor for action, whenever you suspect violations of the U.S. Fair Labor Standards Act, of the U.S. Equal Pay Act, or of any of the other federal wage and hour protections. You can take these steps even though you are also protected by a union (or by a private) contract with arbitration procedures. ( If you are so protected, you should also file a grievance.)

LAW: Title 29 U.S. Code sections 201-219.

ENFORCEMENT: U.S. Dept. of Labor, Wage and Hour Division; civil action.

## INDEPENDENT CONTRACTORS ARE NOT COVERED IN THIS BOOK

Individuals working as "independent contractors" are not employees and therefore are not covered by this book. A growing number of workers are being told by unscrupulous employers that they are "independent contractors", when in fact they are employees. Sometimes workers are forced to sign a statement or agreement that they are "independent contractors" when they are not. This kind of statement or agreement is illegal.

Employers pretend workers are independent contractors because it is beneficial to them: it is much cheaper for an employer to consider a worker an independent contractor rather than an employee. Independent contractors are not covered by Workers' Compensation, Unemployment Insurance, State Disability Insurance, or Social Security. Independent contractors do not get benefits such as vacation, sick leave, medical coverage, or retirement. Independent contractors are not covered by state or federal wage and hour protections. Employers do not pay payroll or other taxes on independent contractors. Unless a worker is truly an independent contractor, it is always to his/her disadvantage to work as one.

There is no definitive legal description of an independent contractor. Instead, there are "tests" which are applied. In separating bona fide independent contractors from employees, the key "test" is the right to control the work. Does the employer have the right to control the methods and manner of the work? Is the work supervised by the employer? Can the employer say anything about the work, aside from the ultimate result? If the employer has the right to control how the work is done, then the worker is an employee, not an independent contractor.

Other questions are also asked. Does the employer have the right to discharge the worker? If so, the worker is probably an employee. Who furnishes the tools? Who furnishes the place to work? For how long is the worker employed? How is the worker paid? Is payment made on an hourly rate or by specific project? Can the work be done by assistants or replacements? Is there a special skill involved in the work? How regular or permanent is the work? Does the worker hold a professional or contractor's or business license?

Most workers who think they are "independent contractors" are not. They are actually employees, and all of the rights described in this book protect them.

If your employer wrongly treats you as if you were an "independent contractor", then important legal results occur. You are entitled to receive Unemployment Insurance, State Disability

Insurance, and Social Security benefits, even though the proper taxes were not paid. You are entitled to receive full Workers' Compensation benefits, and you can probably sue your employer for fraud and conspiracy. Your employer will likely end up paying your back Social Security and income taxes, as well as her/his own. An employer who fails to deduct and pay these taxes can be made to pay them for the worker, along with interest and penalties.

If you think that you are being treated as an "independent contractor", but may actually be an "employee", then you must keep accurate records. (See **Preparing to Enforce Your Rights**, this chapter.) When you are ready to act, contact all of the enforcement agencies, not just one. Each agency will apply a slightly different test; each agency will be interested in different problems (back wages; overtime and other rules; unpaid taxes, federal and state; unpaid Social Security contributions; etc.). And remember that your rights may last for a long time. When you retire or are disabled, and need to maximize your Social Security payments, you can go back many years to count time worked under a false "independent contractor" set-up. Keep good records! When you are laid off or fired and need to draw Unemployment Insurance, you can base eligibility on time worked as a so-called "independent contractor." If there is a union at the workplace, be sure to discuss this issue with the union.

LAW: Labor Code sections 3351, 3353 and 3357; Unemployment Insurance Code sections 2101, 2101.5, 2106, 2108, 2109, 2110.5, and 1093; Title 26 U.S. Code sections 3121(d), 3306(i), 3401(c), 3402, 3101, 3111, 6601, 6671, 6672, 7202, 7204, 7215, 7501, 7512, 6051, 3102, and 1401; Title 26 Code of Federal Regulations sections 31.3121(d)-1, 31.3306(i)-1, and 31.3401(c)-1.

ENFORCEMENT: Labor commissioner; Internal Revenue Service; California Franchise Tax Board; California Employment Development Department (unemployment); U.S. Social Security Administration; Workers' Compensation Appeals Board; civil action.

## OTHER EMPLOYEE GROUPS NOT COVERED IN THIS BOOK

Since this book focuses on California rights, and the State of California has no authority to control the federal government, federal workers are not included in most of the protections outlined. Therefore we have not spelled out "federal workers" in the "exceptions" listed for each right. You should assume federal workers are not covered, unless otherwise stated.

This book does not discuss special protections which apply to limited groups. We do not deal with the special organizational protections given farm workers by California law. We do not deal with the specific statutes protecting all the various groups of government (public sector) workers.

This book does not discuss the many special protections given to minors (workers under 18) by both state and federal law. All the protections we list apply to minors. You have all of the rights we describe; in addition, if you are under 18 you have numerous other rights.

There are many other provisions of California law which we have been unable to include. Almost every industry is affected by very narrow laws or regulations. The only way to learn all of the protections which apply to you is to work with a union that represents workers in your industry or occupation.

# CHAPTER 2

## HIRING RIGHTS

### YOU HAVE A RIGHT TO A COPY OF YOUR JOB APPLICATION FORM

If you are an applicant for a job and are required to sign an application form, the employer must file a copy of that form with the Labor Standards Enforcement Division.

If you are required to sign an application form (or any other form) in the process of obtaining employment, or while employed, you have a right to receive a copy of that form upon request.

LAW: Labor Code sections 431-432; Labor Standards Enforcement Division Memo 75-1; Government Code sections 18720-18720.5.

ENFORCEMENT: Labor commissioner; district attorney; civil action.

EXCEPTIONS: Railroad workers covered by the Railway Labor Act.

### NO EMPLOYER MAY INFLUENCE A WORKER TO MOVE BY MISREPRESENTING JOB CONDITIONS

Before you change your place of residence, even for a temporary job, you have the right to be told the truth about job conditions.

The employer, or anyone acting for the employer, must not misrepresent:

(1) the kind of work involved in the job;

(2) the existence and number of jobs available;

(3) the length of time the job will last;

(4) the wages or benefits paid;

(5) the health, safety, or sanitary conditions of the work;

(6) the housing available;

(7) the existence or nonexistence of any labor dispute affecting the work.

This law prohibits employer misrepresentations, whether they are spoken or written or appear in advertisements. This law protects any move, whether from one place in California to another within the state, or from California to a place outside the state, or from outside the state to a job within California.

LAW: Labor Code sections 970-972; Title 29 U.S. Code sections 1821(f), 1831(e), 1843, 1851, and 1854.

ENFORCEMENT: Labor commissioner; district attorney; civil action.

Any employer or employer's agent who violates this law is subject to six months in prison and a $500 fine. Any employer or agent who violates this law may be sued in court and forced to pay double damages.

## DISCRIMINATION IN HIRING IS ILLEGAL: SOME QUESTIONS YOUR EMPLOYER CANNOT ASK

To ensure that employers, employment agencies, and apprenticeship or training programs do not reject job applicants for illegal reasons, limits are put on the kinds of questions they may ask. Except where your employer can show special extenuating circumstances, s/he cannot refuse to hire you because of your:

- age
- race
- nationality
- national origin
- ancestry

- sex
- sexual orientation
- marital status
- religion or creed
- physical handicap

In addition, your employer may not question you about the topics listed in Chapter 8, DISCIPLINE AND DISCHARGE. If it is illegal to fire you for a certain characteristic or activity, it is illegal to refuse to hire you for the same reason.

Questions regarding these subjects cannot be asked on written job applications or questionnaires. They cannot be asked in personal or telephone interviews with you or your references. If they are asked, you cannot be fired or disciplined for not having answered them or, in some cases, for having answered them falsely, incompletely, or incorrectly. If you are denied a job because you refuse to answer illegal questions, or because of how you answer them, there is a good chance that you can sue for the job or its equivalent (in addition to lost wages and benefits).

**Age** -- It is unlawful to discriminate against workers who are 40 or older. A policy is illegal even if it **also** discriminates against younger people. A policy against hiring anyone "over 30" or "over 35" or who is retired is illegal because it affects those 40 and over.

(1) You cannot be asked for your age or your birthdate. (However, the employer can ask your age or birthdate after hiring.)

(2) You cannot be asked when you attended high school or when you graduated.

(3) You cannot be asked for any information which would tend to identify you as over 40 years old.

(4) You can be asked if you are over 18. You can be asked if you can show proof of this if hired. If you are under age 18, you can be asked to submit a work permit after being hired.

(5) You cannot be asked your age in applying for an apprenticeship program (except that you can be asked if you are over 18).

LAW: Government Code sections 11135, 12941, 12990, 18932, and 19700; Fair Employment and Housing Dept. Guidelines; Title 2 California Administrative Code sections

7295.2, 7295.3, 7295.5 and 8101-8312; Title 22 California Administrative Code sections 98230-98238, 98000-98111 and 98300-98413; Labor Code section 3077.5; Title 29 U.S. Code sections 621-631; Title 29 Code of Federal Regulations sections 860.1-860.120; Title 31 U.S. Code sections 6716 and 6721.

ENFORCEMENT: Fair Employment and Housing Dept.; Equal Employment Opportunity Commission; Apprenticeship Standards Division; civil action.

EXCEPTIONS: Employers with fewer than five employees; religious organizations with fewer than 20 employees (except those with state government contracts or grants).

Even workers under age 40 are protected against age discrimination by employers receiving state government funds.

BFOQ.*

**National Origin, Nationality, Ancestry, and Race** -- It is unlawful to discriminate against you because of national origin, nationality, race, or ancestry.

(1) You cannot be asked your birthplace, or the birthplace of your parents, spouse, or other relatives.

(2) You cannot be asked if you are a U.S. citizen. You cannot be asked to indicate your citizenship or the citizenship of your parents, spouse, or other relatives.

(3) You cannot be required to produce naturalization papers or first papers or a "green card" prior to being hired. The employer is allowed to make a statement that these papers will be required after you have been hired. The employer can ask you if you will be able to submit verification of your right to work.

(4) You cannot be asked to specify your mother tongue.

(5) You cannot be asked what language you commonly use or speak. Your employer may ask what languages you speak, read, or write, but not how you learned the language.

(6) You cannot be asked the name and address of a relative to be notified in case of an emergency. You can be asked the name and address of your parent or guardian, if you are a minor (under 18). You can be asked the home and address of a **person** to be contacted in an emergency.

(7) You cannot be asked or required to attach a photograph to a job application or questionnaire. The employer may state that a photograph is required after you are hired.

(8) You cannot be asked any questions about your race or color.

(9) You cannot be asked the color or complexion of your skin, eyes, or hair.

(10) You cannot be asked your height or weight.

**LAW**: Government Code sections 11135, 12940, 12990, and 19702-19704; Labor Code sections 1735 and 3095; Title 2 California Administrative Code sections 8101-8312; Title 22 California Administrative Code sections 98000-98111, 98200-98211, and 98300-98413; Fair Employment and Housing Guidelines; Title 31 U.S. Code sections 6716 and 6721; Title 41 Code of Federal Regulations section 60-1.1 to 60-1.4 and 60-50.1 through 60-50.5; Title 42 U.S. Code sections 2000e-2000e-12.

**ENFORCEMENT**: Fair Employment and Housing Dept.; Equal Employment Opportunity Commission; Apprenticeship Standards Division; civil action.

**EXCEPTIONS**: Employers with fewer than five employees; religious organizations with fewer than 15 employees (except those with government contracts).

Employers with certain federal contracts may require U.S. citizenship for work on those contracts, but not for all positions with the company. Where a security clearance is required for the specific job, you may be asked for additional information after you are hired.

BFOQ.*


**Sex** -- It is unlawful to discriminate against you because of your sex.

(1) You cannot be asked your sex (gender) on the application form or pre-employment questionnaire. The only exception is that the employer may compile this information for recordkeeping purposes.

(2) You cannot be asked how many children you have or care for.

(3) You cannot be asked any questions about your family responsibilities (dependents, childcare, child support, housework).

(4) You cannot be asked questions about childbearing or fertility, pregnancy or birth control, abortions or sterilizations.

(5) If you are asked about prior work experience, you can include in your answer information about prior unpaid or volunteer work experience. The employer must consider volunteer work as well as paid work.

LAW: Government Code sections 11135, 12940, 12945.5, 12990, and 19702-19704; Labor Code sections 1735 and 3095; Health and Safety Code sections 25955 and 25995.3; Title 2 California Administrative Code sections 7290.9 and 7291.0, 8101-8312; Title 22 California Administrative Code sections 98000-98111, 98240-98244, and 98300-98413; Title 31 U.S. Code sections 6716 and 6721; Title 42 U.S. Code sections 2000e-2000e-12; Title 41 Code of Federal Regulations sections 60-1.1 to 60-1.4 and 60-20.1 through 60-20.6.

ENFORCEMENT: Fair Employment and Housing Dept.; Equal Employment Opportunity Commission; Apprenticeship Standards Division; civil action.

**EXCEPTIONS**: Employers with fewer than five employees; religious organizations (except those with government contracts).

BFOQ.*

**Sexual Orientation** -- It is illegal to discriminate in employment on the basis of open disclosure of sexual orientation. The State Supreme Court has ruled that refusal to hire openly gay or lesbian workers violates their right to be free of political coercion. Violation is a crime.

You cannot be asked questions which explore your sexual orientation.

LAW: Labor Code sections 1101, 1102 and 1103; Civil Code sections 51-52; Government Code sections 12930(f)(2) and 12948; Volume 66 California Attorney General's Opinions, p. 486.

ENFORCEMENT: District attorney; civil action.

**Marital Status** -- You cannot be asked questions about your marital status. It is illegal to discriminate against you because you are married, single, divorced, widowed, or a single parent, or living with a partner to whom you are not married.

(1) You cannot be asked your "maiden name". You may be asked if you have used another name or if any of your records (of work history or education) are filed under other names.

(2) You can be asked if you have a spouse who presently works for the employer. However, this information can only be used for two purposes:

(a) The employer can refuse to place one spouse under the direct supervision of the other spouse, for legitimate business reasons (safety, supervision, morale, or security).

(b) The employer can refuse to place both spouses in the same department for legitimate business reasons. The employer can do this only if the kind of work being done involves potential conflicts of interest or other hazards which are greater for married couples than for other persons.

(3) You cannot be asked if you are living with someone to whom you are not married.

(4) You cannot be asked dates of any marriages or divorces.

(5) You cannot be asked where or if your spouse works.

**LAW**: Government Code sections 11135, 12940, 12990, and 19702-19704; Title 2 California Administrative Code sections 7292.4 and 8101-8312; Title 22 California Administrative Code sections 98240-98244, 98000-98111 and 98300-98413; Labor Code section 1735; Title 29 Code of Federal Regulations section 1604.4.

**ENFORCEMENT**: Fair Employment and Housing Dept.; civil action.

**EXCEPTIONS**: Employers with fewer than five employees; religious organizations.

**Religion** -- It is unlawful to discriminate against you on the basis of your religion or lack of religious belief.

(1) You cannot be asked if you have a religion.

(2) You cannot be asked what religion you are.

(3) You cannot be asked what religious days or holidays you observe.

(4) You cannot be asked if your religion prevents you from working weekends or holidays. The employer can state the regular days, hours, or shifts which are to be worked. When the job requires it, the employer may ask about your availability for work on weekends or evenings. However, employers must explore every available reasonable alternative means of accommodating your religious observances, beliefs and practices.

LAW: Government Code sections 11135, 12940, 12990 and 19702-19704; Labor Code sections 1735 and 3095; Title 2 California Administrative Code sections 7293.4 and 8101-8312; Title 22 California Administrative Code sections 98000-98111, 98220-98223 and 98300-98413; Title 31 U.S. Code sections 6716 and 6721; Title 42 U.S. Code 2000e-2000e-12; Title 41 Code of Federal Regulations sections 60-1.1 to 60-1.4 and 60-50.1 through through 60-50.5.

ENFORCEMENT: Fair Employment and Housing Dept.; Equal Employment Opportunity Commission; Apprenticeship Standards Division; civil action.

EXCEPTIONS: Employers with fewer than five employees; religious organizations.


## OTHER PROHIBITED QUESTIONS

**Bonding** -- You cannot be asked if you have ever been refused bonding or if you have ever had a bond cancelled. The employer may state that bonding is a condition of hire.

**Arrest** -- You cannot be asked if you have ever been arrested. The employer can ask if you have ever been convicted of a felony or, within a specified time period, of a misdemeanor which resulted in your imprisonment -- but that question must be accompanied by a statement that a conviction will not necessarily disqualify you from the job. (See also Chapter 3, BLACKLISTING, INVESTIGATIONS AND POLICE RECORDS.)

**Credit Rating** -- You cannot be asked about your current (or past) credit rating, your assets or liabilities or debts, or about any bankruptcies or garnishments. You cannot be asked if you own or rent your home. (See also Chapter 4, WAGES, FRINGE BENEFITS AND WORKING CONDITIONS.)

**Military Discharges** -- You cannot be asked when, or if, you served in the military, or when you were discharged. You cannot be asked what type of discharge you had. You cannot be asked about service in foreign military forces. You may be asked about relevant job skills obtained in the military service.

**Membership and Associations.**-- You cannot be required to list the organizations to which you belong. You can be asked to list job-related organizations, but **not** labor organizations. You cannot be asked if you have ever belonged to a union. You cannot be asked how you feel about unions or strikes, or whether you would support a union. You cannot be asked anything about your union beliefs or activities. You cannot be asked anything about your politics. You cannot be asked anything about the race, nationality, or sex of your friends.

LAW: Labor Code sections 923, 432.7 and 1735; Government Code sections 11135, 12940, 12990 and 19702-19704; Fair Employment and Housing Dept. Guidelines; California Constitution Article I, sections 1 and 8; Title 42 U.S. Code 2000e-2000e-12; Public Utilities Code section 453; Title 11 U.S. Code section 525.

ENFORCEMENT: Labor commissioner; Fair Employment and Housing Dept.; civil action.

Federal preemption may occur, in which case coverage of union rights may be enforced by the National Labor Relations Board (NLRB).

EXCEPTIONS: Some employers with fewer than 15 employees may not be covered for some of the above listed questions. Consult with your union or your attorney.

Independent contractors are protected against discrimination under the Unruh Act. (Civil Code sections 51-53. Triple damages and attorney's fees available.)

## YOU CANNOT BE DENIED A JOB BECAUSE OF CHILD OR FAMILY SUPPORT ORDERS

A court can issue an order forcing an employer to deduct child support or family support payments from your wages. Some employers dislike the additional paperwork involved in processing these orders. However, it is unlawful for an employer to deny you a job (or discharge or discriminate against you in any way) because of a child support or a family support order.

LAW: Civil Code section 4701.

ENFORCEMENT: Civil action.

## YOUR EMPLOYER CANNOT DISCRIMINATE AGAINST YOU BECAUSE OF CUSTOMER PREFERENCE

The laws that protect you from discrimination also protect you against discrimination because of customer preference or request (see above). In addition, it is against the law for a customer of your employer (or potential employer) to ask that you be denied employment, terminated, transferred or otherwise discriminated against because of your sex, race, color, religion, ancestry, or national origin or because you have traveled to or lawfully conducted business in a foreign country (e.g., Israel, South Africa, etc.). It is also illegal for your employer to give information about you to anyone in order to assist in this kind of a boycott of a foreign country (unless the U.S. government is also boycotting that country).

LAW: Business and Professions Code sections 16721-16722; Title 50 Appendix U.S. Code sections 2407 and 2410; Title 15 Code of Federal Regulations Part 369; Civil Code sections 51.5 and 52.

ENFORCEMENT: Civil action.

## CONDITIONS UNDER WHICH YOUR EMPLOYER CAN ACCEPT A CASH BOND FROM YOU

Any money which you give or advance to your employer (as part of the employment relationship) is considered a cash bond. For example, if you must pay a deposit for keys or equipment, that is a cash bond. A note (or other legal paper which obligates you to pay money) is considered a cash bond. Any investment made by you is considered to be a cash bond. Any property which is put up by you is considered to be a cash bond. There are only two situations in which your employer may legally accept a cash bond:

(1) when you are entrusted with property of an equivalent value; or

(2) when the employer advances merchandise to you which you are to sell or deliver.

If your employer accepts a cash bond, it must be kept in a separate savings account (which cannot be attached or garnished). It must be returned to you with interest, immediately upon your return of the employer's property.

**LAW:** Labor Code sections 400-410.

**ENFORCEMENT:** Labor commissioner; district attorney; civil action.

Any employer who violates these rules is subject to six months in jail and a $500 fine. If an employer takes any of the cash bond for his/her own use, or even mingles it with his/her other property, s/he may be guilty of theft and may face a lengthy prison sentence.


## YOUR EMPLOYER MUST PAY FOR FIDELITY BONDS

Your employer is legally bound to pay for any fidelity bond required of you. This also applies to any bond required of you if you are a job applicant.

For example, if you must be bonded for $50,000 (to protect against job losses), your employer must pay for that bond.

**LAW:** Labor Code sections 401 and 408.

**ENFORCEMENT:** Labor commissioner; district attorney; civil action.

Any employer who violates this law is subject to six months in jail and a $500 fine.

**EXCEPTIONS:** Your employer may sometimes accept a cash bond; see above. An employee of a savings and loan association may have to sign for a bond, but the employer must still pay the cost. Financial Code sections 6200 and 6203(b).

## PAYING OR POSTING MONEY IN ORDER TO APPLY FOR A JOB IS ILLEGAL

It is against the law in California for an employer to require a prospective employee to pay money in order to have his/her job application considered or processed. It is also illegal for anyone to charge an application fee for any apprenticeship program. (Reasonable costs may be charged to apprenticeship applicants **after** they have been accepted into a state-approved apprenticeship program. This post-acceptance fee is **not** allowed for any other job application situation.)

LAW: Labor Code sections 400-410, 450, 451, and 3091; Business and Professions Code section 9912.5.

ENFORCEMENT: Labor commissioner; Apprenticeship Standards Division; district attorney; civil action.

Any employer or employer's agent who requires payment for processing or considering a job application is subject to six months in jail.

## YOU CANNOT BE FORCED TO PATRONIZE YOUR EMPLOYER'S PLACE OF BUSINESS

It is illegal for your employer to make you shop at his/her store (or any other specific store), or make you buy any particular brand of goods.

These prohibitions apply to anything of value: food, services, tools, apparel, office supplies. They also apply to lodging, board, vehicles, and transportation.

LAW: Labor Code sections 450-452; Title 29 U.S. Code sections 1822 and 1832.

ENFORCEMENT: Labor commissioner; district attorney; civil action.

Any employer or employer's agent who violates this law may be subject to six months in jail and a $500 fine.

EXCEPTIONS: Your employer can specify the style and the brand of your uniform. (See also Chapter 4, WAGES, FRINGE BENEFITS AND HOURS OF WORK on tools, uniforms, meals and lodging.)

## YOUR EMPLOYER CANNOT REQUIRE INVESTMENT TO GET OR TO KEEP WORK

Your employer cannot require you to buy part of a business in order to get work, or in order to be considered for a position. S/he cannot require you to make any investment or loan, or to buy any stock.

This law applies to businesses, worker-owned cooperatives, and all other operations. This law protects those already working, as well as those applying for a position.

This law prohibits your employer from advertising this sort of scheme and it also prohibits any scheme where you take part of your wages (or salary, or commission, or compensation) in the form of a share of the business.

LAW: Labor Code sections 407, 408, and 410; Title 29 Code of Federal Regulations section 531.32(b).

ENFORCEMENT: Labor commissioner; district attorney; civil action.

Any employer who violates this law is subject to six months in jail and a $500 fine.

## JOB RIGHTS AND BANKRUPTCY PROTECTIONS

You cannot be discriminated against because of bankruptcy or because of participation in a wage-earner protection plan. This law applies to all employers.

You are protected in all areas of employment: hiring; firing; discipline; all terms and conditions of work. You cannot be fired for any bankruptcy-related reasons. You cannot be refused a job or license or permit for this kind of reason.

You cannot be discriminated against because:

(1) you filed bankruptcy;

(2) your spouse filed bankruptcy;

(3) you or your spouse entered a wage earner protection plan or are otherwise protected under the Bankruptcy Act;

(4) you were insolvent (broke, not paying your bills, in debt) before you used the Bankruptcy Act;

(5) you have not paid one or more debts (which you dealt with under the Bankruptcy Act).

LAW: Title 11 U.S. Code section 525.

ENFORCEMENT: Civil action.

EXCEPTIONS: This law applies to all employers.


## YOU CANNOT BE FORCED TO RESIDE WITHIN YOUR PUBLIC EMPLOYER'S JURISDICTION

No city or county, or other local or regional public employer, can impose a residency requirement on its employees (or job applicants). You cannot be required to be a resident of the city, county, or district.

LAW: California Constitution, Article 11, section 10(b).

ENFORCEMENT: Civil action.

EXCEPTIONS: You may be required to reside within a reasonable and specific distance from your place of employment (or other location). After you obtain a job, the public employer may require that you live no more than a specified commuting distance away, if this requirement is reasonably related to your duties.

## THE COST OF REQUIRED PHOTOGRAPHS MUST BE PAID BY THE EMPLOYER

Your employer must pay for any photo s/he requires of you as an applicant or as an employee.

LAW: Labor Code sections 401 and 408; Title 2 California Administrative Code section 7287.3(c)(2).

ENFORCEMENT: Labor commissioner; district attorney; civil action.

## YOUR EMPLOYER MAY NOT USE YOUR PHOTO FOR ADVERTISING PURPOSES WITHOUT YOUR CONSENT

In general, your employer may not use your photograph in any advertising or solicitations without your consent. This law protects your name and likeness, as well, and it applies to both employers and non-employers.

LAW: Civil Code section 3344.

ENFORCEMENT: Civil action.

If your employer violates this law, s/he is liable to you for any damages. (That is, you could collect for loss of reputation, invasion of privacy, etc.) In addition, your employer must pay you $300.

EXCEPTIONS: News photos and pictures of very large groups.

## PRE-EMPLOYMENT PHYSICAL EXAMS: YOU HAVE A RIGHT TO AN UNBIASED MEDICAL EVALUATION

If your employer requires you to take a medical examination, you have a right to a fair one. Your employer may condition a job offer on passing a physical **only** if **all** of the following rules and conditions are followed:

(1) No physical exam can be required until after you have been chosen for the job in question.

(2) All employees entering similar positions must be similarly subjected to a medical exam. It is illegal to require a physical exam only of those over the age of 40, or only of those with a record of physical disability. The exam standards must be no more stringent or difficult for those over 40 or those with a disability than the standards used for younger or healthier applicants.

(3) Exams, tests, or interviews must be made reasonably accessible to you if you have a handicap or disability (or if you have religious or military restrictions on when you are available). For instance, exam rooms must be accessible to wheelchairs; interpreters must be provided for the hearing-impaired.

(4) The exam results must be treated as confidential medical records. The exam results must be maintained separately from other employment and application records. (See also Chapter 10, EMPLOYEE RECORDS: COLLECTING, STORING AND ASSESSING INFORMATION.)

(5) You have a right to a physical exam geared to the specific duties of your prospective job. The employer must use different medical standards for different jobs. The physical requirements must be for the particular position you seek. No test or exam of physical agility or strength can be used unless the physical strength or agility being tested is related to the actual work you will do on the job, and no alternative test is available which does not discriminate against the handicapped or disabled. It is illegal to deny you a position because of your general health or physical condition, or because you may be more likely than others to get sick or hurt, or because the employer may have to pay higher insurance premiums.

(6) The employer must consider and explore ways in which your physical handicap might be accommodated **before** making an adverse employment decision.

(7) You must be given the right to contest unfavorable exam results. You must be given the right to submit independent medical opinions to the employer **before** a final decision is made.

**LAW, ENFORCEMENT, EXCEPTIONS:** *See final entry, this chapter.*

## YOUR EMPLOYER DOES NOT HAVE UNLIMITED ACCESS TO YOUR MEDICAL RECORDS

Tight rules control the information that a doctor can divulge to the employer. Unless you sign a release (or authorization), the doctor can only report to the employer (1) a "functional limitation" that may limit your "fitness to perform" the job duties and (2) any "functional limitations" that may entitle you "to leave work for medical reasons." Even then, the doctor **cannot** report to the employer any reason or cause for the "limitations". For example (without a release or authorization) the doctor could say that you cannot lift more than 60 pounds on a regular basis, but s/he could **not** tell the employer what condition led her/him to that conclusion. (See Chapter 10, EMPLOYEE RECORDS: COLLECTING, STORING AND ACCESSING INFORMATION for more information regarding the limitations on your employer's access to medical records.) Be sure that the "limitations" apply only to the present job duties. You may not be denied work because a future job or promotional possibility has different requirements.

Remember that a doctor hired and paid by your employer to examine you is working for your employer, and may consequently believe that s/he owes more consideration to the employer than to you. If you are denied a job because of that doctor's report, and the doctor was negligent in examining or diagnosing you, then you can sue the doctor and/or employer for damages.

LAW, ENFORCEMENT, EXCEPTIONS: *See final entry, this chapter.*

## YOUR EMPLOYER CANNOT REQUIRE YOU TO SIGN A MEDICAL RELEASE

Many employers circumvent these laws by asking prospective employees to sign an authorization for release of medical information as part of the job application process. Although it is illegal for an employer to retaliate against you for refusing to sign such a release, if you do refuse and then are not chosen for the job, it may be hard to prove that your refusal was the cause of the job denial. To avoid this problem, it is best for you to sign the release. Then, **after** you have been examined by the employer's doctor, but before you leave her/his office, hand the doctor a signed copy of this note:

*"I hereby cancel any and all authorizations for the release of medical information concerning me. Please restrict your communications about my medical condition to those authorized by law in the absence of a release. See Civil Code sections 56.10(c)(8)(B) and 56.15."*

Keep a copy of this note.

This strategy will help discourage your employer from illegally discriminating against you: You were already in the final stage of being given the job; it will be hard for the employer to prove that your legal restriction of medical information did not cause any later change of mind. (You can use this kind of note for any physical, medical, or psychiatric exam.)

LAW: Civil Code sections 56-56.37.

ENFORCEMENT: Civil action.

Any violation which results in economic loss (or physical injury) is a crime. You can sue for damages and attorney's fees and $3,000 in punitive damages.

EXCEPTIONS: See Chapter 10, EMPLOYEE RECORDS: COLLECTING, STORING AND ACCESSING INFORMATION.

## AN EMPLOYER CANNOT REFUSE TO HIRE YOU BECAUSE YOU MIGHT GET A DISEASE OR SUFFER INJURY

Your employer cannot deny you a job because s/he thinks that some pre-existing condition of yours exposes you to a high degree of risk. This means that genetic or medical screening cannot be used to deny you work. You have the right to insist on taking a job, even though it endangers your health.

An employer can deny you a position only if your health condition immediately endangers you or others. It must pose an imminent and substantial degree of risk. This applies to hiring, promotion, job transfer, job bidding and assignment, reclassification, and other employment selection procedures.

If an employer uses one (or more) of the following characteristics to screen people out of jobs, assignments, or promotions, there is a good chance that unlawful discrimination is occurring: eye color; skin color; physical size; blood pressure (hypertension); diabetes; sickle cell trait; color blindness; hearing loss; chronic liver disease; seizure disorder (epilepsy; abnormal EEG); lumbar sacralization; obesity; use of tobacco, alcohol, drugs; age; diet; exercise habits; reproductive status, childbearing plans; region of birth or residence. If you think you have been a victim of such discrimination, you have the right to examine all of the employer's files about you. (See Chapter 10, EMPLOYEE RECORDS: COLLECTING, STORING AND ACCESSING INFORMATION.)

These items are statistical indicators; any or all of them might be used in predicting future insurance or other costs. You cannot legally be denied an opportunity because of them. If you have questions, be sure to discuss them with your fellow workers, your union, the enforcement agencies, and special organizations concerned with occupational health or discrimination issues.

**LAW, ENFORCEMENT, EXCEPTIONS**: *See final entry, this chapter.*

## AIDS SCREENING CANNOT BE USED TO DENY YOU A JOB

No employer or potential employer can legally test your blood for AIDS antibodies. (The AIDS antibodies test reveals exposure to the AIDS virus.)

No employer can even ask you to authorize an AIDS antibodies test.

No one (except you yourself) can tell an employer any of your AIDS antibodies test results.

No employer can use any AIDS antibodies test results to determine whether you will be hired or fired.

**LAW**: Health & Safety Code sections 199.20-199.23.

**ENFORCEMENT**: District attorney; civil action.

Violation is a crime punishable by up to a year in jail and $10,000 fine. Violators may also be sued for damages, psychological harm, and civil penalties.

**EXCEPTIONS**: The law protecting the confidentiality of AIDS screening is very new. The legality of the following questions has not been determined: "Have you been given a diagnosis of AIDS, pre-AIDS, ARC, or an AIDS-related condition?" "Have you been exposed to AIDS or engaged in high-risk practices?" If you answer "yes" to this kind of question, your chances of being hired will not be improved. It is not legal to deny you employment because you might get sick. The only proper question is: "Can you do this particular job at this particular time?" If you give an employer any other medical information or authorize blood tests, any deviation from the norm found in that information will probably be used against you (and you will find it very hard to prove the information was used illegally).

## YOU MAY NOT BE DENIED A JOB BECAUSE OF A PHYSICAL HANDICAP

California law prohibits discrimination on the basis of physical handicap or medical condition.

You may not be denied a job because:

(1) of any physical handicap (including cosmetic disfigurements);

(2) you are thought to have a handicap;

(3) you have cancer which has been controlled;

(4) you have high blood pressure or a history of back trouble or a special sensitivity to smoke;

(5) you have sight, hearing, or speech impairments;

(6) you have any history of a physical handicap or disability.

You can be denied a job only if you have a handicap that keeps you from doing the major functions of the job, or which would endanger your safety or that of others. The employer must "reasonably accommodate" your disabilities, including assigning special shifts or schedules. (See Chapter 8, DISCIPLINE AND DISCHARGE.)

The basic state law protects only those with physical disabilities (including neurological and endocrinological problems). Mental and emotional disabilities which do not have a physical basis are not protected. However, if the employer is a federal or state contractor, or a direct or indirect recipient of federal or state government funds (including Medi-Cal or Medicare funds), then mental and emotional disabilities are protected, and none of the questions listed below may be asked about mental or physical conditions. (In any case, you should be very careful about answering questions about mental or emotional disabilities. See Chapter 10, EMPLOYEE RECORDS; COLLECTING, STORING AND ACCESSING INFORMATION.)

You cannot be asked:

(1) general questions about your physical condition;

(2) to describe your general medical condition;

(3) if you have any handicaps or physical disabilities;

(4) if you have any illnesses;

(5) to list any of your hospitalizations or to list your doctor's name;

(6) if you have any particular disabilities;

(7) if you have ever been treated for any of a list of diseases or conditions;

(8) if you are now receiving or have ever received Workers' Compensation;

(9) if you have ever received disability payments or insurance;

(10) if you have a driver's license (unless driving is an essential part of the job).

You can be asked about your present physical condition or your medical history only in a very limited way. The employer can ask questions if they are **directly related** to determining whether you would endanger your own safety or the safety of others if you got the job.

You can be asked if you have any physical condition or handicap which may limit your ability to perform the job applied for, and if you answer yes, you may be asked what can be done to accommodate your limitation.

The employer can state that job offers may be made contingent upon your passing a job-related physical examination.

LAW: Government Code sections 11135, 12926, 12940, 12990, 19253.5, 19701 and 19702; Title 2 California Administrative Code sections 7287.4, 7293.6, 7293.9, 7294.0, 7294.1, and 8101-8312; Fair Employment and Housing Dept.

Guidelines and Questions and Answers; Title 22 California Administrative Code sections 98250-98263, 98000-98111 and 98300-98413; Labor Code sections 132a and 1735; Title 29 U.S. Code sections 706(7), 793 and 794; Title 38 U.S. Code sections 2011-2013; Title 28 Code of Federal Regulations sections 41.1-41.58; Title 41 Code of Federal Regulations sections 60-741.1 through 60-741.54; Health and Safety Code sections 150-154; Title 31 U.S. Code sections 6716 and 6721.

**ENFORCEMENT:** Labor commissioner; Fair Employment and Housing Dept.; Office of Federal Contract Compliance Programs; Workers' Compensation Appeals Board; district attorney; civil action.

**EXCEPTIONS:** Employers with fewer than five workers and religious non-profit employers are covered only in the following cases:

(1) If the employer has state or federal contracts, or receives state or federal funds (including Medi-Cal or Medicare), then all of the above rules apply.

(2) The restrictions on asking about past industrial (occupational) injuries, about disabilities related to job injuries, and about Workers' Compensation claims always apply.

(3) Basic privacy rights prohibit overly intrusive questions from any employer.

(4) Laws protecting the confidentiality of medical information apply to all employers. See Chapter 10, EMPLOYEE RECORDS: COLLECTING, STORING AND ACCESSING INFORMATION.

(5) If you are harmed as a result of a doctor's negligence in examining or diagnosing you or reporting to an employer, you are protected no matter how small the employer.

(6) Specific protections in connection with AIDS, drug, alcohol, psychiatric, and other special types of information apply in all cases. See also Chapter 10, EMPLOYEE

# RECORDS: COLLECTING, STORING AND ACCESSING INFORMATION.

## CHAPTER 3

## BLACKLISTING, INVESTIGATIONS, AND POLICE RECORDS

### BLACKLISTING IS AGAINST THE LAW

It is unlawful for your former employer to lie about you or to in any way misrepresent you or your work history. This is sometimes known as "blacklisting" and is against the law (whether you left your former employer voluntarily or were discharged).

Your employer may, upon special request, give to a prospective employer a truthful statement of why you left a job. However, if your former employer submits a statement to a prospective employer without being asked, that will be considered evidence of blacklisting and a violation of the law.

If your employer submits a statement which contains a secret mark or code (conveying information different from the information expressed in the words of the statement), that will be considered evidence of blacklisting and a violation of the law.

**LAW:** Labor Code sections 1050, 1052, 1053, and 1054.

**ENFORCEMENT:** Labor commissioner; district attorney; civil action.

An employer who violates the law is subject to jail, fines, treble damages, and punitive damages.

**EXCEPTIONS:** Employees of public utilities have special protections. Any public utility employee who leaves his/her job has the right to request and receive a letter stating his/her period of employment and the type of work s/he performed. A public utility violating this law may be fined. Labor Code sections 1055 and 1056.

## PHOTOGRAPHS AND FINGERPRINTS MAY NOT BE GIVEN TO A THIRD PARTY

No one may require an employee or job applicant to be photographed or fingerprinted for the use of a third person, if there is a chance that those photos or prints could be used to the detriment of the worker.

An employer may require photos or prints only if they are kept completely "in house" and are never communicated to any outside party. No employer may require that prints or photos be taken by any police department or by any third person.

LAW: Labor Code sections 1051, 1052, and 1054; Volume 10 California Attorney General's Opinions, p. 19; Title 2 California Administrative Code section 7287.3(c)(2).

ENFORCEMENT: Labor commissioner; district attorney; civil action.

An employer who violates this law is subject to six months in jail and a $500 fine. Violators may also be sued for treble damages.

EXCEPTIONS: No photos or prints may be communicated to any law enforcement or other government agencies, except as outlined in the arrest/police records sections of this chapter. Legally required federal or state licensing and security clearance applications are also excepted.

## EMPLOYERS DO NOT HAVE LEGAL ACCESS TO MOST FILES KEPT ABOUT YOU

Your employer (or prospective employer) cannot obtain information about you from:

(1) insurance companies;

(2) public or private schools, junior colleges, colleges or universities;

(3) alcohol abuse or drug abuse programs;

(4) providers of mental health services;

(5) anyone with results of AIDS antibodies tests.

Employers have only limited access to information in the files of federal government agencies. Most medical information about you is also protected. (See Chapter 10, EMPLOYEE RECORDS: COLLECTING, STORING, AND ACCESSING.)

LAW: Civil Code sections 56-56.37 and 1798-1798.76; Education Code sections 49060-49078 and 67100-67147.5; Health and Safety Code sections 199.20-199.23, 11970.5-11978 and 25250-25257; Insurance Code sections 791-791.26; Penal Code section 11105.05; Welfare and Institutions Code sections 5328-5330; California Constitution, Article I, section 1; Title 5 U.S. Code sections 551-552a; Title 20 U.S. Code section 1232g; Title 21 U.S. Code section 1103; Title 42 U.S. Code sections 290dd-3, 290ee-3, and 9501(1)(H); Title 34 Code of Federal Regulations sections 99.1-99.67; Title 42 Code of Federal Regulations section 2.38.

ENFORCEMENT: Civil action.

In most cases punitive damages and/or attorney's fees are available.

EXCEPTIONS: Personal and confidential information can be released if you give a written authorization. If you sign such a release as part of the job application process, you can still preserve your privacy. Immediately send a letter to the agencies (schools, insurance companies, etc.) telling them that you are cancelling any authorizations for release of personal information. Once this cancellation is received, it is illegal for information to be released to your employer.

## INVESTIGATIONS: EMPLOYEES AND JOB APPLICANTS MUST BE PROMPTLY NOTIFIED

If your employer or prospective employer has an investigating agent interview someone to gain information about you, then these rules apply: The employer must notify you in writing about the investigation. This written notice must be given or mailed to you within three days after the investigation is requested. This written notice must tell you that you can ask for details of the investigation. It must also tell you that you have a right to inspect the files of the agency investigating you.

If you respond to this notice with a written request for details, then the employer must tell you the exact nature and scope of the investigation.

LAW: Title 15 U.S. Code sections 1681d, 1681n, and 1681o; Civil Code sections 1786.16(a)(2), 1786.50, and 1786.52.

ENFORCEMENT: Civil action.

You may sue for damages, punitive damages, costs and attorney's fees, invasion of privacy, and distress.

EXCEPTIONS: Investigations by the employer's own staff may not be covered. You need not be told of an investigation if you are being considered for a position for which you have not applied.

Investigations conducted by government agencies are controlled by other laws.

## YOU MUST BE TOLD IF YOUR JOB DENIAL, DISCHARGE, OR LACK OF PROMOTION IS THE RESULT OF AN INVESTIGATION OR CREDIT REPORT

The employer must promptly tell you if a job denial, discharge, promotion or transfer denial was based, in whole or in part, upon information from an investigation or credit report.

The employer must also tell you the name and address of the investigation or credit agency.

These rights apply both to investigations and to mere paperwork reviews of your credit records.

**LAW**: Title 15 U.S. Code sections 1681m, 1681n, and 1681o; Civil Code sections 1785.20, 1785.20.5, 1785.31, 1786.40, 1786.50, and 1786.52.

**ENFORCEMENT**: Civil action.

You may sue for damages, punitive damages, and attorney's fees.

**EXCEPTIONS**: Certain investigations conducted solely by the employer's own staff may not be covered; but you can see any reports from "in house" investigations. Labor Code section 1198.5. (See Chapter 10, EMPLOYEE RECORDS: COLLECTING, STORING AND ACCESSING INFORMATION.)

Investigations conducted by government agencies are controlled by other laws.

## YOU HAVE THE RIGHT TO INSPECT INVESTIGATION AND/OR CREDIT RECORDS

Your right to see any investigation or credit report about you applies to any report given to your employer, or an employer to whom you have applied for work. You have a right to see any report which an employer has received for employment purposes:

(1) in connection with deciding whether to hire you;

(2) or to fire you;

(3) or to promote or transfer you.

You have the right to inspect all files about you which are held by the reporting agency. Only the names of the people interviewed may be denied to you. You may see all the agency learned about you, as well as what it sent to the employer.

The investigating or credit agency must tell you the name of every non-employer who has received a report on you in the last six months and every employer who has received a report on you in the last two years.

The agency must show you your file when you appear in person, during normal business hours, after giving it reasonable notice. The agency must explain to you, in writing, any coded information in the file. You may be accompanied by a person of your choosing when you examine your file.

If you make a written request, with proper identification, then the agency must send a copy of your report to any addressee you specify (and the agency must use certified mail).

The maximum amount you can be charged for a copy of the agency's report on you is $8.00. If (1) you have been denied a job (or fired) because of the agency's report, and (2) you request to see and copy your file (within 30 days of being told that you lost the job because of the report), then the agency cannot charge you any amount.

**LAW**: Title 15 U.S. Code sections 1681g, 1681h, and 1681j; Civil Code sections 1785.10, 1785.15, 1785.17, 1786.10, 1786.22, and 1786.26.

**ENFORCEMENT**: Civil action.

You may sue for damages, punitive damages, and attorney's fees.

**EXCEPTIONS**: Provisions of these laws may not apply to investigations conducted solely by the employer's own "in house" investigators; but you have the right to see all such "in house" reports. In addition to the above specified rights to see agency files, you have the right to see (at your workplace) any reports sent to your employer. Refusal to let you see them is a crime. Labor Code section 1198.5.

Government records about you are controlled by other laws, but once your employer receives copies you have the right to inspect them at your workplace. (See Chapter 10, EMPLOYEE RECORDS: COLLECTING, STORING AND ACCESSING INFORMATION.)

## YOU HAVE THE RIGHT TO CORRECT INVESTIGATING AND CREDIT AGENCY INFORMATION ABOUT YOU

You have certain rights to disagree with and to correct the files about you which are held by investigation and credit agencies. If you think that your file contains anything which is (1) false, or (2) out of date, or (3) misleadingly incomplete, then you should write to the agency and demand a correction.

The agency has three options:

(1) The agency can immediately do what you demand.

(2) The agency can reinvestigate the disputed facts. After this reinvestigation, it must record the current, correct information. It must do this within a reasonable period of time.

(3) The agency can decide that your complaint is frivolous or irrelevant. It cannot base this decision on the fact that its information is different from your version of the facts.

If the agency investigates your complaint and finds that its original version (1) was wrong, or (2) that the information can no longer be verified, then it must take certain steps. It must delete the inaccurate (or unverifiable) information from its file. It must notify you that it has done this. Next, if you request it (and you should make this request, in writing), the agency must send out a correction. This correction must be sent to every employer who has received a report on you within the last two years. (It must also go to every non-employer who has received a report within the last six months.)

If the agency refuses to investigate your complaint, or if it does investigate but does not agree with your version of the truth, it has certain duties. It must notify you of its refusal to correct. You then have the right to insert a brief statement into your file. This should be in writing. This statement of yours should explain the dispute and give your version of the truth. Once you do this, the agency has certain other duties. It must include your version in any future reports about you. You should also request that your version be sent out to past recipients of reports. If you do this, the agency has to send your version to every employer who received a report within the last two years (and to every non-employer who received one within the last six months).

> **LAW, ENFORCEMENT, EXCEPTIONS:** *See entry below on obsolete information.*

## YOU HAVE ADDITIONAL RIGHTS REGARDING CREDIT REPORTS

If you have complained about a credit report or the file it was based on, and the agency is investigating your complaint, then you should demand in writing that the agency give notice of the dispute while it is investigating. This means that the agency must include, in any reports about you that it sends out while it is investigating your complaint, a statement that the data you complained about is currently in dispute. And once you have filed your version of the disputed facts, the agency must send your statement with any reports (even if it has not finished its own investigation). There is a time limit on the agency. If it has not confirmed its original information within 90 days, you can require it to delete the disputed data from its reports. It has only 90 days. If it hasn't verified its version of the facts by then, your version wins by default.

> **LAW, ENFORCEMENT, EXCEPTIONS:** *See section below on obsolete information.*

## OBSOLETE INFORMATION MUST BE REMOVED FROM INVESTIGATING AND CREDIT AGENCIES' FILES

You are protected against investigating and credit agencies keeping obsolete information about you. There are limits on what the agency can include in its reports about you even if the information is correct.

Unless the job you are seeking involves an annual salary of $30,000 or more, no credit or investigating agency can include any of the following data in reports about you:

(1) bankruptcy more than 14 years old;

(2) unsatisfied (unpaid) legal judgments more than 10 years old;

(3) lawsuits against you or satisfied (paid) judgments more than 10 years old;

(4) debts more than 7 years old;

(5) arrest or conviction records more than 7 years old (see sections on police and arrest records in this chapter; an agency reporting such criminal history information may well be in violation of other laws);

(6) any other adverse information about you more than 7 years old.

If the job you seek involves a salary of less than $20,000 per year, then no bankruptcy can be reported unless it is less than 10 years old.

Any report which requires an interview or contact with another individual has an additional limit. Any information not derived from official public records must have been verified within the last three months.

**LAW**: Civil Code sections 1785.13, 1785.16, 1785.18, 1785.30, 1786.18, 1786.24, 1786.26, 1786.28, and 1786.30; Title 15 U.S. Code sections 1681c, 1681d, and 1681i.

**ENFORCEMENT**: Civil action.

If you lose a job because of a report that contains any false information, or that is seriously incomplete or misleading, or that invades your privacy or your rights to associate with others, or is in any other way improper, you may sue. You may also sue if the credit or investigating agency refuses to follow the legal procedures outlined above, even if you have not otherwise been harmed.

You cannot legally be denied a job because of bankruptcy or a wage-earner plan, or any debts discharged in bankruptcy. See Chapter 2, HIRING RIGHTS.

EXCEPTIONS: Your rights concerning investigations conducted (and files kept) by your employer's own "in house" investigators may differ. (See Chapter 10, EMPLOYEE RECORDS: COLLECTING, STORING AND ACCESSING INFORMATION.) Your rights concerning files about you which are kept by government agencies are controlled by other laws. (You have similar rights to inspect, dispute, and correct, however.)

## MANDATORY LIE DETECTOR TESTS ARE ILLEGAL

You cannot be required to take a lie detector test. This law applies whether you are seeking a job or already have one. This law applies to any form of so-called lie test: polygraph, voice analyzer, lie detector, or any other test or questioning which is claimed to detect truth or falsehood.

It is a crime for the employer to demand or require a lie detector test. Veiled threats are illegal. Any retaliation against you for refusing to take the test is also illegal.

If an employer wants you to take a lie detector test, s/he must do certain things. You must be given written notice before you are asked to take the test. The notice must tell you that you have an absolute right to refuse to take the test.

You cannot be punished in any way for refusing to take a lie detector test.

If you already have a job, and are asked to take a test, you should refuse. No lie detector tests are accurate. Almost all courts and arbitrators refuse to consider lie detector test results because they are so inaccurate. If you agree to the test, and the machine operator decides that you are lying, the employer can fire you.

If you are applying for a job, and the employer asks you to take a lie detector test, what should you do? It is best not to take the test. The employer often tries to suggest that s/he will only hire people who take the test. Even to suggest this is illegal. If it is true that only test takers are hired, then the employer is guilty of a crime and may be sued for damages.

If you do take a lie test, the rules on what questions can be asked applicants still apply. (See Chapter 2, HIRING RIGHTS.) If you are asked illegal questions, you do not have to answer and you should write the questions down immediately after the test (so that you won't forget them).

You should be aware that lie detector operators almost always try to unnerve you. At some point, usually at the end of the test, they will accuse you of flunking the test. Often this is after they have said that the test is finished and they are starting to put their gear away. They want to see how you react to their surprise announcement.

Other test givers use card tricks: they give you marked or rigged decks of cards, and then pretend to figure out which cards were picked--making you think that the "machine" told which answers were true. The purpose is to get the test-taker extremely nervous and convinced that the test is accurate.

A polygraph is a machine which measures your rate of breathing, your pulse or blood pressure, and your sweating.

Before any polygraph test is given, you must be told the subject matter or area of inquiry of the test. All of the questions to be asked must be read aloud to you **before** the polygraph is hooked up to you. It is illegal for the examiner to throw in any question which is not read in advance.

> LAW: Labor Code sections 432.2 and 433; Evidence Code section 351.1; U.S. Constitution, 5th and 14th Amendments; California Constitution, Article 1, section 15; Business and Professions Code sections 9300-9319.

> ENFORCEMENT: Labor commissioner; Polygraph Examiners Board, Dept. of Consumer Affairs; district attorney; civil action.

> An employer may be subject to six months in jail for violating these rules.

> EXCEPTIONS: These laws do not apply to railroads covered by the Railway Labor Act or to any local or state employers. Other restrictions, however, cover those employers. For example, police officers have much stronger

protections against lie detector tests. A court challenge to lie detector tests for non-police government employees is pending. Currently, for those local or state government workers who are not protected by the regulations explained above, the following rules apply. (These rules apply to any local or state government worker who is **forced** to answer questions, whether a lie detector test is involved or not).

(1) The government employee must be told that the questions will relate specifically and narrowly to the performance of his or her official duties.

(2) The government employee must be told that the answers cannot be used against him or her in any subsequent criminal proceedings.

(3) The government employee must be told if the penalty for refusing to answer will be discharge.

(4) If the government employee asks to have his or her union representative present during the questioning, this request must be honored.

## MANDATORY VOICE STRESS ANALYSIS AND/OR VOICE PRINTS ARE ILLEGAL

No employer can use a voice stress analyzer on you without your permission. Some people claim that analyzers indicate emotional stress in the voice, which might indicate falsehoods or give other information about the person speaking. It is a crime to use this kind of device without the express written permission of the person analyzed. This written authorization must be obtained before any use of the analyzer.

It is also a crime to make a voice print without a person's permission. It is illegal to have or to use a voice print without permission. This authorization must also be in writing and be obtained in advance. (Voice prints can be used to identify the speaker. They can also be used for the same purposes as the analyzer.)

It is a crime for an employer to require you to give permission for use of a voice analyzer or print. You cannot be refused a job, or fired, or disciplined for refusing.

> **LAW:** Penal Code section 637.3; Labor Code sections 432.2 and 433.

> **ENFORCEMENT:** Labor commissioner; district attorney; civil action.

> You may sue for damages, punitive damages, emotional distress, and invasion of privacy.

> **EXCEPTIONS:** Government agencies operate under different rules; some law enforcement uses are allowed.

## SECRET RECORDINGS ARE ILLEGAL

It is illegal for an employer or any other person to secretly record a private conversation. This is so even if the person doing the recording is a party to the conversation. This applies whether the conversation is face-to-face or over a telephone.

The only way to legally record a private conversation is to clearly announce the intention in advance and obtain permission from all parties.

> **LAW:** Penal Code sections 632 and 637.2; Title 18 U.S. Code sections 2510-2520; Title 47 U.S. Code section 605.

> **ENFORCEMENT:** District attorney; U.S. Attorney; civil action.

> Violation of these laws is a crime. It also subjects the violator to civil penalty. The violator may be sued for three times the amount of actual damages suffered by the person taped, or $3,000 per taping incident, punitive damages and attorney's fees.

> **EXCEPTIONS:** Law enforcement agencies.

## YOUR RIGHTS REGARDING POLICE AND ARREST RECORDS

Your employer cannot seek, possess, or use any information about arrests for which you were not convicted.

Your employer cannot seek, possess, or use any information about two year old (or older) marijuana convictions.

Your employer cannot seek, possess, or use any information about any arrests which led to your participation in a diversion program.

It is illegal for your employer to **ask** you about any arrests which did not lead to a conviction. This applies whether you are applying for a job or already work for the employer. This applies to private and government employers. The one basic exception is that your employer **can ask** if you have been arrested and are out on bail (or on your own recognizance [O.R.]) still awaiting trial. You must tell your employer about this kind of arrest, but only if you are asked.

**Definitions** -- What is an arrest which **did** lead to "conviction"? This means any arrest where the prosecutor actually decides to file formal charges, **and** then you plead guilty, or you plead "no contest," or you plead "nolo contendere," or you go to trial and are found guilty by a jury or judge.

But, if you went into any diversion program, then that arrest may **not** be counted as one which led to "conviction." This rule applies whether the "diversion" was before trial or was after trial and conviction.

What is an "arrest"? This means any time you were arrested, or stopped, or interrogated, or held, or detained by the police (or any other law enforcement agency). Also, if you went to jail, or to the police station, that is an arrest. For this purpose, a detention is the same as an arrest. No matter what you did, or what someone said you did, or what the police thought you did, the employer cannot ask you about it (or discipline you for it), if the "arrest" did not lead to a "conviction."

**Marijuana Convictions** -- A marijuana conviction which is two years old (or older) is treated like an arrest which did not lead to conviction. The employer cannot ask you about it and you do not have to answer if s/he does ask. (Legal developments under the Constitution make your protections broader than those in Labor Code section 423.8).

**Diversion Programs** -- Any referral to or participation in any diversion program is treated in the same way. The employer cannot ask you about it and cannot use any information about it against you.

**Employer Restrictions** -- The employer cannot lawfully ask you about these kinds of arrests (or convictions) or require that you answer any questions about them. If your employer, in violation of the law, asks these kinds of questions, you may be protected even if you lie in response. If your employer asks this kind of question and you answer truthfully, your answer cannot be used against you.

In addition, the employer is forbidden to find out, in any way, about these arrests or convictions. And if the employer nevertheless does find out, s/he may not use that knowledge against you.

**What To Do If You Are Arrested** -- Workers who are arrested understandably become upset. Not only is the arrest disturbing, but much time and money is involved in contesting the charge. It is usually made very easy to simply enter a guilty plea and escape any further cost and hassle. But if you do so, you may give up important rights.

The laws explained here give you strong protections. But, if you do enter a guilty or "no contest" plea, you will lose most of these protections. And then you might lose your job. Before pleading guilty to any charge, you should discuss these protections with your lawyer and with your union.

Employers with five or more employees (except religious organizations) may not ask about convictions which have been legally sealed, expunged, eradicated, or dismissed.

**LAW:** Labor Code sections 432.7 and 432.8; California Constitution, Article I, section 1; Title 2 Calif. Administrative Code section 7287.4(d)(1).

**ENFORCEMENT**: District attorney; civil action.

You can sue for actual damages, plus costs, plus attorney's fees. If the employer has intentionally violated these laws, then you can get treble damages, plus attorney's fees. For instance, if you lost a year's wages because of a violation, and the employer refused to reinstate you even after being told about the law, then you could get three years' wages and benefits. Any intentional violation is also a misdemeanor.

**EXCEPTIONS**: Most of these rules do **not** apply to you if you work for (or are seeking work with) a criminal justice agency. If the employer is a railroad covered by the Railway Labor Act, then the Labor Code sections do not apply. But your protections under the State Constitution and other statutes are similar; you should consult your union and lawyer.

**Special Circumstances: Employment in Health Facilities --** If the employer is a health care facility, then you may be asked about certain arrests in certain special circumstances.

These special rules apply **only** if the employer is one of the following types of health care facilities:

(1) a general acute care hospital;

(2) an acute care psychiatric hospital;

(3) a skilled nursing hospital;

(4) an intermediate care facility;

(5) a special hospital (for maternity or dentistry care);

(6) a general acute care/rehabilitation hospital;

(7) an intermediate care facility/developmentally disabled (habilitative or not).

If you are applying for **a position with regular access to patients**, then this rule applies: The employer can ask if you were ever arrested for one of the sex crimes listed in Penal Code section 290. The employer can ask about sex crime arrests even if they did not lead to conviction. (The health facility can get police records about such arrests.)

If you are applying for **a position with access to drugs and medication**, then a second rule applies: The employer can ask you if you were ever arrested for one of the **drug crimes** listed in Health and Safety Code section 11,590. The employer can ask about drug crime arrests even if they did not lead to conviction. (The health facility can obtain police records about such drug arrests.)

But these health care facilities cannot ask you about any other kind of arrest, regardless of the position for which you are applying.

**LAW:** Labor Code section 432.7(e).

**ENFORCEMENT:** District attorney; civil action.

**EXCEPTIONS:** Railroads; criminal justice agencies.


## SPECIAL RULES REGARDING POLICE RECORDS

These special rules apply in the following cases: job applicants for positions with supervisory or disciplinary power over minors; community care facilities; intermediate care facilities/developmentally disabled; public utilities; government agencies; commercial banks, savings and loan associations, and credit unions.


**Commerical Banks, Credit Unions, Savings and Loan Associations** -- Certain financial institutions may ask you to allow your fingerprints to be taken and your police records obtained. The law allows only these employers to make such requests:

(1) commmercial banks (state or federal);

(2) savings and loan associations (state or federal);

(3) credit unions (state or federal).

The financial institutions can use this procedure **only**:

(1) if you are applying for employment; and

(2) if you give your written consent.

Even if you give written permission, the institution is still forbidden to ask about arrests which did not lead to conviction. All it can do is send your fingerprints to a law enforcement agency, along with your written consent, and ask for information. It can only ask about **convictions** (or arrests for which you are still awaiting trial). Even then, it can only ask for this information about **certain crimes**.

The crimes about which the institution can ask include most property offenses: embezzlement, counterfeiting, burglary, bookmaking, robbery, forgery, computer fraud, credit card offenses, receiving stolen property, theft, obtaining funds by bad checks or false pretenses, and false financial statements.

What this law allows the institution to do is to check your **theft-related conviction record**, by sending in your fingerprints.

The state cannot legally tell a financial institution about any arrests which did not lead to conviction.

**LAW:** Financial Code sections 777, 6525, 8600, and 14,409.2; California Constitution, Article I, section 1.

**ENFORCEMENT:** Attorney General; district attorney; civil action.


**Certain Jobs With Supervisory or Disciplinary Power Over Minors** -- Certain employers can obtain **conviction** records of applicants for certain jobs.

The only employers that are able to do this are nonprofit corporations that have employees or volunteers in positions with supervisory or disciplinary power over one or more children (under 18). The State Attorney General can also specify other employers that can obtain those data, so long as their employees or volunteers have this kind of power over minors.

The state then legally can send the employer records of convictions and of commitments as a mentally disordered sex offender. The state must send the applicant a copy of the information sent to the employer. The state cannot legally send any records of arrests which did not lead to conviction.

The employer can take your fingerprints in order to obtain your conviction records.

**LAW:** Penal Code section 11105.3; California Constitution Article I, section 1.

**ENFORCEMENT:** Attorney General; district attorney; civil action.

**Community Care and Daycare Facilities** -- Most employees of community care facilities must submit conviction records and prior employment histories. This must be done within 20 days of being hired. The worker has to declare, under penalty of perjury, any criminal **convictions**.

Community care facilities are places which provide care for children or adults, either residential or daycare. (This does **not** include health facilities.) Examples are daycare centers, foster homes, and homes for the mentally or physically handicapped.

If the worker has ever been convicted of a sex crime against a minor, or child abuse, or a violent felony, the state will require his or her termination. If the worker was convicted of another offense (except for a minor traffic violation), then the worker will either be terminated or the employer will seek an exemption. The State Department of Social Services determines whether the worker can stay on the job until a decision is made about the exemption.

**LAW:** Health and Safety Code sections 1502, 1522, 1524, 1564 and 1596.871.

**ENFORCEMENT**: Community Care Licensing Division, State Department of Social Services; civil action if waiver or exemption is denied (short time limit).

**EXCEPTIONS**: **None** of these rules apply to non-supervisory employees who are not residents of the facility, **unless** they provide client assistance in dressing, grooming, bathing, or personal hygiene, or unless they have frequent and routine contact with the clients. Fingerprints are **not** required of employees of most social rehabilitation facilities (residential facilities providing assistance, guidance, or counseling) **unless** they are supervisors or reside in the facility. (But **all** employees of social rehabilitation facilities serving minors with alcohol or drug abuse problems must be fingerprinted.)

**Intermediate Care Facilities/Developmentally Disabled Habilitative** -- Within 20 days of being hired, certain employees of "intermediate care facilities/developmentally disabled habilitative" must submit fingerprint cards. The State Department of Health Services will then check the worker's **conviction** (not arrest) records. If the employee has been convicted of a crime which is substantially related to his or her job duties, then the State Department may require her or his termination. (As with all governmental determinations, this action may be appealed.)

An "intermediate care facility/developmentally disabled habilitative" is a facility which provides 24 hour care to, and helps educate and train, developmentally disabled people. By law, this category applies only to facilities with 4 to 15 beds, no more than 15 disabled clients, and medical certification that the clients do not need continuous, skilled nursing care.

**LAW**: Health and Safety Code sections 20, 1250, 1265.2, and 1265.5.

**ENFORCEMENT**: Licensing and Certification Division, State Department of Health Services; civil action (if waiver or exemption is denied; short time limit).

**EXCEPTIONS**: This law applies to (1) workers who are residents of the facility, or (2) are direct care staff. Direct care staff means all facility staff who are trained and experienced in the care of persons with developmental disabilities and who directly provide program and nursing services to clients. Administrative and licensed personnel shall be considered direct care staff when directly providing program and nursing services to clients.

**Public Utilities** -- There are two sorts of jobs which may allow a public utility (one covered by Public Utility Code section 216) to receive certain police records: jobs at **nuclear power facilities** and jobs which involve entrance to **private residences**.

*Nuclear Power Stations* -- If you apply for a job which involves working **on site** at a nuclear energy facility, then the utility can ask a local or state police agency for your police record. If the utility is given this information, then the police agency must also give a copy to you. The restrictions of Labor Code section 432.7 **still apply**. That is, the utility **cannot** even consider any arrests which did not lead to conviction (except for those where you are still awaiting trial). The police agency cannot lawfully send any information about nonconviction records.

**LAW**: Penal Code sections 11,105(c)(1) and 13,300(c)(1); California Constitution Article I, section 1.

**ENFORCEMENT**: Attorney General; district attorney; civil action.

*Access to Private Residences* -- If you apply for a job (or if you already hold a job) which involves access to private residences, then the utility can request police records of convictions (and arrests where you are still awaiting trial). If a local or state police agency gives the utility these data, it must also give a copy to you. The utility must not disclose the information it receives. It must destroy all copies of this information not more than 30 days after employment (or promotion or transfer) is granted or denied. (If you are awaiting trial, this time limit is 30 days after your case is resolved.)

The police agency cannot legally send any data about arrests which did not lead to conviction (except where you are still awaiting trial).

LAW: Penal Code sections 11,105(c)(9) and 13,300(c)(9); California Constitution Article I, section 1.

ENFORCEMENT: Attorney General; district attorney; civil action.

If the utility or the police agency violates any of these rules, a crime has been committed. The guilty person can be sentenced to six months in prison. And you can sue for damages.

**Government Agencies** -- Law enforcement agencies can ask job applicants about arrests and can obtain arrest and conviction records.

LAW: Labor Code section 432.7(d); Penal Code sections 11,105(b)(1-6, 14) and (c)(2), and 13,300(b)(1-6, 13) and (c)(2).

Other state and local agencies are in a different situation. These government units may receive and use conviction information, but only under certain rules. (They can ask about or receive arrest information, where the arrest did not lead to a conviction, **only** about arrests where you are still awaiting trial, and about drug or sex arrests if the government unit is also one of the health facilities discussed above.)

To obtain conviction records, the government agency's governing board must pass a statute, a regulation, or an ordinance. That statute or ordinance must meet the following requirements:

(1) It must refer to specific criminal conduct. That is, it has to spell out certain specified criminal law convictions.

(2) It must spell out job requirements or exclusions based on the specified convictions.

(3) There must be a rational relationship between the job duties, the job requirements or exclusions, and the specified convictions.

For example, a government unit can legislate that its school bus drivers must not have been convicted of child molesting. It has to pass a statute or ordinance specifying that criminal record information, containing any convictions for molesting, can be sought by the unit. After this law is passed, the government unit can ask driver applicants about such convictions and can obtain data about molesting convictions. The agency has to specify what kind of convictions it is interested in, and what will happen if an applicant has that kind of conviction. There must be a reasonable connection between the type of conviction and the job sought. For example, the agency cannot lawfully refuse to hire a gardener because of a draft refusal conviction.

It is important to note that Labor Code section 432.7 still applies. The government unit cannot use any arrests which did not lead to conviction. The state and local police agencies **cannot** send any nonconviction data (Labor Code section 432.7(h) notwithstanding). And the local government unit cannot use any convictions except for those which were spelled out in its statute or ordinance.

LAW: Penal Code sections 11,105(b)(9, 10) and 13,300(b)(9, 10); Labor Code section 432.7; California Constitution, Article I, section 1; Title 11 Calif. Administrative Code sections 701-708.

ENFORCEMENT: Attorney General; district attorney; civil action.

## CRIMINAL CONVICTIONS MAY AFFECT YOUR ABILITY TO BE LICENSED OR CERTIFIED

Criminal conviction records may also affect employment as a result of the licensing process. Many occupations require some form of state licensing or certification: school bus driver, security guard, teacher, lawyer, etc.

Often your employer will take and process the application for your license or certification. Some state government licensing agencies check police records. (This process is controlled by various state and federal constitutional and statutory safeguards, but sometimes the licensing body is unaware of these provisions.)

If the licensing agency refuses to license you, this may affect your job. Sometimes the agency tells your employer the reason for its refusal to license. This reason might be a criminal conviction which the licensing agency thinks is part of your record.

(1) If this happens, the agency and/or your employer may be in violation of the law. See the sections on police records and consult your union and your lawyer.

(2) You have the right to challenge a license refusal. Even if you have convictions on your record, they may have nothing to do with your ability to do the job. Consult your union and your lawyer.

(3) Even if you are not licensed, this may not mean that you must lose your job. Consult your union and your lawyer.

LAW: Specific statutes governing occupations which require licensing.

ENFORCEMENT: Civil action.

## POLICE RECORDS ARE CONFIDENTIAL: YOUR EMPLOYER MAY NOT OBTAIN OR POSSESS YOUR RECORD

It is a crime for your employer (or prospective employer) to obtain your police record or "rap sheet." It is a crime for anyone to give your record to your employer (or prospective employer). It is a crime for your employer to possess such records.

Your employer cannot legally use your rap sheet to discipline or discharge you, or refuse to hire or promote you.

No one can lawfully tell your employer (or prospective employer) about your arrests which did not lead to conviction. (See the arrests sections in this chapter.)

It is a crime for your employer to possess any arrest information of this sort. It is a crime for anyone to communicate this kind of information to your employer. It is a crime for a police officer or any other law enforcement employee to disclose any arrest information with the intent of affecting your job.

Arrest information includes any data about:

(1) the fact that you were arrested;

(2) the alleged offense for which you were arrested;

(3) the outcome of the arrest or charge.

These rules apply to all information about arrests, whether the data comes from "rap sheets" or from any other law enforcement source.

LAW: Labor Code sections 432.7, and 433; Penal Code sections 11,140-11,143 and 13,302-13,304; Title 11 California Administrative Code sections 701-708.

ENFORCEMENT: Attorney General; district attorney; civil action.

An employer may be liable to treble damages, attorney's fees, six months in prison, and a $500 fine.

EXCEPTIONS: See the other arrest and police records sections in this chapter.

## YOUR EMPLOYER MAY NOT REQUIRE YOU TO OBTAIN A COPY OF YOUR POLICE RECORD

As an individual, you have a right to see and copy police records concerning yourself. In most cases, however, it is unlawful for your employer to obtain police records about you. To get around this law, an employer might require you to get a copy of your own record (and show it to the employer.)

Or an employer might require you to ask for a copy of your record, so that you could prove that you do not have a police record.

Neither requirement is legal. Moreover it is illegal for an employer to base hiring, firing, promotion, or transfer--in whole or in part--upon obtaining or not obtaining police records.

LAW: Penal Code sections 11,125 and 13,326.

ENFORCEMENT: Attorney General; district attorney; civil action. (Labor Code section 432.7 may also apply, allowing recovery of treble damages and attorney's fees.)

Violation is a crime. An employer is subject to six months in prison for each violation.


## YOU HAVE THE RIGHT TO NOT HAVE YOUR EX-FELON OR PAROLE STATUS COMMUNICATED TO YOUR EMPLOYER OR PROSPECTIVE EMPLOYER

It is in the interests of society that ex-offenders be able to earn a decent living. No one benefits if people are forced to turn to crime to earn a living. Therefore, the laws prohibit communicating ex-offender information with the purpose of depriving the person of work.

These laws apply if you are an ex-felon or if you are on parole.

No one can inform your employer of your ex-felon status in an effort to get you fired or demoted. No one can inform a prospective employer of your status in an effort to keep you from being hired. No one can inform a non-employer of your status, hoping that the information will be passed on to an employer.

The law applies to people you met in jail, to police, district attorneys, court and probation personnel, in fact, to everyone.

**LAW:** Penal Code sections 2947 and 3058.

**ENFORCEMENT:** District attorney; civil action (for damages).

Violation is a misdemeanor, punishable by six months in jail and a $500 fine.

**EXCEPTIONS:** There are no exceptions. Anyone who communicates any ex-felon information to your employer, with the intent of depriving you of work, is in violation of the law. This intent may be inferred from the person's actions. No one has the legal duty to contact your employer and tell her or him of your ex-felon status: such an act is a crime.

The Department of Corrections may provide information concerning your parole status to the police chief or sheriff where you reside, so long as you are on parole. (See also the sections on police and arrest records in this chapter.)

## CHAPTER 4

## WAGES, FRINGE BENEFITS, AND HOURS OF WORK

### WAGES ARE YOUR PROPERTY

Wages in California are a special kind of property. Once you earn your wages, you are entitled to receive them in full. Once your employer agrees to pay you a certain wage or salary for your work, s/he cannot then (retroactively) pay you a lesser amount. Any benefits your employer agrees to grant you in addition to your cash wages are also your property and are protected in the same manner as your cash wages. For example, your employer may agree to pay commissions, bonuses, fringe benefits, pensions, paid time off (leave, vacation, sabbatical, mental health days, sick leave, disability leave, paid leave of absence, paid holidays), call-back pay, reporting pay, stand-by pay, etc. Once earned, those benefits become your property and are also defined as "wages."

LAW: Labor Code sections 200, 216, and 219-225; California Constitution, Article I, section 9.

ENFORCEMENT: Labor commissioner; civil action.

### WAGE CLAIMS AND COMPLAINTS TO THE LABOR COMMISSIONER

You should keep a diary of your wage rate and actual hours of work. In the event that you do not immediately recognize a violation, you will have records on which to base a complaint at a later date (as long as it is within the time limit).

Complaints and claims for wages must be filed in the county in which the wages were earned or where the violation of law occurred. Complaints are filed on a form, DLSE 1, which can be obtained from any deputy labor commissioner's office.

The complaint form may be filled out in the office of the deputy labor commissioner, or completed at home and then mailed or hand-carried back.

When you file a complaint, you may request subpenas from the deputy labor commissioner to ensure that a certain person or a certain record will be present at the hearing on your complaint.

You may want to subpena both friendly and unfriendly witnesses. If you need another employee to testify, the subpena will give your co-worker additional protections against retaliation. This may make him or her feel more comfortable about giving honest testimony against your employer.

After you file your complaint, the deputy labor commissioner will send a notice to your employer. The deputy labor commissioner conducts an investigation of the complaint and then schedules one of two kinds of hearings: a 98(a) hearing or a 98.3 hearing.

Hearings conducted by the deputy labor commissioner are informal. You may choose to be represented by an attorney, but this is not required. The hearings are tape recorded and witnesses are required to testify under oath. You have the right to cross-examine the employer as well as other opposition witnesses.

The major difference between the two types of hearings concerns compliance and appeal:

For a 98(a) hearing, the decision of the deputy labor commissioner is final and binding and can be enforced as a court order unless appealed within 10 days.

For a 98.3 hearing, the decision of the deputy labor commissioner is not binding: compliance is voluntary. If the employer does not comply with the deputy labor commissioner's decision, the commissioner must then take the issue(s) to the courts. If you are dissatisfied with the decision or actions of the labor commissioner, you may pursue your complaint in court.

LAW: Labor Code sections 92, 93, and 98-98.3; Title 8 California Administrative Code sections 13500-13510; Labor Standards Enforcement Division Memo 76-15.

## WAGE CLAIMS AND COMPLAINTS TO THE LABOR COMMISSIONER: TIME LIMITS

It is important to file wage claims and complaints in a timely manner. If you do not have a written contract of employment, you generally have two years in which to file a wage claim with the labor commissioner. If you are filing a complaint under the Equal Pay Act, you have two years to file. If you have a written employment contract, you have four years to make a wage claim.

Complaints of retaliation made under Cal-OSHA have very short time limits (30 days). (See Chapter 5, WORKING CONDITIONS: SAFETY, HEALTH AND SANITATION.) Complaints of retaliation for making a complaint to the labor commissioner also have a 30-day time limit.

**LAW:** Code of Civil Procedure sections 337-339; Labor Code sections 98.6, 98.7, 1197.5, 6311, and 6312.

**EXCEPTIONS:** There are many exceptions to all time limits. Even if you think you might have delayed too long, file anyway and discuss your case with your union or lawyer.

## PAID WORK TIME

You must be paid for all hours that you work. This includes any time that you are "under the control" of your employer, even if you are only answering the phone or waiting for work. In other words, you must be paid for all time that you are "on duty," whether or not you are performing the specific functions of your job. You are off-duty only when **all** of the following apply:

(1) You have no job functions at all.

(2) The off-duty period of time is lengthy enough to be used effectively for your own purposes.

(3) You can leave the premises and do whatever you want.

(4) You know beforehand when the off-duty time will begin and when it will end.

In addition to regular work time, you must usually be paid for all time spent in the following activities:

(1) Meetings, lectures, and training programs required by your employer.

(2) Travel time used in the course of your employment (other than time spent commuting to and from your regular work location).

(3) Writing reports or completing paperwork related to your job.

(4) Civic or charitable functions, when required by your employer.

(5) Suggestion systems, quality of worklife circles, and grievance committees (unless waived by collective bargaining agreement).

(6) Rest breaks.

(7) Some van pooling programs.

(8) Washing or changing clothes (under some circumstances).

(9) Other preparatory and concluding activities (under most circumstances).

(10) Waiting for and receiving medical attention or exams on your employer's premises or at his/her direction during working hours.

Your employer must pay you for all the time you work, even if it is outside of regular hours. You must be paid whether you work at home, or at the worksite, or while traveling. Your employer has this responsibility even if s/he has a rule or instruction against this kind of work. S/he has this responsibility, even if s/he does not request you to do this work. In fact, you must be paid for all the time you work, even if your employer has a rule against working after hours (if after-hours work is allowed, despite the rule).

It is unlawful for your employer to retaliate against you for making a demand for payment. If you have any questions about hours worked in your specific industry, contact your union and the labor commissioner and the U.S. Department of Labor, Wage and Hour Division. (See APPENDIX for the appropriate addresses and telephone numbers.)

> **LAW**: Labor Code sections 200 and 1195.5; Industrial Welfare Commission Orders section 2 (G, H, M, N, O); Title 29 U.S. Code sections 201-219 (Fair Labor Standards Act); Labor Standards Enforcement Division Memo 84-6 (Revised).

> **ENFORCEMENT**: Labor commissioner; U.S. Dept. of Labor, Wage and Hour Division; civil action.

> **EXCEPTIONS:** White collar*; fire protection and law enforcement employees of a public agency with fewer than five such employees; outside salespersons.*

## YOU MUST BE PAID AT LEAST THE MINIMUM WAGE

Both the State of California and the federal government set a legal minimum wage. You must be paid at least the higher of the two rates (if they differ). The current rate for both the federal and state minimum wage is $3.35 per hour. It is unlawful for your employer to pay less than the minimum wage.

Some workers may be entitled to a higher minimum wage. If your employer is receiving state or federal funds, or if you work in a convalescent hospital or other long term care facility receiving MediCal funding, contact your union or enforcement agency to determine your legal minimum wage.

It is illegal for any amount to be credited or off-set against the minimum wage. For example, in California there is no tip credit; your employer cannot reduce your wage by the amount of tips you receive.

**LAW:** Labor Code sections 210, 1197, 1197.1, and 1199; Title 8 California Administrative Code section 11,000; Industrial Welfare Commission Orders, section 4; Title 29 U.S. Code section 206 (Fair Labor Standards Act).

**ENFORCEMENT:** Labor commissioner; U.S. Dept. of Labor, Wage and Hour Division; civil action.

Your employer is subject to a fine (for each underpaid employee) of $50.00 per pay period and $100 for each subsequent violation.

**EXCEPTIONS:**

(1) Apprentices (in certain industries) regularly indentured under the state Apprenticeship Standards Divison .

(2) Certain handicapped workers in sheltered workshops licensed by the state under Labor Code sections 1191-1193 and the Industrial Welfare Commission Orders section 6 (for state exemption) and licensed by the U.S. Department of Labor (for federal exemption).

(3) Certain learners*, minors, and white collar* workers.

(4) Outside salespeople*.

(5) Attendants, babysitters and companions*.


**PROMISED WAGES MUST BE PAID**

When your employer agrees to or promises to pay a certain wage, that is a binding contract.

No employer may lawfully hire a worker, knowing that agreed wages and benefits will likely not be paid

No employer may lawfully hire a worker who has been encouraged to accept the job by false or misleading statements.

It is evidence of intent to defraud if the employer hires any worker without advising that person of:

(1) every wage claim against the employer due and unpaid, and

(2) every judgment that the employer has been unable to pay. In other words, if the employer has not paid some worker in the past, s/he must inform each new worker of that fact. If the employer does not do so, and then does not pay the new worker on time and in full, that employer has committed a serious crime.

**LAW:** Labor Code sections 206, 216, 222, 223, and 225; Penal Code section 484(a).

**ENFORCEMENT:** Labor commissioner; district attorney; civil action.

**EXCEPTIONS:** Public employees.

Note that unless your wage agreement is for a specific length of time (such as the usual collective bargaining agreement), your employer can give you notice and unilaterally change your future wage rate.


## WAGES MUST BE PAID ON TIME

Your employer must post a notice, where you can see it, stating the schedule of paydays. Your employer must adhere to this schedule. Unless you are covered by a collective bargaining agreement which provides otherwise, you must be paid at least twice a month. For work which you do between the first and fifteenth of the month, you must be paid between the sixteenth and the last day of the same month. For work that you do between the sixteenth and the last day of the month, you must be paid between the first and the tenth day of the following month.

You must be paid not more than seven calendar days following the close of the pay period if you are paid on a weekly basis. Your employer may be fined for failure to pay on time. If you are covered by a collective bargaining agreement, the pay provisions of the agreement apply.

It is unlawful for your employer to pay with a voucher or out-of-state check which cannot be immediately turned into cash.

**LAW**: Labor Code sections 204, 205.5, 207, 212, and 220.

**ENFORCEMENT**: Labor commissioner; civil action.

**EXCEPTIONS**: Public employees; farm laborers and domestics who receive meals and lodging from their employers (must be paid at least monthly); white collar* employees (must be paid at least monthly); vehicle sales commissions (must be paid monthly).

All overtime wages must be paid no later than the payday for the next regular pay period.

For wage payments upon discharge, quitting, or layoff, see Chapter 8, DISCIPLINE AND DISCHARGE.


## YOU ARE ENTITLED TO AN ITEMIZED WAGE STATEMENT

At the time of each payment of wages, your employer must furnish an itemized wage statement. For wages paid by check, draft, or voucher, the statement must show:

(1) gross wages earned;

(2) total hours worked (by each employee whose compensation is based on an hourly wage);

(3) all deductions (all voluntary deductions may be shown as one total);

(4) net wages earned;

(5) the inclusive dates of the period for which you are paid;

(6) your name or social security number; and

(7) the name and address of your employer.

For cash wages, the statement must show:

(1) all deductions;

(2) total hours worked (by each employee whose compensation is based on an hourly wage);

(3) the dates of the period for which you are paid;

(4) your name or social security number; and

(5) the name of the employer.

**LAW:** Labor Code sections 226-226.6; Industrial Welfare Commission Orders, section 7.

**ENFORCEMENT:** Labor commissioner; civil action.

You may collect actual damages or $100 (whichever is greater), plus attorney's fees, from your employer for any violation. Your employer may be fined $1000 and is subject to one year in jail.

**EXCEPTIONS:** Public employees.


## PAYMENT OF UNDISPUTED WAGES IS MANDATORY

Your employer must pay the wages due you. If you and your employer do not agree on the amount of wages due, your employer must **immediately** pay you the portion of the wages you both agree is due. S/he **cannot** hold back the money s/he admits owing you and wait until the "whole thing is straightened out." If you say that you are owed $450 and your employer says that you are owed $400, s/he **must** pay you the undisputed $400 at once.

These are your rights even if you sign a release or settlement or paycheck which says "payment in full," or "for all wages," or any other similar words. It is illegal to force you to sign any statement of this kind.

**LAW:** Labor Code sections 206, 206.5, 216, 218 and 220.

**ENFORCEMENT:** Labor commissioner; district attorney; civil action.

**EXCEPTIONS:** Public employees.

## IT IS ILLEGAL TO MISREPRESENT THE SALARY OR COMMISSION OF SALESPEOPLE, BROKERS, OR AGENTS

If you are going to work as a salesperson, or a broker, or an agent, you have a right to know the commission or compensation you may earn. This right exists whether you are going to work as an employee or as an independent contractor.

It is illegal for anyone to misrepresent the commissions or compensation which prospective salespeople, brokers, or agents will earn or the method of calculating the compensation.

**LAW:** Labor Code sections 976 and 977.

**ENFORCEMENT:** Labor commissioner; district attorney; civil action.

**EXCEPTIONS:** A newspaper or magazine publisher who accepts an ad in good faith is not guilty of misrepresentation.

## YOU HAVE A RIGHT TO EQUAL PAY FOR EQUAL WORK

It is illegal for an employer to pay you less than is paid to other workers, if the difference is on account of your sex. This is the law under state and federal Equal Pay Acts. It is unlawful for you to be paid less than a member of the opposite sex, if all of the following conditions are met:

(1) The job content of the work is substantially equal.

(2) The jobs require substantially equal skill (experience, training, or education).

(3) The jobs require approximately equal effort (mental or physical energy).

(4) The jobs have a comparable degree of accountability (responsibility).

(5) The jobs have similar working conditions (a comparable physical and psychological work environment and hazards).

The five tests listed above are applied to the **actual** content of the jobs (requirements and performance), not to the job descriptions. The two jobs (your job and the job held by a member of the opposite sex) do **not** have to be held simultaneously for this law to apply.

The two jobs being compared **do** have to be in the same establishment. (This means either in the same location or under a central administration with some connection of work or employees.) The employer can pay a wage differential based on seniority, quantity or quality of production, bona fide differences in job tasks, or a bona fide merit system.

It is illegal to reduce a worker's pay in order to comply with this law. For example, the employer cannot lower a man's pay to achieve equality for a woman; the woman's pay must be raised.

LAW: Labor Code sections 98.7, 1197.5 and 1199.5; Government Code section 12940; Title 29 U.S. Code sections 206 and 201-219; Title 42 U.S. Code section 2000e-2; Title 29 Code of Federal Regulations Part 1620; Title 2 California Administrative Code section 7291.1; Labor Standards Enforcement Division Memo 79-2; Fair Employment and Housing Case 81-12 (CEB #24 80-81).

ENFORCEMENT: Labor commissioner; Equal Employment Opportunity Commission; district attorney; civil action.

Violation may be a misdemeanor. A civil action can obtain double back pay plus attorney's fees.

EXCEPTIONS: Unlike many federal wage and hour laws, the federal Equal Pay Act **does** cover administrators, executives, professionals, outside salespersons, and state and local government workers. Those few employees not covered by the federal Act are covered by the state Act.

## LAWFUL DEDUCTIONS FROM YOUR WAGES

Your employer may lawfully deduct money from your wages only if the deduction is for one (or more) of the following reasons:

(1) federal or state taxes which are legally required to be withheld;

(2) Social Security or state disability insurance (SDI) contributions which are legally required to be withheld;

(3) court-ordered wage garnishments or wage "assignments" for child support or family support (see also section on child support payments in this chapter);

(4) legal deductions by federal or state tax collectors for back taxes which you personally owe the government;

(5) employee-ordered contributions to charities, purchases of U.S. bonds, and deposits in banks and credit unions;

(6) employee-ordered payment of union dues, assessments, or initiation fees;

(7) legitimate employee-ordered wage assignments (see section on wage assignments in this chapter);

(8) legitimate employee contributions to retirement plans, fringe-benefit plans, insurance, or hospital or medical plans.

**LAW:** Labor Code sections 221-227 and 300; Code of Civil Procedure sections 483.010, 487.020, and 706.011.

**ENFORCEMENT:** Labor commissioner; district attorney; civil action.

## UNLAWFUL DEDUCTIONS FROM YOUR WAGES

It is illegal for your employer or supervisor to require or receive a "kickback" of any amount from your wages. Your employer can never require that you pay back any amount of legitimate wages already paid to you.

Employers are not allowed to collect debts by deductions or withholding from wages. If your employer thinks that you owe him/her a certain amount, the employer is in exactly the same situation as anyone else: s/he can try to reach a voluntary settlement with you in which you agree to pay the owed amount. If no agreement is reached, the employer can go to court and sue you. If you and the employer are already in court, or are before a labor commissioner, then s/he can try to convince the judge or labor commissioner that you owe the money. What your employer **cannot** do is deduct her/his claim from your wages (or deposit, or bonus, or commission, or fringe benefit).

Your employer **cannot** deduct or withhold from your pay, or require that you pay (before receiving your wages), any of the following:

(1) money supposedly owed for negligence, or theft, or losses or shortages, or errors, or no-shows, or fines, or penalties, or breakage, or customer walkout;

(2) money you borrowed from the employer or from a fellow worker;

(3) money which the employer advanced to you against wages;

(4) wages which were paid to you in error or as an overpayment;

(5) money you spent, on the employer's account, which you were not authorized to spend;

(6) money which you owe the employer as the result of a stock purchase plan, or for purchase of goods or services from the employer or any company store;

(7) money owed for rent or other employer-provided services;

(8) money supposedly due for lost or non-returned tools, or safety gear, or uniforms, or merchandise, or any other equipment or advances;

(9) any amount for delays in computing or claiming wages.

LAW: Labor Code sections 200-203, 216, 221-227, 300, and 400-410; Code of Civil Procedure section 483.010, 487.020, and 706.011; Wage-Hour Division Opinion Letters 1219 and 1303; Title 29 Code of Federal Regulations sections 531.35, 531.39, and 531.40.

ENFORCEMENT: Labor commissioner; district attorney; civil action.

In many cases violation is a crime.

EXCEPTIONS: The state Labor Commissioner has issued a memo, 85-3, suggesting that some employer deductions may be allowed. The memo indicates that labor commissioners will allow employers to deduct amounts allegedly due as a result of dishonesty, willful misconduct, or gross negligence (provided the employer can prove this at a hearing). The memo also indicates that labor commissioners will allow employers to deduct regular repayment amounts from your regular paychecks, if you have signed an agreement providing for this, in order to pay back money you have been advanced by the employer. But labor commissioners will not allow employers to collect the total amount still owed from your final paycheck if you leave or are terminated, and will collect up to 30 days extra pay for you if this is done.

If your employer has deducted money for one of these reasons, you may want to go to small claims court or consult an attorney or your union, rather than go to the labor commissioner.

## YOU CANNOT BE REQUIRED TO SIGN WAGE RELEASES OR WAIVERS

Your employer can never require you to sign or agree to any release, assignment, waiver, or settlement of wages. This law protects wages you have already earned. It even protects money which your employer advanced or loaned to you (before you earned it). Any wage release or waiver of this sort is null and void.

Your employer **can** have you sign a receipt for money or a paycheck received by you. This receipt cannot, however, include any waiver or any statement that is a compromise of other claims.

LAW: Labor Code section 206.5; Business and Professions Code section 7110.1; Harbors and Navigation Code section 864.

ENFORCEMENT: Labor commissioner; district attorney; civil action.

Any employer or supervisor who violates this law and makes you sign a release or waiver is guilty of a crime.

EXCEPTIONS: Public employees.

## YOUR EMPLOYER CANNOT SECRETLY PAY YOU LESS THAN SCALE

Your wages may be set by law (for example, the minimum wage or the prevailing wage); or by a union contract; or by agreement between yourself and the employer. It is illegal for your employer to agree to pay you a certain wage or salary, and then to actually pay you a lesser amount.

It is illegal for your employer to withhold any part of the wages due under a union contract.

LAW: Labor Code sections 216, 222, 223, 225 and 225.5.

ENFORCEMENT: Labor commissioner; district attorney; civil action.

If your employer knows that you are owed a certain amount of wages, but denies this; or if your employer knows that you are owed a certain amount of wages, but refuses to pay you, s/he is guilty of a crime and is subject to six months in jail and a $500 fine.

**EXCEPTIONS:** The criminal penalties do not apply to public sector employers.

## BONUSES ARE SUBJECT TO THE SAME PROTECTIONS AS OTHER WAGES

Sometimes an employer may attempt to get around the laws by redefining wages. For example the employer may state (in a contract or notice) that the workers' wages are the minimum wage (or some similarly small amount), and that every dollar paid above that minimum is a "bonus" or is paid "solely within the discretion" of the employer. Therefore, the employer says, s/he can deduct fines out of the bonus, or can collect large amounts for meals or lodging, or otherwise treat the bonus as if it were not wages.

But laws apply to the reality of a situation, not just to the words used. If in fact there is an agreement, or an understanding, or a practice to pay the bonus, then the bonus is legally considered wages.

All fines, deductions, or charges used to reduce the bonus or the discretionary wages are illegal. Affected workers should be sure to keep careful records of all such deductions.

**LAW:** Labor Code sections 200, 206.5, 216, 219, 221, 225 and 225.5.

**ENFORCEMENT:** Labor commissioner; district attorney; civil action.

**EXCEPTIONS:** Public employees.

## ALL WAGE FINES AND PENALTIES ARE ILLEGAL

Your employer can **never** "fine" you. S/he cannot take a fine out of your paycheck. S/he cannot make you pay a fine out of your pocket. Fines and penalties are illegal, whether they go to your employer, a supervisor, a fellow worker, a charity, the coffee fund, or even to a fund which may be repaid to you. You cannot be fined for swearing or for any other acts or omissions.

LAW: Labor Code sections 221, 224, 225 and 225.5.

ENFORCEMENT: Labor commissioner; district attorney; civil action.

Collecting any fines or penalties is a crime. The supervisor or employer responsible for any fine is subject to six months in jail and a $500 fine.

EXCEPTIONS: The criminal penalties do not apply in the public sector.

## YOUR EMPLOYER MUST REIMBURSE YOU FOR MOST LOSSES YOU SUSTAIN ON THE JOB

You do not have to subsidize your employer's business. Therefore, if you have to spend money or use up your property in order to carry out your job duties, you have a right to be reimbursed by your employer.

The key is whether or not the money you spent was "necessarily" expended. If you could have done the job without the expenditure, then you may not get your funds back (unless you have either a personal or a union agreement that such expenses will be reimbursed). If you necessarily spent the money, however, your employer must reimburse you.

The same rule applies to anything you lose as a direct consequence of your job. If your employer tells you to do something, and that directly causes a loss, your employer must make it up to you.

A similar rule applies when you suffer any harm or loss due to your employer's "want of ordinary care." For example, if your car is parked in the company lot, and the company negligently releases smoke which damages your car's paint, then the company owes you a new paint job. Or, if your employer arranges for you to leave your tools at work in a locked area, but then forgets to lock up one night, and your tools are stolen--the employer owes you a new set of tools.

**Musical Instruments and Equipment** -- A special rule protects this type of property. Whoever controls the premises where an employed musician leaves such gear is responsible for its safe-keeping. If such gear is damaged or stolen as a result of a failure to take reasonable and necessary precautions, the person in control of the premises is liable for the repair or replacement of the gear. This is broader than the rules outlined above. It applies the usual employer responsibility to (1) the actual employer of the musician, (2) any purchaser of musical services (even if not technically an "employer"), and (3) the owner of the premises upon which an employed musician is working (even if the owner is not an employer and is not the purchaser of the services).

LAW: Labor Code sections 2800, 2800.1, 2802, and 2804.

ENFORCEMENT: Labor commissioner; civil action.

No contract or agreement can waive or give away these rights.

EXCEPTIONS: The rules apply to any loss resulting from obedience to the directions of the employer, even if those directions are unlawful. The only exception is that if the worker **knew**, at the time s/he obeyed the orders, that they were unlawful, then s/he cannot collect reimbursement for resulting losses. For required tools see **In Most Cases Your Employer Must Furnish Tools and Equipment** in this chapter.

## GENERALLY YOU ARE NOT RESPONSIBLE FOR YOUR EMPLOYER'S LOSSES

Except for the areas described below, you are **not** financially responsible for your employer's business. You cannot be made responsible for losses outside your control. You cannot be made responsible for losses caused by mere negligence. If customers walk out without paying, or if merchandise is unaccountably missing, or if the usual hustle and bustle results in spillage and/or breakage, each is the employer's loss, not yours. The employer cannot demand reimbursement for these kinds of losses. The employer cannot base your pay on a formula which reduces your pay when there are losses, or shortages, or breakage.

In certain circumstances, however, you **may** be responsible to your employer for some losses.

(1) Dishonest or willful acts: If you steal from the employer, or help someone else to do so, or destroy the employer's property **on purpose**, you are responsible.

(2) Gross negligence: If your employer can prove gross negligence, as opposed to an error or a mistake, you may be liable for the loss. But in general, losses due to recording incorrect prices, or making errors in addition, or failing to include all items in a bill are **not** considered gross negligence. Generally you are **not** responsible for shortages in your cash box or till.

It is important to remember that even though your employer may not demand reimbursement for losses, s/he may fire you for even an honest mistake, if you do not have the protection of a union contract. If your employer fires you for dishonesty and you are innocent, you may have grounds for a "wrongful discharge" suit. (See Chapter 8, DISCIPLINE AND DISCHARGE.)

LAW: Labor code sections 200-203, 216, 221, 225, 225.5 and 400-410; Code of Civil Procedure section 483.010, 487.020, and 706.011; Labor Standards Enforcement Division Memo 82.2 and 85-3. Industrial Welfare Commission Orders on this topic are enjoined and not enforced.

**ENFORCEMENT**: Labor commissioner; district attorney; civil action.

## YOUR EMPLOYER MUST PAY YOUR LEGAL EXPENSES IF YOU ARE SUED FOR JOB-RELATED REASONS

If you are sued because of your job, your employer normally must pay for your legal defense. If you lose the law suit, the employer must usually pay the damages, costs, and other amounts which the court tells you to pay. These rules apply to any law suit which is based on something you did--or neglected to do--in the course of doing your job.

Usually when you are sued in connection with your work, your employer will also be sued. It is better for you to have a separate attorney, and not share a lawyer with your employer. The employer (or the employer's insurance company) is usually responsible for paying this separate attorney, but **you** have the final say about legal strategy no matter who is paying the bill.

It is hard for an attorney to represent two interests at once. Usually there will be a conflict between your interests and those of the employer (or insurance company). If you have any questions about these matters, be sure to talk with an **independent lawyer**, not one who is suggested by your employer's attorney. The latter may simply repeat what s/he has heard from your employer's lawyer.

These rights always apply; you cannot give them up or lose them. Even if you have signed a release, a contract, a settlement, or an agreement to the contrary, you still have these rights. Even if you have agreed with your employer that you are an independent contractor, you still have these rights.

LAW: Labor Code sections 2802 and 2804; Government Code section 825; Civil Code sections 2338 and 2772; State Bar of California Rules of Professional Conduct Rule 5-102.

ENFORCEMENT: Civil action; complaint to the State Bar of California; complaint to the judge hearing your case;

malpractice action against attorney (there are lawyers who specialize in suing other lawyers).

## YOUR TIPS AND GRATUITIES ARE YOUR PROPERTY

A tip left by a patron is your property, and yours alone. This applies to cash tips and to credit card tips. Your employer cannot credit any part of that tip or gratuity against your wages. Your employer cannot give any part of that tip to anyone else. Your employer cannot make a private agreement with you or any other employee or labor union which violates the intent of this law. Your employer must keep an accurate record of all tips and gratuities which s/he receives (either as credit card tips, to be passed on to you, or otherwise).

Credit card tips must be paid by the next regular pay day, even if the employer has not yet collected from the credit card company.

LAW: Labor Code sections 350-356; Business and Professions Code section 17200; Wage and Hour Division Opinion Letter 1571; Labor Standards Enforcement Division Memo 85-4.

ENFORCEMENT: Labor commissioner; district attorney; civil action.

Violation is a crime; the employer is subject to 60 days in jail and a $500 fine.

EXCEPTIONS: This law does not apply to employees of certain unique operations. To be exempt, the operation must make **no charge at all** to its patrons; the employees must be guaranteed their wages irrespective of tips. This exemption is for operations such as valet parking concessions where the customer's cars are parked for free. The **only** income received by the concession operator is the "tips."

Tip sharing is allowed only if all the involved employees agree to share. No one can be forced to participate in a tip sharing pool.

## SERVICE CHARGES MUST BE SHARED AMONG THE WORKERS

A service charge is not a "tip." A service charge is a fixed, mandatory fee, subject to sales tax, charged to the patron by the establishment. The entire amount of the service charge must be distributed among those actually providing the following services: setting up, preparing food and beverages, serving, and cleaning up. No more than 25% may be distributed to employees involved in the selling, planning, or arranging of the function. No one having greater than 5% ownership or interest in the establishment may share in the distribution of the service charge.

**LAW**: Labor Code sections 350-356; Labor Standards Enforcement Division Memo 82-5.

**ENFORCEMENT**: Labor commissioner; civil action.

**EXCEPTIONS**: (1) A valid collective bargaining agreement can specify a different distribution of service charges.

(2) If the collective bargaining agreement is silent on distribution of service charges, then existing labor-management practice applies, as long as it is known and accepted by the union representing the employee.

(3) In a non-union establishment, the employer may vary the 75%/25% rule only after notifying patrons how the service charge will be distributed.

(4) An employee who is actually involved in the function can be excluded from the distribution only if: (a) s/he earns at least one and three-quarters times the minimum wage; and (b) has received advance written notice of his/her exclusion.

## IN MOST CASES YOUR EMPLOYER MUST FURNISH TOOLS AND EQUIPMENT

When you need tools or equipment to do your job, or when tools and equipment are required by your employer, they must be provided by your employer.

Your employer may require a deposit as security for these tools and/or equipment. This kind of a deposit is considered a "cash bond" and is subject to the regulations governing cash bonds. The amount of the bond cannot exceed the value of the tools; and you must be given a receipt. (See also Chapter 2, HIRING RIGHTS.) If the tools and/or equipment are worn and must be repaired or replaced, your employer must pay for them.

Your employer must furnish any tools and/or equipment which are necessary for safety under Cal/OSHA. For example, if heavy-duty insulated gloves are required for safety to do certain kinds of electrical work, those gloves must be provided by the employer. (See Chapter 5, WORKING CONDITIONS: SAFETY, HEALTH, AND SANITATION.)

Your employer may not deduct the cost of lost or unreturned tools or equipment from your pay, even though you have signed a prior authorization to that effect. However, you may owe your employer for the cost of the tools and s/he may take legal action to receive payment from you.

LAW: Labor Code sections 216-222, 96(g), 400-410, 98.3(a), 2802, 2804, 6306, 6401, and 6403; Code of Civil Procedure section 483.010, 487.020, and 706.011; Title 8 California Administrative Code section 3380-3412 and 3556; Industrial Welfare Commission Orders section 9; Title 29 Code of Federal Regulations sections 531.32(c) and 531.35.

ENFORCEMENT: Labor commissioner; civil action.

EXCEPTIONS: Lawfully indentured apprentices; public employees; barbers and beauticians; employees whose wages are at least two times the minimum wage; and IWC exceptions.*

There are no exceptions to the deposit/cash bond rules, the safety equipment rules, or the pay deduction rules.

Exceptions only apply to the rule stated in the first paragraph.

## IN MOST CASES YOUR EMPLOYER MUST REIMBURSE YOU FOR USING YOUR CAR

If your employer requires you to furnish your own car or truck, to be used in the course of your job, you must be paid for all costs necessarily incurred in its use. The rate of reimbursement can be agreed to by you and your employer; otherwise the labor commissioner or court will determine a reasonable amount. You must be reimbursed for: gas, oil, and servicing required for the job; any additional insurance you must obtain; any deductibles or other uninsured losses resulting from work-related uses; and a reasonable amount for depreciation.

**LAW:** Labor Code sections 2802 and 2804; Labor Standards Enforcement Division Memo 84-7; Title 29 Code of Federal Regulations section 531.32(c).

**ENFORCEMENT:** Labor commissioner; civil action.

## IN MOST CASES A REQUIRED UNIFORM MUST BE PROVIDED AND MAINTAINED BY YOUR EMPLOYER

A uniform is defined as wearing apparel or accessories of distinctive design or color. If your employer requires you to wear a pink dress or a certain style and color jacket, or any other distinctive article of clothing, that is a uniform. If your employer requires you, as a condition of employment, to wear a uniform, s/he must provide that uniform. In addition, your employer must "maintain" that uniform. Maintenance includes dry cleaning, ironing, or separate laundering. Instead of providing maintenance, your employer can pay you a weekly maintenance allowance of at least $3.35 (the minimum wage). If your uniform requires only minimal care, such as washing and tumble or drip drying, you may be responsible for the maintenance yourself, with no allowance. If the uniform becomes worn or torn and must be replaced or repaired, your employer must pay for it.

Your employer may not deduct the cost of a lost or unreturned uniform from your pay, even though you have signed a prior authorization to that effect. However, you may owe the cost of the uniform to your employer, and s/he may take legal action to receive payment from you.

If your employer requires a deposit as security for the uniform s/he provides, the deposit is considered a "cash bond" and is subject to the regulations governing cash bonds. The amount of the bond cannot exceed the value of the uniform(s). (See also Chapter 2, HIRING RIGHTS.)

Certain types of work clothes which are normally thought of as uniforms may not be covered by the law which requires your employer to provide uniforms. These include:

(1) Some types of nurses' uniforms: Classic white nurses' uniforms which can be worn in any hospital or institution may be exempted. However, required pastel uniforms or uniforms distinctive in some way are covered.

(2) Food servers' "black and whites": If an employer specifies white blouse or shirt and black shirt or pants, that uniform may be exempt. If the employer specifies anything more distinctive than just "black and whites" (for example, the style or kind of fabric), then that uniform is covered by this law.

If you are required to wear a uniform which, because of its style or cut, exposes you to sexual harassment, that is a violation of the law. (See also Chapter 8, DISCIPLINE AND DISCHARGE.)

LAW: Labor Code sections 216-222, 400-410, 452, 2802 and 2804; Industrial Welfare Commission Orders section 9; Code of Civil Procedure sections 483.010, 487.020, and 706.011; Labor Standards Enforcement Division Memos 82-2 and 85-3; Title 29 Code of Federal Regulations section 531.32(c).

ENFORCEMENT: Labor commissioner; civil action.

EXCEPTIONS: Public employees; IWC exceptions.* (For purposes of the Industrial Welfare Commission Orders,

RNs are **not** professionals and **are** covered by the wage orders; these uniform rules thus apply to RNs who are not exempt under another exception.)

Your employer must supply protective apparel. (See Chapter 5, WORKING CONDITIONS: SAFETY, HEALTH, AND SANITATION.).

## RULES GOVERNING EMPLOYER-PROVIDED MEALS AND LODGING

In some work environments, it may be necessary or desirable for meals and/or lodging to be provided by your employer. The cost of meals or lodging **cannot** be credited against the minimum wage unless a collective bargaining agreement so provides or you voluntarily agree. If you make a personal agreement with the employer, then (1) it must be in writing, (2) you must get a copy, and (3) you must have the right to cancel it (in writing) at any time (the cancellation to be effective within a month).

When credit for meals and lodging is used as part of the minimum wage, the cost of those meals and lodging is regulated and maximum charges are set by the Industrial Welfare Commission. If you are required to live on the employer's premises, the amount charged for meals and lodging (regardless of the wage paid) is also regulated by the Industrial Welfare Commission. The maximum charges allowed for meals and various kinds of lodging are specified in the Industrial Welfare Commission Orders for each industry.

Meals and lodging provided by employers must meet certain minimum standards. Meals must be nutritious and well-balanced. Lodging must be available to the employee on a full-time basis and must be sanitary and adequate according to customary standards. In general, you cannot be charged for meals that you do not eat.

LAW: Industrial Welfare Commission Orders sections 10 and 11; Title 29 Code of Federal Regulations section 531.29-531.33.

**ENFORCEMENT**: Labor commissioner; civil action.

**EXCEPTIONS**: Public employees; IWC exceptions*; resident apartment managers (Labor Code section 1182.8).

## YOU HAVE A RIGHT TO OVERTIME PAY

**State Law Rules** -- Most workers are protected by state law overtime rules, federal law overtime rules, or by both. You have a right to be paid at one and one-half times your "regular rate of pay" for all hours you work in excess of 8 hours a day and/or in excess of 40 hours a week. You must be paid double your regular rate of pay for time worked in excess of 12 hours in one day and for time worked in excess of 8 hours on the seventh day worked in a week.

It is possible for an employer and a group of employees to agree on an alternative work week based on four 10-hour days. Under this kind of an agreement, overtime at one and one-half times the regular rate of pay must be paid for the time worked in excess of 10 hours a day or 40 hours per week, and for the first eight hours worked on the fifth, sixth or seventh day of work. You must be paid double your regular rate of pay for time worked in excess of 12 hours in one day and for work in excess of eight hours on the fifth, sixth, or seventh day of work. The 4-10 work week schedule must provide at least two consecutive days off per week. In order to adopt a 4-10 work week, the employer and at least two-thirds of the affected employees must voluntarily enter into a written agreement. This agreement will stand for at least 12 months. If after 12 months the employees wish to revoke this agreement, they must present a majority petition to the employer who will conduct a vote of all affected employees. If two-thirds of the employees vote to eliminate the 4-10 work week, the employer has 60 days to reschedule a normal work week.

**Federal Law Rules** -- You must be paid at one and one-half times your "regular rate of pay" for all hours you work in excess of 40 hours in a week.

**State Law. Use of Compensatory Time Off (Comp Time) Instead of Overtime** -- The Division of Labor Standards Enforcement will allow the use of compensatory time off (comp time) rather than overtime pay under the following conditions:

(1) Prior to working overtime, the employee must voluntarily request in writing that s/he be granted compensatory time off in lieu of overtime compensation. In making such a request, the employee must clearly state in writing that s/he wishes to be compensated at the overtime rate in the form of time off from work, rather than in the form of monetary compensation.

(2) The time off must be given at the rate at which it is earned, e.g., one and one-half hours off for one hour of overtime worked from the 8th to the 12th hour in a day and two hours off for one hour of overtime worked after the 12th hour in one day.

(3) The time off must be given in the same work "week" in which it is earned, or before the end of the pay period if the pay period exceeds one work week.

(4) The time off must be given during what would normally be work time.

(5) Records must be kept which accurately reflect overtime earned and taken.

In some cases you will be due overtime pay under federal law which requires time and one-half your regular rate of pay, for all hours in excess of 40 in one week (with no comp time exception).

**Federal Law. Overtime Rights of Public Employees** -- Effective April 15, 1986, public employees will have the right to be paid at the rate of time and one half for hours worked in excess of forty hours a week. (Some public employees are entitled to overtime pay for work **before** April 15, 1986; consult your union or enforcement agency.) The use of compensatory time off (earned at the rate of time and one half for time worked over 40 hours a week) will also be allowed under the following circumstances:

(1) If employees are represented, there must be agreement with their labor organization before the compensatory time option can be allowed.

(2) If employees are not represented by a labor organization, the employer must secure individual agreements with those employees before the work is performed. However, if prior to April 15, 1986, the employer had a regular practice of allowing the accumulation of compensatory time, no individual agreement is necessary for those employed prior to that date.

(3) Employees may not accrue more than a maximum amount of accumulated comp time. The maximum number of hours allowed for safety, emergency and seasonal employees is 480; for all other employees, the maximum is 240 hours. Additional overtime worked must be paid in cash.

(4) An employee who has accumulated compensatory time must be allowed to take the time off within a reasonable period after making the request (so long as the request does not **unduly** disrupt the operation).

It is unlawful to discriminate against an employee or group of employees because they assert the right to receive overtime pay.

LAW: Labor Code sections 510-556; Industrial Welfare Commission Orders, section 3; Labor Standards Enforcement Division Memo 84-2; Title 29 U.S. Code sections 201-219.

ENFORCEMENT: Labor commissioner; U.S. Dept. of Labor, Wage and Hour Division; civil action.

EXCEPTIONS: If you are covered by the state law, all the above protections apply. If you are not covered by the state law, but are covered by federal law, then you must be paid time and one-half for time worked in excess of 40 hours a week.

Exempt from state law only (but protected by federal law): Public employees; on-site construction, logging, mining and drilling employees (except clerical); student nurses.

Exempt from federal or state law or both: white collar* exceptions; outside salespersons*; attendants, babysitters, and companions*; students, apprentices and learners*; certain family members; minors working in agriculture; taxi cab drivers; motion picture theater projectionists; certain employees whose hours are regulated by the U.S. Dept. of Transportation; certain employees of small broadcast stations; certain employees of camps, amusement parks, and ski establishments; employees covered by a union contract in an industry under the Railway Labor Act; fire and law enforcement, or correctional employees of a public agency; seamen and fishermen*; certain salespersons who earn more than one-half of their salary as commissions; hospital workers with approved 8 and 80 back-to-back work week.

## RULES ABOUT A SEVENTH DAY OF WORK

Normally your employer cannot require that you work more than six days in seven. When this is so, your employer cannot legally discipline or discharge you for refusing to work on the seventh day of your work week.

Usually when you do work seven days straight, your employer must pay you one and one-half times your regular rate of pay for all time worked on the seventh day. If you work more than eight hours on that seventh day, your employer must pay you at least twice your regular rate of pay. These seventh-day overtime rules do not apply when your total hours worked that week do not exceed thirty (30) hours and you do not work more than six (6) hours on any one day of that week.

**LAW:** Labor Code sections 510-556, 1182.2, 1182.4, and 1198.3; Industrial Welfare Commission Orders, section 3.

**ENFORCEMENT:** Labor commissioner; district attorney; civil action.

**EXCEPTIONS**: The requirement of at least one day off in seven does **not** apply if any of the following conditions exist:

(1) Your total hours of work do not exceed 30 hours in one week.

(2) Your total hours of work do not exceed 6 hours in any one day.

(3) Your job is covered by a union-negotiated collective bargaining agreement which specifically allows seven straight days.

(4) There is a valid work-related emergency.

(5) The Chief of the Division of Labor Standards Enforcement gives an exemption to your employer.

(6) You work in the railroad industry.

(7) The seventh day of work is the necessary care of animals, crops, or agricultural lands.

(8) The seventh day's work is the protection of life or property from loss or destruction.

(9) The nature of your work reasonably requires that you work seven or more consecutive days, and in each calendar month you receive total days off equal to one day off in seven.

(10) You are a public employee (in most cases).

(11) You handle and prepare agricultural products (in most cases).

(12) You work at an organized camp or a ski establishment.


The overtime rules governing pay for work done on the seventh workday in a week are different from those given above for:

(1) Public employees.

(2) IWC exceptions.*

(3) Workers handling agricultural products after harvest.

(4) Most workers covered by union contracts providing for overtime premiums and a regular rate of pay of at least $4.35 per hour.

(5) Employees making at least one and one-half times the minimum wage, if more than 50% of their pay comes from commissions.

(6) Employees of a hospital with a legal 8 and 80 back-to-back work week.

(7) Ambulance drivers and attendants with employer-provided dormitories and kitchens and a written agreement.

(8) Irrigators.

(9) Employees in an organized camp or ski establishment.

(10) Airline workers who have requested a temporary change of schedule.

(11) Motion picture projectionists.

(12) Certain broadcasting industry workers in small cities.

(13) Certain workers in the motion picture and television film and video tape industry.


The following workers receive at least one and one-half times their regular rate of pay for all hours worked on the seventh consecutive workday (but no mandatory double time required by law):

(1) Resident managers of homes for the aged having fewer than eight beds.

(2) Employees with direct responsibility for children under 18 who receive 24-hour-a-day care in an institution or similar establishment.

(3) Personal attendants employed by a nonprofit organization to babysit or supervise, feed or dress a child or person needing supervision because of age, disability, or mental deficiency, so long as the attendant does "no significant amount" of other work.

## YOU HAVE A RIGHT TO REST BREAKS AND MEAL PERIODS

You have a right to a 10 minute paid rest break for every four hours you work. The rest break should be taken in the middle of the four hour period.

When you work a shift in excess of six hours, you have a right to a 30 minute unpaid meal period. If your job is such that some duties must continue through the meal period, or you must be available to handle emergencies, you must be paid for the whole meal period. (You must agree in writing to an on duty meal period.)

If your total work period is not more than six hours, you and your employer may waive your right to a meal period.

**LAW**: Industrial Welfare Commission Orders, sections 11 and 12.

**ENFORCEMENT**: Labor commissioner; civil action.

**EXCEPTIONS**: IWC exceptions.*

In the motion picture and television film and video tape industries you cannot work more than six hours without a meal period.

## SPLIT SHIFT PREMIUM PAY

If your employer requires you to take an unpaid break, other than a bona fide rest or meal break, you are working a split shift. If your employer requires you to work a split shift and you are paid minimum wage, you must be paid a premium of $3.35 for that shift. If you are paid above minimum wage, what you earn per shift above minimum wage is deducted from the $3.35. For example, if you earn $3.55 per hour and work an 8-hour shift, the amount you earn above minimum wage for that shift is $1.60. That is deducted from the $3.35, leaving a total premium of $1.75 per shift.

LAW: Industrial Welfare Commission Orders, section 4.

ENFORCEMENT: Labor commissioner; civil action.

EXCEPTIONS: IWC exceptions*; lawfully indentured apprentices; employees who reside at the place of employment. If you are covered by a union contract paying a higher premium, this rule does not apply.


## YOU MUST BE PAID IF YOU REPORT TO WORK

If you report to work for your regular shift and are given less than one-half the usual hours of work or are furnished no work at all, you must be paid for at least one-half your regular shift hours or at least two hours, whichever is greater. If you report to work a second time in one workday, for instance, reporting for the second part of a split shift, or reporting (after a break) for overtime work, you must be paid for at least two hours.

If you are called in, at any time, for an unspecified number of hours but are not furnished any work, you must be paid at least two hours for reporting in.

LAW: Industrial Welfare Commission Orders, section 5.

ENFORCEMENT: Labor commissioner; civil action.

EXCEPTIONS: IWC exceptions*.

If the lack of work is caused by some unexpected or unusual occurrence (such as a power failure), and if your employer made a reasonable attempt to notify you not to report, then reporting time pay may not apply.

When you are receiving "stand by" pay and are called in to work, reporting time pay may not apply (unless covered by Industrial Welfare Commission Order 15).

If you report to a regular shift of more than eight hours, you may not receive more than four hours reporting time pay unless you work more than four hours or are covered by a union contract granting additional reporting time pay or are covered by Industrial Welfare Commission Order 15, Household Occupations.

## YOU MUST BE PAID FOR TIME SPENT ADJUSTING GRIEVANCES

If you spend time helping to resolve a workplace problem, that is considered "hours worked" and you must be paid at your regular rate. If your hours worked, including this grievance adjustment time, exceed eight hours a day or 40 hours a week, then the overtime hours must be paid at the overtime rate (e.g., one and one-half times your regular rate).

LAW: Labor Code sections 200, 1174 and 1195.5; Title 29 Code of Federal Regulations section 785.42.

ENFORCEMENT: Labor commissioner; U.S. Dept. of Labor, Wage and Hour Division; civil action.

EXCEPTIONS: Where a collective bargaining relationship exists, whether or not this time is paid is determined by the language of the agreement and past custom or practice. (See above, **You Have a Right To Overtime Pay**, for overtime pay exceptions.)

## IN SOME CASES YOU ARE ENTITLED TO PAID WORK TIME TO VOTE

You have the right to vote at every election. At every statewide election, you have special rights. If you do not have sufficient time to vote outside of working hours, then your employer must allow you to use part of your working hours. S/he cannot punish or discipline you for doing this.

At a statewide election, if you need to use part of your working hours to vote, you have the right to be paid for that time. You must be paid for up to two hours of working time. If you need to miss more than two hours, you will only be paid for the first two hours you miss.

In order to receive this paid time for voting, you must meet the following requirements:

(1) You have to **need** the working time. This can be because of a particular shift, or because of long lines at your voting precinct, or because you cannot vote at any other time owing, for example, to childcare limitations. If you have enough time to vote before or after your shift, you cannot get this paid voting time (unless your union and employer have agreed to it).

(2) You must take the paid-time for voting at either the end or the beginning of the shift. To get paid for it, the voting time cannot be in the middle of the shift.

(3) In choosing whether to take time off at the start or at the end of the shift, you must select the shortest absence.

(4) If you know (at least three working days before the election) that you will need this paid time to vote, you must give your employer at least two working days' notice. You have to tell her/him in advance if you want to get paid. However, if long lines at the precinct or another problem arises, you need not give advance notice to get paid.

**LAW:** Elections Code sections 14350 and 14352.

**ENFORCEMENT:** Labor commissioner; civil action.

EXCEPTIONS: None.

## YOUR EMPLOYER CANNOT PENALIZE YOU FOR JURY DUTY

Your employer cannot discriminate against or discharge you for jury duty. This protection applies to trial juries, inquest (coroner's) juries, and being called for jury service even though you never actually serve. To be fully protected, be sure to notify your employer as soon as you know you may have to miss work.

If you are a school district or community college district employee, it is illegal for your district to encourage or solicit you to seek exemption from jury duty. Your district must make up the difference between your fees as a juror and your regular earnings.

LAW: Labor Code section 230; Education Code sections 44037 and 87036; Title 28 U.S. Code section 1875.

ENFORCEMENT: Complaint to the court or coroner; district attorney; civil action.

In addition to all lost wages and benefits, and reinstatement, special rights apply if your jury was in federal court. Attorney's fees and civil penalties are available. If you cannot hire a lawyer, you may apply to the U.S. district court where your employer has her/his business, and that court will appoint an attorney for you.

EXCEPTIONS: None.

## YOUR EMPLOYER CANNOT PENALIZE YOU FOR APPEARING AS A WITNESS

It is illegal for your employer to discriminate against you or to discharge you for appearing as a witness as required by law. If you are subpenaed to a hearing, or ordered to appear in court (even without a subpena), or ordered (by notice) to a deposition, you may attend as required, even if your attendance is required during your normal working hours. To be fully protected from possible disciplinary action, be sure to notify your employer as soon as you know that you may have to miss work.

**LAW**: Labor Code section 230.

**ENFORCEMENT**: Labor commissioner; civil action.

**EXCEPTIONS**: None.

## PAID TIME FOR SUBPENAED PUBLIC EMPLOYEES

If you work for the state of California or any political subdivision of the state, you have a special right. Normally, someone subpenaed as a witness to appear in a legal matter may demand witness fees (which are quite low). The witness must get these fees from the party who subpenas her/him. A private sector worker will not be paid for her/his lost wages (unless s/he has a union contract which protects her/him).

However, if you work for any part of state or local government (including school districts or special districts), you will not lose wages. The only exceptions are (a) if you are called as an expert witness (in which case you will be paid for your time by the party calling you) or (b) if you are subpenaed in a case where you are a "party." You are a party if you are a named plaintiff or defendant in the legal action. That is, you are a party if you are suing someone or are being sued by someone.

If you are not a party and are not an expert witness, then your government employer is required to give you a leave of absence with no loss of pay. You must be paid the full amount you would have earned if you had not been subpenaed, subtracting only those witness fees which you actually are paid. Be sure to give your employer advance notice that you have been subpenaed.

**LAW**: Government Code sections 1230 and 1230.1.

**ENFORCEMENT**: Civil action.

**EXCEPTIONS**: None.

## PROMISED BENEFIT PAYMENTS MUST BE MADE

Your employer violates the law if s/he agrees to make payments into a benefit fund, and then willfully fails to make those payments. This kind of an agreement might be contained within a contract between your labor union and your employer, or if your workplace is not organized, the agreement might be a promise or a benefits pamphlet from your employer to you and other employees. The protections in the law apply to health or welfare funds, pension funds, vacation plans, or any other employee benefit plan.

LAW: Labor Code section 227; Title 29 U.S. Code sections 1101-1104 and 1131.

ENFORCEMENT: Labor commissioner; U.S. Department of Labor; civil action.

Violations may be a misdemeanor or a felony.

## YOUR EMPLOYER MAY NOT CANCEL YOUR MEDICAL BENEFITS WITHOUT NOTICE

Your employer is not required by law to provide medical benefits (see Chapter 6, WORKERS' COMPENSATION). However, once provided your employer may not cancel medical benefits without at least 15 days' notice. (This may not apply to those benefit plans covered by the Employee Retirement Income Security Act of 1974 [ERISA].)

If your employer terminates your group medical coverage (or if you lose your job), you have the right to "convert" that group policy to an individual policy which provides at least minimum benefits. If your group policy covers dependents, you have the right to an individual policy which covers dependents.

Dependents who lose their coverage for any reason (except those listed below) also have the right to an individual policy.

You do not have the right to convert the policy if:

(1) The group policy is replaced by similar coverage under another group policy within 60 days; or

(2) The policy was terminated because you failed to make a required payment when due; or

(3) You were not covered any time during the three months prior to termination of the policy.

**LAW**: Labor Code section 2806; Insurance Code sections 12670-12692.

**ENFORCEMENT**: Labor commissioner; Insurance Commissioner; civil action.

**EXCEPTIONS**: Employee Retirement Income Security Act provides different federal rights under certain plans.

## YOUR WAGES CAN BE GARNISHED ONLY UNDER SPECIAL CIRCUMSTANCES

Your wages are subject to garnishment **only** if someone has won a judgment against you in court (or you owe back taxes or family support) **and** you have not yet paid the judgment.

Both federal and state laws limit the amount that a garnishment can take from any given paycheck. Usually 25% is the most that can be taken out of your take-home pay. You may reduce the amount taken by showing that you and/or your family need more than 75% of your earnings to live on. (Your employer must give you a form that tells you how to apply for special treatment.)

There are also other legal procedures that may help you. Wage-earner protection plans and bankruptcy proceedings will stop garnishments and protect your job and wages. Many unions have legal services plans. Local legal aid societies and bar associations provide free or low-cost legal advice. If you have any serious troubles, you should consult a lawyer.

Some employers dislike the bookkeeping involved in garnishments. If you are not protected by a union contract, then your employer may attempt to discharge you because of garnishments. But the following legal restrictions apply:

(1) You cannot be discharged because of garnishments based on one debt. (This applies no matter how many times garnishments are served for that one debt.)

(2) You cannot be discharged because of garnishments based on one court judgment against you. (This applies no matter how many debts were combined in that one court proceeding.)

(3) You cannot be discharged because a garnishment has been threatened.

(4) If you are given a warning or a suspension by your employer (because of a garnishment), that warning or suspension cannot be used to support a later discharge (i.e., there can be no "progressive discipline" based on garnishments).

(5) If you file for bankruptcy or a federal wage-earner protection plan, you cannot be disciplined or discharged for your debts or your bankruptcy, and the garnishments will stop.

**LAW:** Labor Code section 2929; Code of Civil Procedure sections 706.010-706.154; Title 15 U.S. Code sections 1671-1677; Title 11 U.S. Code section 525.

**ENFORCEMENT:**Labor commissioner; district attorney; civil action; U.S. Department of Labor, Wage and Hour Division.

Any employer who violates these rules is subject to one year in prison and a $1,000 fine. It is in your best interest to complain to **both** the labor commissioner and the Department of Labor. If you notify your employer within 30 days of discharge that you are going to the labor commissioner and then file a complaint within 60 days, the labor commissioner can get you reinstatement and back pay. If you go to the U.S. Department of Labor or use your own lawyer, then you will be entitled to full back pay and reinstatement. If you are challenging a suspension, rather than a discharge, then the U.S. Department of Labor may be a better choice.

## NO DISCIPLINE OR DISCHARGE FOR CHILD OR FAMILY SUPPORT DEDUCTIONS

In certain cases a special kind of court order for child support or family support can be served on your employer. Your employer **cannot** discharge you because of this kind of court-ordered wage assignment, no matter how many times such an order has been served.

If your support obligations are more than you can pay, consult a lawyer about having them lowered. Support payments are subject to modification (up or down), depending on the needs and resources of the children and parents. If your divorce lawyer isn't helpful, get another lawyer. In this kind of case, as in any other, you can always change attorneys.

**LAW:** Civil Code sections 4700.1, 4701, and 4801.6; Code of Civil Procedure section 1699; Probate Code section 3088.

**ENFORCEMENT:** Civil action.

## MOST WAGE ASSIGNMENTS ARE UNLAWFUL

In the past, when a worker bought something "on time," or borrowed money, the loan or sales contract would include a direction to the worker's employer, authorizing the employer to deduct a certain amount from the worker's wages (i.e., a wage assignment). Now this practice is more strictly controlled. The rules are outlined below.

These rules do **not** apply to special court-ordered support "assignments"; to court-ordered garnishments; to deductions for taxes or social security or state disability insurance; to legitimate fringe benefit and retirement plan deductions; or to legitimate charitable deductions. But, if any money is taken out of your paycheck for any other reason, then it is considered an "assignment," and these rules do apply. If they are not strictly followed, you can get back all of your deducted money .

You **cannot** assign future wages for any loan, or for the purchase of anything other than necessities. You cannot tell your employer to pay (to someone else) wages which you have not yet earned. You can only "assign" part of the wages already earned, that is, money which your employer already owes you. Don't let your employer deduct wages for an illegal assignment. If you want to pay off a loan or a purchase, do it yourself.

**Exception**: You can assign your future wages **only** if (1) if you are paying for necessities of life; and (2) nothing else is included with those necessities for payment; and (3) the assignment is made directly to the person who furnished those necessities.

You **cannot** assign more than 50% of your take-home pay. You must always have at least half of your pay (after deductions) left over for you.

You **cannot** make more than one assignment in connection with one transaction (or series of transactions). Any assignment must include a notarized statement to that effect. For example, you can legally sign only one assignment to pay off your account with a merchant or landlord.

You **cannot** assign any wages if you are paid by a central payment plan. In some industries, people work for more than one employer, but get one combined paycheck from a common wage payment center. If you are paid this way, you cannot make any assignments.

You **can always** cancel or stop any assignment. You can do this at any time. You can always revoke a power-of-attorney. Give your employer a written note saying that you are cancelling and renouncing all assignments and powers-of-attorney. Date it and make a copy for yourself.

There can only be one wage assignment in effect. You cannot have two assignments from your wages at the same time.

Your employer **cannot** make a wage deduction or withholding legal just by having you sign a wage assignment or power-of-attorney. In fact, you can **never** legally make any assignment to your employer, or to anyone acting for her/him.

Any wage assignment is automatically stopped by a garnishment or support order. For so long as the garnishment (or support order) continues, no money can be taken out of your wages for any other assignment.

No wage assignment is valid unless it is in writing and is signed by you, personally. (Again, this does not apply to court ordered family support assignments.)

No wage assignment is valid **unless**:

(1) it is in a separate written agreement (it cannot be included in a sales, or loan, or rent contract); and

(2) it specifically identifies the transaction (it must accurately spell out what you are paying for).

If you are under 18, no wage assignment is valid unless it is signed by your parent or legal guardian (and his/her signatiure is authenticated by a notary public). If you are over 18, the assignment must include your written notarized statement that you are over 18.

If you are not married, the assignment must include your notarized written statement that you are single. If you are married, the assignment is not valid unless it is also signed by your spouse (and his/her signature is authenticated by a notary public).

**Exception**: If you are legally separated by a court order, or if you are living apart after an interlocutory judgment of dissolution, and if you include a notarized statement of this fact in the assignment, then you do not need your spouse's signature.

**LAW**: Labor Code sections 206.5 and 300; Title 29 Code of Federal Regulations sections 531.35, 531.39, and 531.40.

**ENFORCEMENT**: Labor commissioner; civil action.

If money has been taken from your pay because of an illegal or defective assignment, you can get it all back. If your employer has had you assign wages to her/him, the employer is guilty of a crime.

**EXCEPTIONS**: Only as explained above.


## ASSIGNMENTS AS "LOANS"

If you do make a wage assignment in return for money, or for credit, or for any goods or services, or for housing or rent, then the Consumer Finance Lender Law applies.

**Exception**: The law does not apply to loans or puchases for your business. But you **cannot** assign any as-yet-unearned wages for business purposes.

Legally, the amount of wages you assign is considered a "loan." The amount by which your wage assignment is more than the regular price or value of what you have received is considered "interest."

Whoever gets your wage assignment **must** have a license from the California Commissioner of Corporations. S/he must give you a written statement with her/his name, address, and loan license number; with the rate of interest being charged; with the exact amount of wage assignment you have made; and with a statement of how and when the assignment will be paid off. There are very strict regulations limiting what "interest" may be charged. Other rules strictly control what "charges" may be added on.

The person who gets your money cannot have you sign a paper if it has any blanks not yet filled in. S/he cannot have you sign any power-of-attorney or confession-of-judgment.

If any of these rules are violated, then the wage assignment is not valid and no money can be collected. You do not **owe** any money (no matter what you may have gotten in return for the assignment); **and** you can get back any money taken from your wages.

LAW: Financial Code sections 24000-24653 and 24471; Uncodified Measures, California usury initiative 1919-1, section 3.

ENFORCEMENT: Corporations Commissioner; State Attorney General; district attorney; civil action.

Any person who accepts an illegal wage assignment is guilty of a crime and is subject to six months in jail.

EXCEPTIONS: Only as explained above.


## YOU HAVE THE RIGHT TO CANCEL A WAGE ASSIGNMENT OR POWER-OF-ATTORNEY AT ANY TIME

A power-of-attorney is **revocable at any time**. In fact, to be good at all, it must say (in writing) that you can renounce it at any time. To cancel a power-of-attorney, give your employer a written note saying, "I hereby renounce and revoke all powers of attorney and wage assignments." Sign the note; date it; and make a copy for yourself.

You cannot give a power-of-attorney to your employer to cash your paycheck. Your employer cannot require you to sign a power-of-attorney or any other release of wages due (or wages which will later be earned or even uncarned wages which have been advanced to you). Any such power-of-attorney or release is invalid and the employer is guilty of a misdemeanor.

Anyone who has a power-of-attorney must take special care to protect your interests. S/he must use the "utmost good faith" to act for your benefit. If s/he does anything to harm you or take advantage of you, you can sue for **damages and attorneys' fees**.

LAW: Labor Code sections 206.5 and 300; Civil Code sections 2355 and 2356; Penal Code sections 507 and 514.

ENFORCEMENT: Labor commissioner; district attorney; civil action.

## YOU CANNOT BE HARASSED AT YOUR WORKPLACE BY DEBT COLLECTORS

Anyone trying to collect a debt **cannot** legally harass you at work. This applies to a collection agency and also to those who regularly collect debts owed them. Stores, doctors, hospitals, credit companies, and collection agencies are all covered by this law.

A debt collector can call your employer **once**. In that one call, s/he can verify your employment and nothing else. S/he can write to your employer once, but **only** if it is necessary to obtain the following information: your home address and telephone number, and your place of employment. (It is very hard to imagine a debt collector who does not have this information already--especially if s/he knows your employer's address.) A debt collector **cannot** tell your employer that you owe money, or say anything else about you, either by letter or phone.

Any letter sent to you at work by a debt collector must be addressed to you personally and say "Personal and Confidential" on the envelope. The envelope **cannot** show the name of the collection agency or make any reference to debt.

No debt collector can call you at work, if you tell her/him that you are prohibited from receiving such personal calls. S/he cannot call you at work, if you tell her/him that you do not want to be called there.

The debt collector **cannot** threaten to tell your employer that you owe money, or threaten anything else which might harm your employment or reputation.

No debt collector can call you at home or at work without disclosing her/his identity. S/he cannot call in a way intended to annoy or harass.

**LAW:** Civil Code sections 1788-1788.30; Business and Professions Code section 6947; Title 16 California Administrative Code section 627; Title 15 U.S. Code sections 1692b, 1692c, and 1692k.

**ENFORCEMENT:** Civil action.

You can collect actual damages, punitive damages, penalties for each violation, and attorney's fees. Consult with the Federal Trade Commission and the Collection and Investigative Services Bureau.

## YOUR EMPLOYER CANNOT DISCRIMINATE AGAINST YOU OR DENY YOU BENEFITS BECAUSE YOU ARE PREGNANT

You cannot be discriminated against in any way because of pregnancy, miscarriage, abortion, or any related medical condition.

Your employer (or potential employer) cannot ask you any questions about birth control, family planning, or childcare. S/he may not ask who will take care of your child, or who is the father of your child, or whether the parents are married. The employer may not test your blood or urine for signs of pregnancy or birth control.

So long as you are "able to perform the major functions necessary to the job," an employer cannot refuse to hire you because you are pregnant.

A pregnant applicant or employee cannot be denied participation in a training program because of her pregnancy. For private sector "for profit" employers (and non-religious "nonprofit" employers) with five to fourteen employees, California law gives a clear rule: If you will complete the training program at least three months before you anticipate beginning your pregnancy leave, then your condition cannot be used to deny you the training. For other employers, it is up to the employer to prove that your pregnancy will unreasonably interrupt the training, in order to deny you the opportunity. To avoid problems, it is best to not tell an employer about your condition. The employer may not legally ask, and you should not tell.

You can never be required to be sterilized in order to get or to keep a job.

You cannot be disciplined or in any way penalized for an abortion, an absence due to an abortion, or medical complications from an abortion. If medical coverage is provided, it must include coverage for medical complications resulting from abortions.

You cannot be forced to take a leave based solely on the stage of your pregnancy.

Your employer can require reasonable notice of the date your pregnancy leave will begin, and its estimated duration. But your employer must give you reasonable advance notice of this requirement, and you do not have to give notice until you can determine (with reasonable certainty) the expected date that your leave will begin.

Short absences due to your pregnancy are considered part of your pregnancy leave. If disabilities associated with your condition (e.g., morning sickness) cause you to miss work, and you are later able to return, your employer must allow you to return to your original job (even though you will later be taking another leave to give birth).

If your employer has a policy, or practice, or union contract requiring or permitting temporarily-disabled workers to transfer to light duty (or to less strenuous work, or to less hazardous work), then your employer must allow a pregnant worker to make this kind of transfer if she so requests. When she is no longer pregnant, the worker must be allowed to return to her original job with no loss of seniority, and with the pay and benefits attributable to the job classification at the time she returns. If you do transfer to less hazardous or strenuous work, this does not eliminate your other rights. You still have the leave of absence rights discussed below.

For private sector "for profit" employers (and non-religious "nonprofit" employers) with five to fourteen employees, California law provides an additional rule. Even though one of these employers does not have any policy or practice or union contract allowing transfers of temporarily-disabled workers, you are nevertheless protected by the following law:

(1) If you are pregnant and request a transfer to light duty or less strenuous or less hazardous work; and

(2) your request is based on the advice of your physician; and

(3) the transfer can be reasonably accommodated;

(4) then you must be given the transfer.

When you have recovered, you must be allowed to return to your **original job** with no loss of seniority and with the pay and benefits attributable to the job classification at the time you return.

No employer can require a physician's certification that a pregnant worker is disabled, or that she has recovered, or that she will probably need such-and-such time off, unless the employer also requires that kind of medical certification to verify other (non-pregnancy) temporary disabilities or illnesses.

Your employer must allow you at least a four month leave for a disability due to pregnancy, childbirth, or related medical conditions. (This basic four month rule refers to unpaid disability leave. For paid leave, see other rules below.)

If you choose, you must be allowed to use all of your accrued paid leave time prior to any unpaid portion of your pregnancy leave. This includes all your paid sick leave, paid vacation time, paid disability leave, and any other accrued paid leave you may have.

You cannot be penalized in any way for taking this four month pregnancy leave. You must be allowed to continue accruing seniority and other benefits in the same way as any other (non-pregnant) worker on a leave of absence.

If your employer allows other (non-pregnant) workers to take leaves of absence longer than four months, then a worker disabled by pregnancy or a related condition must also be allowed a longer leave of absence.

For any public sector employer, and for any private sector employer with fifteen or more employees, the paid portion of a pregnancy leave must always be at least at long as the paid sick or paid disability leave provided for other (non-pregnancy) disabilities.

California law gives a different rule for private sector "for profit" employer (and for non-religious "nonprofit" employers) with five to fourteen employees If these employers provide paid sick leave (or paid disability leave) for non-pregnant temporarily disabled workers, then paid leave must also be provided for workers disabled due to pregnancy. If the worker has a normal pregnancy, then the paid pregnancy leave can be shorter than the other disability leaves. Unless a union contract calls for more, the paid portion of the pregnancy leave can be limited to six weeks. (In all cases, the employer must allow at least four months pregnancy disability leave, paid or unpaid.) If the worker has an abnormal pregnancy, or if she suffers any complications, then the paid portion of her pregnancy can no longer be restricted to six weeks. The paid portion must then be at least as long as the paid disability leave (or paid sick leave) given to other (non-pregnant) workers. (All that you need is a note from your doctor saying that your pregnancy is "abnormal" or saying that you are disabled for more than six weeks due to complications.)

If you have left work due to pregnancy, but are not on paid leave, you should apply at once for State Disability Insurance. (Apply at your local unemployment office, the Employment Development Department.) A worker disabled by pregnancy or childbirth can receive up to 39 weeks of disability insurance. Get a doctor's note that you are disabled from your regular work, but apply as soon as possible. You have already paid for this insurance. (It is the "SDI" deduction on your paycheck stub.)

You must notify your employer when you are ready and able to return to work. Your employer must reinstate you in your **original job**. Normally you must be reinstated within two weeks.

You cannot be forced to accept a "waiting period" before returning to work after childbirth, unless the same "waiting period" is applied to all other employees returning to work after a disability or illness. Even then, no "waiting period" is allowed if it exceeds two weeks, unless the employer can prove that it is a business necessity.

Even after a new mother is medically able to work, under certain conditions she must be allowed to remain on leave of absence, to care for her infant, if she so requests. This is true if the employer allows workers to take leaves of absence for travel, or for education which is not work-related, or for other personal reasons. If such personal leaves are allowed, then they must also be allowed for infant care.

You and your dependents cannot be denied any insurance coverage or fringe benefits, nor have your coverage or benefits reduced, nor have your coverage or benefits cancelled, because you are an unwed mother.

**Original Job:** When you have taken a leave, or have been transferred to different job duties, because of pregnancy, childbirth, or related medical conditions, your employer must return you to your **original job**, with the same pay, working conditions, benefits, and opportunities for advancement, unless that position is no longer available due to **business necessity**.

There is a rebuttable presumption that your job can be left open or can be filled by a temporary employee. If your job is no longer open, your employer must make a reasonable, good faith effort to return you to a substantially similar job. This means a job with equal pay and benefits, and one which is performed under similar working conditions, and which provides similar opportunities for advancement.

**Business Necessity:** A **business necessity** is something which is necessary to the safe and efficient operation of the business and something for which there is no alternative which would accomplish the same result with a lesser discriminatory impact.

LAW: Government Code sections 12940, 12943, 12945, 12945.5 and 19702; Labor Code sections 1735 and 1777.6; Unemployment Insurance Code section 2626(a); Title 42 U.S. Code section 2000e(k); Title 29 Code of Federal Regulations section 1604.10 and Appendix; Title 2 California Administrative Code sections 7286.7, 7290.8, 7290.9, 7291.0(c), 7291.1(d), and 7291.2; Title 10 California Administrative Code section 2560.3; Title 22 California Administrative Code sections 98240-98244.

**ENFORCEMENT:** Fair Employment and Housing Dept.; Equal Employment Opportunity Commission; U.S. Dept. of Labor Office Federal Contract Compliance Programs; civil action.

**EXCEPTIONS:** The above rules (with the exceptions given) apply to all public employers, to all private sector "for profit" employers with five or more employees, to all non-religious "nonprofit" employers with five or more employees, to all "nonprofit" employers with fifteen or more employees, and to virtually all employers who are recipients of government funds, perform government contracts, or perform public works.

No employer, no matter how small, can legally allow harassment because of pregnancy.

California State Civil Service employees, and employees of the California State Universities and Colleges, have a special protection. These employees have the right to an unpaid leave of absence for pregnancy, childbirth, and recovery, for a period selected by the employee, for up to one full year. Once you have selected the period of absence, any change requires the approval of your employer. (This right may be modified by a union contract.) Government Code section 19991.6; Education Code section 89519.

An employer challenge to the **Original Job** rule is pending before the U.S. Supreme Court.

## CHAPTER 5

## WORKING CONDITIONS:
## SAFETY, HEALTH AND SANITATION

### YOUR EMPLOYER MUST PROVIDE A SAFE AND HEALTHFUL WORKPLACE

You have the right to a safe and healthful work environment. Your employer is required by law to:

(1) provide and promote the use of safety devices and safeguards to reasonably assure your health and safety;

(2) use methods and processes which are reasonably adequate to insure your health and safety; and

(3) do every other thing reasonable to protect your life, safety and health.

LAW: Labor Code sections 6300, 6400-6407.

ENFORCEMENT: Cal-OSHA has the authority to enforce all laws, standards and orders protecting all workers in Calfornia, except federal employees and other with their own special programs (e.g., maritime and mining industries).

EXCEPTIONS: Cal-OSHA exceptions.*

### HEALTH AND SAFETY STANDARDS

The Cal-OSHA standards board adopts occupational safety and health standards. Your employer is required by law to comply with these standards. The standards specify certain safe work practices. They are also developed to:

(1) describe hazardous conditions or toxic materials;

(2) specify equipment and work practices which must be used to prevent or eliminate those conditions;

(3) limit worker exposure to dangerous substances.

As a worker or interested person, you have the right to propose new standards, or changes or amendments in existing standards, at meetings of the Cal-OSHA standards board. Dates and times of the meetings are available by calling the Standards Board. You also have the right to notice of your employer's request for a variance (a special exemption to a standard), and the right to oppose that request.

LAW: Labor Code sections 140-147.1; Title 8 California Administrative Code sections 403-428.

ENFORCEMENT: Cal-OSHA.

EXCEPTIONS: Cal-OSHA exceptions.*

## YOU HAVE THE RIGHT TO ASK CAL-OSHA TO INSPECT YOUR WORKPLACE

If you believe that there are unsafe or unhealthful conditions where you work, you can ask Cal-OSHA to inspect your workplace. Cal-OSHA will investigate complaints in the following order:

(1) Occupational accidents resulting in fatalities.

(2) Serious hazards or conditions posing imminent danger to the lives or safety of employees.

(3) Other serious violations.

(4) Nonserious violations.

Generally, Cal-OSHA will not give the employer advance notice of the inspection.

LAW: Labor Code sections 6309 and 6321.

ENFORCEMENT: Cal-OSHA.

EXCEPTIONS: Cal-OSHA exceptions.*

## YOU HAVE THE RIGHT TO FILE A CONFIDENTIAL COMPLAINT

If you make a complaint, Cal-OSHA is required to keep your name confidential unless you request otherwise.

LAW: Labor Code section 6309.

ENFORCEMENT: Cal-OSHA.

## DISCIPLINARY ACTION FOR EXERCISING ANY OF YOUR RIGHTS UNDER CAL-OSHA IS ILLEGAL

If you believe that your employer has punished you by:

(1) firing you;

(2) demoting you;

(3) taking away any seniority or benefits you have earned;

(4) transferring you to an undesirable shift; or

(5) threatening or harassing you in any way

because you made a complaint to Cal-OSHA or used any of your other rights under Cal-OSHA, call the labor comissioner immediately.

You must file a complaint with the labor commissioner within 30 days of the disciplinary action. If the labor commissioner agrees that your employer has punished you for exercising any of your rights under Cal-OSHA, s/he will order you returned to your job and given any pay or benefits lost. Be sure to also file a complaint (within 30 days) with the Area Director of federal OSHA. (See also Chapter 9, WHISTLEBLOWING: REPORTING VIOLATIONS OF THE LAW.)

LAW: Labor Code sections 98.7, 6310, 6311 and 6312; Title 29 U.S. Code section 660(c); Title 29 Code of Federal Regulations Parts 1977 and 1978, and section 1954.3(e).

ENFORCEMENT: Labor commissioner; Federal OSHA, Regional Office; U.S. Department of Labor; civil action.

EXCEPTIONS: Cal-OSHA exceptions.* Employees with their own special programs are protected against retaliation but enforcement procedures vary.


## YOU HAVE THE RIGHT TO SPEAK PRIVATELY WITH THE CAL-OSHA REPRESENTATIVE DURING AN INSPECTION

Your right to talk privately with the Cal-OSHA representative is protected by law. You may wish to give the inspector information about your workplace hazards that may not be obvious, such as:

(1) hazardous work areas;

(2) accidents that have occurred in specific areas;

(3) an unusual number of illnesses or health problems among the workers.

You may also tell the inspector whether working conditions are normal during this inspection or whether they have been purposefully modified because of the inspection.

LAW: Labor Code section 6314.

ENFORCEMENT: Cal-OSHA.


## A UNION REPRESENTATIVE MAY ACCOMPANY CAL-OSHA REPRESENTATIVES ON INSPECTIONS

If there is a union representative at your worksite, s/he has the right to accompany the OSHA investigator on the inspection. If more than one union is represented, such as on a construction site, the investigator will attempt to choose a representative satisfactory to all parties and will consult with additional workers on the tour.

If there is no union, you and your co-workers, in conjunction with the OSHA inspector, may select an employee representative. Your employer may **not** designate the employee representative. The employee representative who accompanies the investigator must be paid for time spent on the inspection. If no representative is available, the investigator will consult with a number of workers during the inspection.

**LAW:** Labor Code section 6314.

**ENFORCEMENT:** Labor commissioner; Cal-OSHA.

## YOU HAVE THE RIGHT TO REFUSE TO DO UNSAFE WORK UNDER CERTAIN CONDITIONS

You can refuse to perform work under certain conditions. For you to be fully protected by law, all of the following conditions must be met:

(1) Doing the work violates a Cal-OSHA standard, or violates the Labor Code. (Any work which is not safe and healthful violates Labor Code section 6400.)

(2) Doing the work creates a real and apparent hazard. This means:

(a) A reasonable person would agree that there is a hazard or danger; and

(b) the danger is to the health or safety of you or of another worker; and

(c) there is not enough time to eliminate the danger through regular complaint channels.

**Steps to Take Before You Refuse to do an Unsafe Job --**

(1) Tell your supervisor or employer about the hazard and ask that it be fixed.

(2) Make it clear to the supervisor that the only reason you are refusing to do the work is because you believe that your health or safety would be in danger if you did the work. Tell your supervisor that you believe that doing the work would be a violation of either the state occupational safety and health standards or the Labor Code.

(3) Make it clear to the supervisor that you are willing to do the work as soon as the job is made safe. Tell your supervisor you will do work that is safe in the meantime.

(4) If you are not sure whether a particular job presents hazards, talk to your union steward or business agent and/or other workers. Find out whether they agree with you that the work presents a hazard to you or your fellow workers or violates standards.

(5) If the employer does not immediately eliminate the hazard, call the nearest office of Cal-OSHA. You cannot be disciplined for contacting Cal-OSHA with your complaint.

(6) If your employer fires you or threatens to punish you for refusing to perform unsafe work, immediately call the California Labor Commissioner, as well as your union and the Regional Office of Federal OSHA.

**Time Limits For Filing Your Claim --** If you are laid off or discharged for refusal to do unsafe work, you must file a claim with the labor commissioner within 30 days after being laid off or discharged (this time may be extended for good cause). You should also file a claim within 30 days with Federal OSHA.

Your claim will be investigated by a special "discrimination complaint investigator" who will report back to the labor commissioner. If the labor commissioner determines a violation has occurred s/he will notify you and order your employer to remedy the situation by:

(1) reinstatement;

(2) payment of back wages (with interest);

(3) attorney's fees associated with any hearing held by the labor commissioner in investigating the complaint; and

(4) posting of notices to employees.

If your employer does not comply with the order of the labor commissioner within 10 working days following notification, the labor commissioner must promptly bring a court action against your employer. If the labor commissioner fails to go to court promptly, you may bring action against the labor commissioner. If you win, you will receive court costs and attorney's fees.

If the labor commissioner does not decide in your favor, you may go to court and win relief on your own.

LAW: Labor Code sections 98.6, 98.7, 6311 and 6312; Title 29 U.S. Code section 660(c); Title 29 Code of Federal Regulations Part 1977 and section 1954.3(e); Title 49 Appendix U.S. Code section 2305 (for commercial motor vehicles).

ENFORCEMENT: Labor commissioner; Federal OSHA, Regional Office.

EXCEPTIONS: Cal-OSHA exceptions.* (See also Chapter 9, WHISTLEBLOWING: REPORTING VIOLATIONS OF THE LAW.)

## YOUR EMPLOYER MUST RESPECT CAL-OSHA AND PESTICIDE PROHIBITIONS

The Division of Occupational Safety and Health (Cal-OSHA) can prohibit ("red tag") use of a piece of equipment (or entry to a place). This must be done if use of that gear (or entry to that place) will cause "an imminent hazard." A notice of this prohibition must be posted or attached to the equipment. It is a crime to remove this notice, or to use the equipment (or enter the place) until the hazard is corrected and the equipment (or place) made safe.

It is a crime for anyone to order a worker to enter an area properly posted as dangerous due to pesticide application.

LAW: Labor Code sections 6323-6327.5 and 6406-6407; Food and Agricultural Code sections 12978 and 12985.

ENFORCEMENT: Cal-OSHA; civil action.

Violation may be punished by a year in jail and $1,000 fine.

EXCEPTIONS: Entry may be made to a prohibited place in order to fix the hazard.


## YOUR EMPLOYER MUST POST ANY CITATION GIVEN BY CAL-OSHA

Your employer must post any citation given by Cal-OSHA. It must stay posted for three days or until the condition is corrected (whichever is longer). The posted citation must inform you of the amount of time Cal-OSHA has allowed for correcting the violation(s). It must also explain your rights to request a shorter correction period.

If your employer appeals a citation, your union must be notified of the appeal and of the appeal hearing. If you don't have a union, your employer must post a copy of the appeal, a notice of your rights to participate in the appeals process, and a notice of the appeal hearing.

LAW: Labor Code sections 6408 and 6427-6435; Title 8 California Administrative Code sections 332-332.3 and 353-356.2.

ENFORCEMENT: Cal-OSHA.

EXCEPTIONS: Cal-OSHA exceptions.*

## YOU HAVE THE RIGHT TO PARTICIPATE IN THE APPEALS PROCESS

Your employer has the right to appeal a citation given by Cal-OSHA. Your employer also has the right to appeal the time allowed for correcting a safety violation. You have the right to attend any appeal hearing your employer requests (if you follow the Appeals Board rules). You or your union have the right to appear as a "party," which means that you have the right to subpena and question witnesses and present evidence.

You also have the right to appeal the date fixed for correcting a violation. You can argue that the time is unreasonable, that too much time is being allowed and that workers' safety or health is needlessly endangered.

You should file an appeal, or a request to participate in an employer's appeal, as soon as possible.

In any appeal hearing, you or your union can be represented by a lawyer, by a non-lawyer, or you can act as your own representative.

LAW: Labor Code sections 6317-6319.5, 6430-6434, and 6600-6633; Title 8 California Administrative Code sections 345-394.

ENFORCEMENT: Cal-OSHA.

EXCEPTIONS: Cal-OSHA exceptions.*

## YOU HAVE THE RIGHT TO KNOW ABOUT HARMFUL SUBSTANCES IN THE WORKPLACE

You (or your representative) have the right to see accurate records of worker exposure to potentially hazardous materials. You have the right to be told if you are (or have been) exposed to potentially toxic materials in concentrations higher than limits set by occupational health and safety standards. You have the right to know what is being done to deal with any exposure problems.

Whether or not exposure has actually occurred, your employer must notify you about the presence of hazardous substances. You must be informed of all hazardous substances in your workplace and trained in the proper procedures for dealing with them. Material Safety Data Sheets (MSDSs) must be readily accessible to you, in your workplace, during each shift. The MSDSs will provide specific information about all hazardous substances and how they should be handled (in normal situations and in emergencies). Your employer must retain old MSDS forms even after the particular substance is no longer present at the workplace. Containers holding hazardous substances must be properly labeled. Your employer must have written procedures ensuring:

(1) that you are informed of (a) hazardous substances in unlabeled pipes and (b) of hazards you may encounter in performing non-routine tasks; and

(2) that employees of contractors will be informed of hazards they may encounter.

LAW: Labor Code sections 142.3, 6360-6399.9, 6408 and 9000-9061; Title 8 California Administrative Code sections 340.2, 3204, and 5194; Title 29 Code of Federal Regulations sections 1910.1200 and 1990.101-1990.152.

ENFORCEMENT: Cal-OSHA.

EXCEPTIONS: Cal-OSHA exceptions*; certain laboratories (partial exemptions). Certain trade secrets need not be revealed to you, but must always be made available to medical personnel if the information is needed. MSDS requirements do not aply to: hazardous waste subject to EPA rules; tobacco and related products; wood and wood products; manufactured articles (formed to a specific shape or design) which do not release or cause exposure to a hazardous substance; food, drugs, or cosmetics (for personal consumption); retail consumer products incidentally used by workers; or retail food sale establishments and any other retail trade establishments (but all processing and repair work areas in such establishments are covered).

## YOU HAVE THE RIGHT TO SEE THE RESULTS OF MONITORING AND MEASURING HARMFUL SUBSTANCES IN THE WORKPLACE

Cal-OSHA standards may require your employer to monitor and measure your exposure to harmful materials in the workplace. If so, your employer must provide the opportunity for you or your representative to watch the monitoring. You or your union must be notified prior to any monitoring. You have the right to see the results and to obtain a copy of the report from your employer at no cost.

You have a right to see **any** medical records about yourself kept by your employer. You have this right even after you leave that place of employment. Your employer must keep medical records for at least 30 years. (See also 9 Chapter 10, EMPLOYEE RECORDS.)

LAW: Labor Code section 6408; Title 8 California Administrative Code sections 340.1 and 3204.

**ENFORCEMENT:** Cal-OSHA.

## YOU HAVE THE RIGHT TO SAFE ASBESTOS-RELATED WORK

Before any work is done which might disturb asbestos-containing material or release asbestos fibers, the owner, contractor, and employer must make a good faith effort to determine if asbestos is present.

For all asbestos-handling jobs, a safety conference must be held **before** the start of actual work. This conference must include representatives of the workers, of the unions, and of the employer, contractor, and property owner. This conference must discuss the employer's safety program and all practices and devices to be used for safety.

Beginning January 1, 1987, anyone engaging in work (involving 100 square feet or more of asbestos-containing material) which might release asbestos fibers must be registered with and certified by Cal-OSHA. A copy of the registration must be posted at the work site. All affected employees must be covered by health insurance and workers' compensation. The insurance must pay for all medical examinations and monitoring. A certified person must be provided to conduct air sampling and respirator-fit tests. The employer must notify Cal-OSHA in advance about every job, the potential asbestos exposure, and the practices to be used. Any changes must also be reported. Every work site must have a sign posted, readable from 20 feet away. It must say: "Danger--Asbestos. Cancer and Lung Hazard. Keep Out."

LAW: Labor Code sections 6501.5-6508.5, 6325.5 and 6436; Health & Safety Code sections 24223 and 24275; Education Code section 49410.7; Business and Professions Code sections 7028.1, 7028.2, 7058.5 and 7118.5.

ENFORCEMENT: Cal-OSHA.

EXCEPTIONS: Other rules apply to the manufacture of asbestos-containing products.


## YOUR EMPLOYER MUST LOG WORK INJURIES AND ILLNESSES

Your employer is required to maintain a detailed log of occupational injuries and illnesses (Form 200). You have a right to inspect that form.

No later than February 1 of each year, your employer must post a summary of the previous calendar year's log. This summary must remain posted, in a place where employee notices usually go, at least until March 1. This summary must record the injury experience at your work place.

You have the right to see and copy the logs and annual summaries of the previous five years. And you have this right even if you have left that job and are now a former employee.

LAW: Labor Code section 6410; Title 8 California Administrative Code sections 14301-14400.

ENFORCEMENT: Cal-OSHA.

EXCEPTIONS: Cal-OSHA exceptions.*

An employer who never, during the entire calendar year preceding the current year, had more than ten employees at any time is exempt. S/he need not prepare the log or summary. (However, s/he still must meet Cal-OSHA reporting requirements and must still make your employee medical and exposure records available to you.) An employer subject to the Federal Mine Safety and Health Act does not need to keep records which duplicate information s/he already keeps under that Act.

## YOU HAVE THE RIGHT TO MAKE A COMPLAINT AGAINST CAL-OSHA

If you believe that Cal-OSHA is not acting promptly or properly to protect the health and safety of workers, you may complain to Federal OSHA. Any person can make a complaint about the administration of Cal-OSHA. Your complaint should be directed to the Assistant Regional Administrator of the federal agency and should contain specific facts showing Cal-OSHA's inadequacies.

The Assistant Regional Administrator must acknowledge receipt of your complaint and must keep your name confidential. S/he may decide to make an investigation of the complaint based on:

(1) the number of people affected by the described problem;

(2) the number of complaints received on the same issue;

(3) whether you exhausted state remedies for correction of the problem; and

(4) the degree to which your complaint relates to federal policy.

If the Assistant Regional Administrator does conduct an investigation, s/he will inform you of OSHA's findings and of the corrective action to be taken.

If no investigation is made, OSHA must explain why they are not investigating your complaint. If you are dissatified with this explanation, you may request a review by the Regional Administrator. Be prepared to back up your request with additional documentation.

LAW: Title 29 U.S. Code section 667; Title 29 Code of Federal Regulations sections 1954.20 and 1954.21.

ENFORCEMENT: Federal OSHA, Regional Administrator.

## YOUR EMPLOYER MUST PROVIDE SAFETY DEVICES

In general, your employer must pay for or provide safety devices and safeguards which are reasonably adequate to make your job safe and healthful. Certain equipment is specifically required by law.

Eye Protection: If eye protection is required, then your employer must provide suitable eye protection devices. If you require vision correction (eyeglasses or contact lenses), then the employer must provide:

(1) safety spectacles with suitable corrected lenses; or

(2) safety goggles designed to fit over spectacles; or

(3) protective goggles with corrective lenses mounted behind protective lenses.

Eye protection is required whenever there is a risk of receiving eye injuries such as punctures, abrasions, contusions, or burns as a result of contact with flying particles or hazardous substances or projections, or as a result of injurious light rays.

Foot and Hand Protection: Your employer must provide appropriate foot or hand protection, when conditions require. Foot protection (e.g., safety shoes/boots) is required when workers are exposed to foot injuries from falling objects; hot, corrosive, or poisonous substances; or crushing or penetrating action; or when they are working in abnormally wet locations. Hand protection is required for employees whose work involves unusual or excessive exposure to cuts, burns, or harmful physical, chemical, or radioactive agents.

Head Protection: Employers must provide helmets or hardhats for workers who are exposed to flying or falling objects or electric shocks or burns.

Safety devices, including protective clothing, cannot be interchanged among workers (unless the equipment has been properly cleaned each time). Protective gear or regular working clothes (provided by the employer) which become wet (or are washed between shifts) must be dry before reuse.

LAW: Labor Code sections 6401 and 6403; Title 8 California Administrative Code sections 3380-3390, and 3401-3412.

ENFORCEMENT: Cal-OSHA.

EXCEPTIONS: Cal-OSHA exceptions.*

## YOUR EMPLOYER MUST PROVIDE MEDICAL SERVICES AND FIRST-AID

Every employer must ensure the ready availability of medical personnel for advice and consultation on matters of industrial health or injury. The employer must provide access to a health-care professional who workers can call for help or information.

If there is no clinic or hospital near the workplace which is available to the workers, then the employer must ensure that someone (at the workplace) is properly trained to give first-aid. This can be done by on-site medical facilities, or by proper equipment to transport an injured worker to a doctor, or by a phone system for summoning a doctor.

Whenever a worker's eyes (or body) may be exposed to any corrosive materials, the employer must provide facilities for quick drenching or flushing of the eyes (or body). These facilities must be within the work area and be available for immediate use.

First-aid materials must be readily available on every job, without charge to the worker. These materials must be kept in a sanitary and usable condition; they must be frequently inspected and replenished or replaced as necessary.

LAW: Title 8 California Administrative Code sections 3400, 3439, 3464, 9780(f), and 9780.2; Labor Code section 2440.

ENFORCEMENT: Cal-OSHA.

EXCEPTIONS: Cal-OSHA exceptions.*


## YOUR EMPLOYER MUST PROVIDE CHANGING ROOMS AND SAFEGUARD YOUR PERSONAL PRIVACY

If your occupation requires you to change your clothing, your employer must provide a room or space for changing. This changing room must give you reasonable privacy and comfort, and it **must** be separate from toilet rooms. It must be kept clean.

In any changing room, you have personal privacy rights. (You also have these privacy rights in **any** restroom, toilet, washroom, bathroom, shower, locker room, fitting room, motel room, hotel room, or sleeping room.) It is illegal for anyone to install or to use or maintain any two-way mirror in any of these rooms. You cannot be spied on in any way when changing clothes or using toilet facilities.

LAW: Industrial Welfare Commission Orders 1-13, section 13; Penal Code section 653n; California Constitution Article I, section 1; Title 8 California Administrative Code section 3367.

ENFORCEMENT: Labor comissioner; district attorney; Cal-OSHA; civil action.

You may sue for actual and punitive damages, distress, invasion of privacy. Anyone who installs or uses a two-way mirror is subject to six months in prison and a $500 fine.

EXCEPTIONS: The law against the installation of two-way mirrors does not apply to law-enforcement buildings, medical or custodial institutions, or educational institutions. Even in these, however, you cannot be spied on when changing or using toilets.

The IWC requirement of a special changing room does not apply to: IWC exceptions*; agricultural occupations; and domestic workers who care for a private household.

No one can legally be spied on when changing clothes or using toilets.

Every permanent place of employment covered by Cal-OSHA must provide changing rooms **whenever** workers are required to change from street clothes into protective clothing. These changing rooms must have lockers or other storage facilities for street clothes, and **separate** storage facilities for protective clothing.


## YOUR EMPLOYER MUST PROVIDE CLEAN AND SANITARY TOILET FACILITES

All workers must be provided with toilet facilities within reasonable access. These toilet facilities must be kept clean and sanitary; no overflow from any toilet or drain can be tolerated; no protruding nails, splinters, loose boards, or unnecessary holes or openings can be tolerated. All refuse and garbage must be removed often enough to avoid creating an unsanitary condition.

Each toilet must occupy a separate compartment equipped with a door and a door latch. The doors and walls or partitions must assure privacy. Sinks or other washing facilities must be provided. They must be equipped with running water and provided with soap or other suitable cleansing agents. Clean individual hand towels or warm-air blowers must be provided.

The toilets must be assessible to the workers at all times. Where practicable, they should be within 200 feet of regular work locations. They should not be more than one floor-to-floor flight of stairs from working areas. Reasonable accommodation must be made for the personal needs of the disabled or handicapped. An adequate supply of toilet paper must be provided for each toilet.

If there are at least five workers at the establishment, and at least one of them is of the sex different from other workers, then there must be at least two separate toilets. No person can be allowed to use a toilet assigned to persons of the other sex. The toilet facilities must be comparable and adequate for workers of both sexes.

The need to provide toilet facilities cannot be used to justify a discriminatory employment or assignment decision.

The toilet facilities must be plainly designated for each sex.

If there are four or fewer workers, then one toilet facility is adequate, provided it can be locked from the inside to assure privacy.

Drinking fountains and water dispensers cannot be located in toilet rooms. Food and beverages cannot be stored or consumed in any toilet rooms.

Where showers are required, there must be separate shower rooms for each sex. (If there are fewer than five workers, then one shower room may be used by both sexes, provided that it can be locked from the inside.) Shower soap or cleanser must be provided; individual clean towels must be provided.

LAW: Health and Safety Code sections 5416 and 5474.20-5474.31; Labor Code sections 2350 and 2354; Title 2 California Administrative Code section 7291.1(e)(2); Title 8 California Administrative Code sections 3361-3368; Title 17 California Administrative Code sections 8000-8013.

ENFORCEMENT: Labor commissioner; district attorney; Cal-OSHA; Health Services Dept.; civil action.

Some violations are punishable by jail and a fine.

EXCEPTIONS: The above standards for toilets apply only to permanent workplaces. Toilets do not have to be provided to mobile crews or at normally unattended work locations, provided that workers at these locations or on mobile crews have immediately available transportation to nearby toilet facilities (which must meet the standards listed above).

Construction job sites must have at least one approved toilet or privy for every twenty workers. Farm workers growing or harvesting fruits, nuts or vegetables must have toilets and handwashing facilities (so long as there are at least five workers and the work lasts at least two hours). Where practicable, the facilities must be within a five minute walk. Clean and private toilets, toilet paper, soap, and clean water must be provided. There must be at least one facility for every forty workers.


## YOUR EMPLOYER MUST PROVIDE READILY ACCESSIBLE DRINKING WATER

Every employer must provide fresh and pure drinking water to the workers. Access to the water must be permitted at reasonable and convenient times and places. No charge can be made for the water.

LAW: Labor Code section 2441.

ENFORCEMENT: Labor commissioner; Health Services Dept.; any city or county health officer.

Anyone who violates the law is guilty of a crime and is subject to 30 days in prison and a $100 fine for each offense.

EXCEPTIONS: No exceptions; this law applies to all workers, public and private: those at permanent job sites; those at temporary job sites; those on mobile crews.

Additional protections at every permanent place of employment covered by Cal-OSHA: Drinkable water must be provided for drinking and for washing and cooking. No drinking water sources can be located in toilet rooms. Common use of a cup, glass, or other vessel is forbidden. Use of barrels, pails, tanks, or similar containers is forbidden. Non-drinkable water must be clearly labeled as such. (Title 8 Calif. Administrative Code section 3363.)

# CHAPTER 6

## WORKERS' COMPENSATION

### YOUR EMPLOYER MUST CARRY WORKERS' COMPENSATION

Workers' compensation is a system set up to compensate employees for work-related injuries. A work-related injury is an injury, disease, or other medical condition incurred by an employee in the course of his or her employment and which arises out of the employment; or a pre-existing injury, disease or condition made worse by the employment.

There are three types of work-related injuries:

(1) Specific: occurring from one accident (e.g., breaking a leg from a fall).

(2) Cumulative: injury caused by repetitive activities over a period of time (e.g., bad back, stress-related illness).

(3) Occupational disease: a disease which occurs because of exposure to hazardous substances or conditions on the job (e.g., allergies).

Normally, a work-related injury occurs at the job site. However, you may be covered elsewhere, as well, if the injury occurs as a result of your employment. For example, if your employer requests or encourages you to engage in some special activity--a class, company soft-ball game, or picnic--you may be covered going to and from the activity as well as while there.

All employers in the state of California must carry workers' compensation insurance through a private carrier, or through the state compensation insurance fund, or be self-insured. The employer must cover all employees. The cost of workers' compensation insurance must be paid entirely by the employer, with no contribution from the employee.

**LAW:** Labor Code sections 2801, 3208, 3208.1, 3351, 3700, and 3710.

**ENFORCEMENT:** Labor commissioner; Industrial Relations, Dept. Director; Workers' Compensation Appeals Board.

An employer who does not provide workers' compensation insurance coverage may be guilty of a misdemeanor.

**EXCEPTIONS:** Workers' compensation exceptions.*

An unlicensed independent contractor doing work which requires a contractor's license is treated as an "employee" for purposes of workers' compensation coverage. Labor Code section 2750.5.

## REGULATIONS GOVERNING SELF-INSURED EMPLOYERS

In order to self-insure, an employer must post a bond of at least $100,000 and receive the consent of the Director of the Department of Industrial Relations. Self-insurers are carefully audited and regulated. Consent to self-insure may be revoked at any time by the Director of the Department of Industrial Relations for "good cause."

"Good cause" for revocation includes but is not limited to:

(1) financial problems of the employer;

(2) frequent violations of state safety and health orders;

(3) habitually attempting to make employees accept less than the compensation amount due them;

(4) habitually forcing employees to resort to legal proceedings against the employer to receive compensation;

(5) dishonesty in the compensation process; or

(6) other "good cause."

LAW: Labor Code sections 3700, 3701, 3702, 3702.3, 3702.5, 3706, and 3707; Title 8 California Administrative Code sections 15200-15437.

ENFORCEMENT: Labor commissioner; Industrial Relations, Dept. Director; civil action.

EXCEPTIONS: Workers' compensation exceptions.*

## YOUR EMPLOYER MUST POST INFORMATION ABOUT WORKERS' COMPENSATION COVERAGE AND NOTIFY YOU OF BENEFITS

In a conspicuous location frequented by workers, every employer must post (and keep posted) a notice that lists: (1) the name of the current compensation insurance carrier (or, if certified as self-insured, a notice of self-insurance), and (2) the name and address of the person responsible for claims adjustment; and (3) a summary of your rights.

Every employer must give to every new employee a written notice that tells the worker of his or her rights. This notice must be given by the end of the first pay period.

The employer must also give you written notice of your rights within five working days of his/her knowledge of your injury or claim and, if benefits are denied, must give you an explanation of the denial.

LAW: Labor Code sections 3550 and 3551; Title 8 California Administrative Code sections 9782, 9880, and 15596.

ENFORCEMENT: Labor commissioner; Industrial Relations, Dept. Director.

Failure to comply is a misdemeanor; it is also prima facie evidence of non insurance. (If the employer is not insured, he may be liable to a very expensive law suit.)

EXCEPTIONS: Workers' compensation exceptions.*

This law does not apply to certain in-house domestic servants and child-care attendants, who work in the employer's own residence.

## TIME LIMITS FOR FILING CLAIMS

Normally, claims must be filed within one year of the industrial injury (or of the date you became disabled from cumulative stress or disease, or of the date you learned the injury was work related). This time limit may be extended under certain circumstances.

For example, the time limit may be extended to one year from the time the employer last provided treatment or the compensation carrier last provided benefits. It is always a good idea to report even the most insignificant injury immediately to establish the fact that it occurred on the job, should complications arise. Always give your employer written notice of an injury within 30 days of its occurrence. Keep a copy of this notice for your records.

The notice should contain:

(1) your name and address;

(2) the time and place the injury occurred; and

(3) the nature of the injury.

**LAW:** Labor Code sections 5400-5405.

**ENFORCEMENT:** Workers' Compensation Appeals Board.

**EXCEPTIONS:** Workers' compensation exceptions.*

## YOU HAVE THE RIGHT TO COMPENSATION FOR AN AGGRAVATED INJURY

If you have a pre-existing condition (e.g., a bad back, allergy, nervous condition) which is made worse by the work you do, you may be eligible for some workers' compensation benefits.

Your employer may have to pay medical costs and some benefits if your condition worsened as a result of your job.

**LAW:** Labor Code section 4663.

**ENFORCEMENT:** Workers' Compensation Appeals Board.

**EXCEPTIONS:** Workers' compensation exceptions.*

## YOU HAVE THE RIGHT TO SELECT YOUR OWN PHYSICIAN

You have the right to use your own health care provider. You can go to your own doctor or chiropractor (and change from that doctor to a new doctor if you so desire). You do **not** have to use an employer-selected physician. You do not have to choose your doctor from an employer-approved list.

Your employer must pay for **all** diagnosis and treatment which is connected with your work-related illness or injury.

This right cannot be limited or waived by any agreement or union contract. You cannot be penalized for choosing your own doctor or other practitioner. If you choose the doctor, then you can make sure that s/he is more interested in curing your problem than in saving money for your employer.

To protect this right, you must file a notice with your employer. This should state that you have a personal physician or chiropractor you intend to see in the event of an industrial injury and should give his/her address. Your employer must provide a form for filing this notice.

Your employer must notify you of this right.

**LAW:** Labor Code sections 3550-3552 and 4600-4603.

**ENFORCEMENT:** Workers' Compensation Appeals Board.

**EXCEPTIONS:** If you have not filed a notice (about your own doctor) with your employer **before** your industrial injury, then your rights may be restricted for the first thirty days.

If your employer has posted your rights, and you have not filed a notice (naming your own physician) before your injury, then the following rules apply:

(1) You can always be treated by your own doctor, but your employer does not have to pay for it, for the first thirty days (when you didn't file the notice before the accident).

(2) If you want your employer to pay, then you must use a doctor named by your employer, for those first thirty days. However, you do not have to use (or you can stop seeing) the first doctor your employer names. If you do not like that doctor, ask your employer for "change of physician." Within five working days, your employer must name a different doctor. And in any case, after the first thirty days, you can go to your own doctor (and have the employer pay for it).

(3) You do not have to do what the employer-chosen doctor tells you. As with any doctor-patient relationship, you must make the final decisions about your health. In any serious case, your employer must pay for a second "consulting" physician or chiropractor, of your choice, even during those first thirty days.

(4) Once those first thirty days are up, you can choose your own doctor (and change from that doctor if you so desire), and the employer pays for all needed treatments. Either you or your new doctor or chiropractor must immediately notify your employer of the change.

To avoid any problems, it is best to file the notice (about your own doctor) before any injuries or illnesses. If any questions come up, and in any case where you have a serious injury or illness, you should contact an attorney specializing in Workers' Compensation. Any time your employer asks you to see a different physician, it is important to check with your attorney.

If your employer has not posted your rights, then you have the same rights as if you had notified your employer of your personal doctor prior to your injury.

Workers' compensation exceptions.*

## YOU HAVE THE RIGHT TO BE REPRESENTED BY AN ATTORNEY

You have the right to be represented by an attorney in the workers' compensation claim and appeal process.

Often employers contest the legitimate claims of their employees. An employer's insurance costs are based on claims: the more successful the claims, the higher the cost. The workers' compensations system is very complex, and even when employers do not contest claims, a worker may not receive all that s/he is entitled to receive. Therefore, it is **always** a good idea to be represented by an attorney in the proceedings.

An attorney is not allowed to charge you a fee for a consultation on a workers' compensation problem which does not lead to a claim and settlement. In fact, an attorney can only charge you a fee based on a percentage of the award. (Set by the Workers' Compensation Appeal Board: normally 9-12% of the final award.)

Because workers' compensation is a very specialized area of the law, it is important to retain an attorney who specializes in this area. Consult your union or county bar association for recommendations.

**LAW:** Labor Code sections 4906 and 5700.

**ENFORCEMENT:** Workers' Compensation Appeals Board.

**EXCEPTIONS:** Workers' compensation exceptions.*

## IN SOME CASES YOU MAY HAVE THE RIGHT TO SUE

In general, you cannot sue your employer for most industrial injuries. But this rule does not keep you from suing other people. For example, you may have been injured in part because the machinery you used was not safely designed. In that case, you may sue the manufacturer of the machinery. Or you may have been hurt on the job because of someone's negligence. Perhaps someone hit you with his car while you were working. In addition to compensation from your employer, you can sue the person who hit you.

If you do recover extra damages from another person (often called a "third party"), you may have to reimburse the employer for part of his/her payments to you. It is important to discuss with an attorney any conditions which may allow you to sue for extra money.

**LAW:** Labor Code section 3852.

**ENFORCEMENT:** Civil action.

**EXCEPTIONS:** You **can** sue your employer for injuries resulting from willful assault; intentional infliction of emotional distress or other intentional acts; fraudulent concealment of injury or risk; removal of safety device from power press. If your injury or disease (emotional or otherwise) results from the act of termination, you are not covered by workers' compensation; therefore you are free to sue your employer for damages.

## YOUR EMPLOYER MUST PAY FOR MEDICAL TESTS IN A CONTESTED CLAIM

You are entitled to reimbursement for all expenses that are reasonable and necessarily incurred for laboratory fees, x-rays, medical examinations, medical records, interpreter's fees, and medical testimony to prove a contested claim. You are entitled to reimbursement whether or not you prevail in proving the claim.

**LAW:** Labor Code sections 4620 and 4621.

**ENFORCEMENT:** Workers' Compensation Appeals Board.

**EXCEPTIONS:** Workers' compensation exceptions.*

## YOUR EMPLOYER IS RESPONSIBLE FOR ALL MEDICAL TREATMENT OF YOUR INDUSTRIAL INJURIES

If you have a genuine workers' compensation claim, your employer is responsible for all treatment, including medical, surgical and chiropractic care, hospitalization, nursing, medicines, medical and surgical supplies, crutches, artificial limbs, etc. You have a right to replacement or repair of artificial members, dentures, hearing aids, medical braces, and eyeglasses injured in a work-related accident. (Eyeglasses and hearing aids are covered only if you are hurt in the accident that broke them.)

In any serious case, you have the right to a second or "consulting" physician or chiropractor of your choice, paid for by your employer.

If referred by your doctor and approved by your employer, you may utilize the services of a marriage or family counselor, child counselor, or clinical social worker.

LAW: Labor Code sections 3208, 4600, and 4601; Title 8 California Administrative Code section 9784 and 9785.

ENFORCEMENT: Workers' Compensation Appeals Board.

EXCEPTIONS: Workers' compensation exceptions.*

## YOUR EMPLOYER HAS ACCESS TO ALL MEDICAL AND OTHER RECORDS RELATING TO YOUR WORKERS' COMPENSATION CLAIM

Your employer has access to all reports and records of doctors, chiropractors, psychologists, psychiatrists, rehabilitation counselors, or any other health care professional involved in your evaluation, treatment, or rehabilitation. Do not answer wide-ranging questions which do not relate to your injury. Ask your attorney what information is appropriate to provide and what sort of information should be kept confidential.

LAW: Labor Code sections 4050-4055.

ENFORCEMENT: Workers' Compensation Appeals Board; civil action.

EXCEPTIONS: Workers' compensations exceptions.*

## YOUR EMPLOYER IS RESPONSIBLE FOR THE COST OF MEDICAL TRANSPORTATION

Your employer is responsible for the cost of transportation to and from medical treatments. If you are required to submit to a medical examination at the request of the employer's insurance carrier or the Appeals Board, you are entitled to transportation, meals, and lodging (if necessary) as well.

LAW: Labor Code section 4600.

ENFORCEMENT: Workers' Compensation Appeals Board.

EXCEPTIONS: Workers' compensation exceptions.*

## YOU HAVE TO RIGHT TO RECEIVE DISABILITY PAY

Disability payments normally do not begin until the fourth day after you leave work as the result of a work-related injury. However, if the injury causes a disability of 21 days or more, you are entitled to coverage from the first day.

If you are hospitalized as a result of a work-related injury, payment begins the first day of the hospitalization.

Your rate of pay for a temporary disability is based on a formula awarding you two-thirds of your weekly pay (within the minimum and maximum set by law). These payments may continue until your condition becomes permanent and stationary, or until your payment period runs out (240 weeks). By that time, you should have recovered fully or have received a permanent disability rating. If you are temporarily disabled, but can do some work, you may be entitled to partial disability payments.

If your workers' compensation claim is being contested and you are not receiving benefits, you are entitled to receive State

Disability Insurance benefits (SDI) pending resolution of your workers' compensation claim.

**LAW:** Labor Code sections 4650, 4650.5, 4651, 4651.1, 4651.3, 4652-4657, 4661, and 4661.5.

**ENFORCEMENT:** Workers' Compensation Appeals Board.

**EXCEPTIONS:** Workers' compensation exceptions.*

Law enforcement, lifesaving and firefighting personnel can receive higher benefits.

## YOU MAY BE ELIGIBLE FOR PERMANENT DISABILITY BENEFITS

Once your medical condition stabilizes and becomes permanent, you are eligible for permanent disability benefits. The amount of money you are entitled to is determined by your permanent disability rating. Your rating is determined by the injury, your age and occupation, and your ability to obtain employment.

A rating chart is used to determine the standard rate for a certain type of injury. For example, the loss an an arm would be rated as a 75% loss; the loss of an index finger, 8%. However, a machinist who loses an arm might be rated higher than a teacher with the same injury, because in the latter case loss of an arm may not so severely limit the teacher's job performance.

**LAW:** Labor Code sections 4658-4662.

**ENFORCEMENT:** Workers' Compensation Appeals Board.

**EXCEPTIONS:** Workers' compensation exceptions.*

## YOUR SURVIVORS ARE ENTITLED TO DEATH BENEFITS

Over 100,000 workers die each year as the result of industrial injuries or occupational diseases. Death benefits and burial allowances are available to survivors.

LAW: Labor Code sections 4700-4706.5.

ENFORCEMENT: Workers' Compensation Appeals Board.

EXCEPTIONS: Members of the Public Employees Retirement System cannot receive death benefits under workers' compensation if they are entitled to benefits under the PERS. If benefits under PERS are less than those paid under workers' compensation, survivors are entitled to the difference. Law enforcement officers may be entitled to additional benefits.

Workers' compensation exceptions.*

## YOU MAY BE ENTITLED TO RETRAINING AND REHABILITATION BENEFITS

Disabled employees who cannot return to their original employment may be entitled to vocational rehabilitation and retraining benefits. Your employer or his/her insurance carrier must give you notice of the right to rehabilitation and retraining benefits in any case where you have been disabled or hospitalized for a total of 28 days or more. This notice must be given in writing.

Retraining and rehabilitation may range from training a righthanded worker to perform job duties with his/her left hand, to education and training for an entirely new career.

As an employee with a work-related disability you are entitled to rehabilitation benefits if:

(1) The disability permanently prevents you, or is likely to prevent you, from being employed in your usual and customary occupation or the position you occupied at the time of the injury; and

(2) You can be expected to benefit from a rehabilitation program.

While you are in a rehabilitation program, your temporary disability benefits will continue, even beyond the 240 week maximum.

It is your employer's responsibility to pay for vocational rehabilitation services through a qualified counselor. You have the right to select a counselor to be paid for by your employer. If you and your employer cannot agree on a counselor or on a rehabilitation plan, you may appeal to the Bureau of Rehabilitation. Decisions of the Bureau may be appealed to the Workers' Compensation Appeals Board.

The retraining and rehabilitation plan is voluntary on the part of the injured worker. You cannot be denied workers' compensation benefits, disciplined or discharged merely because you do not wish to participate in a rehabilitation program.

**LAW:** Labor Code sections 6200-6208.

**ENFORCEMENT:** Workers' Compensation Appeals Board.

**EXCEPTIONS:** Workers' compensation exceptions.*

## JOB PROTECTIONS FOR WORKERS WITH WORK-RELATED INJURIES OR ILLNESSES

Special protections are given to a worker who suffers a work-related injury or illness. The injured worker can miss time from work without losing her/his job, classification, seniority, or other job rights. These rights are sometimes called "Judson Steel" rights.

These protections apply to the initial time missed from work due to the injury or illness, to long absences, to intermittent absences, to reoccurrences of injury or illness, and to absences for treatment or therapy. These rights apply even when years are lost from work. You have this protection whenever your absence is partially or wholly due to the work-related illness or injury. (Your health care professional can help you determine if your illness or condition might be connected with, or made worse by, your job). These rights exist even if a union contract or company policy says the opposite or seems to limit the amount (or frequency) of time which can be missed without penalty.

You can lose your job only if your employer has no work that you can do (or may eventually recover enough to do). It is not appropriate for your employer to treat your disability like other disabilities, or your absence like other absences. You cannot be disciplined for your injury or injury-related absences, nor can these count as part of the basis for discipline. No action penalizing you for an injury or injury-related absence is allowed, unless it is required by your employer's "business necessity." These protections exist even if the injury occurred during previous employment.

**LAW:** Labor Code section 132a.

**ENFORCEMENT:** Labor commissioner; district attorney; Workers' Compensation Appeals Board; civil action;

Violation is a misdemeanor and subjects the employer to six months in jail and a $500 fine.

If the Workers' Compensation Appeals Board finds your employer in violation of this law, your award may be increased by one half (up to $10,000).

**EXCEPTIONS:** The only exception is where the injured worker can never return to work. So long as there is a possibility of recovery, the job-injured worker cannot legally be terminated or denied reinstatement rights.

When a worker is finally determined to be forever unable to return to her/his former position, then the laws on "handicap" or "disability" discrimination apply. If s/he may return to work (at the old job "with reasonable accommodation," or at another position), then the employer has a duty to allow that return. (See Chapter 8, DISCIPLINE AND DISCHARGE, and Chapter 2, HIRING RIGHTS.)

Workers' compensation exceptions.*

## YOU HAVE ADDITIONAL RIGHTS IF YOUR EMPLOYER IS NOT INSURED

If your employer does not carry workers' compensation insurance, you have several important rights which are described below.

**Stop Orders** -- The Director of the Department of Industrial Relations can serve a stop order upon your employer. Once this is done, your employer cannot legally use any employee labor. S/he cannot legally have anyone work for her/him.

If you are laid off because of a stop order, the employer has to keep paying your full wages. You are entitled to full pay, as if you had kept working, for as long as the stop order shuts your employer down (but only up to 10 days' pay).

LAW: Labor Code sections 3700.5, 3710.1, 3710.2, and 3712; Title 8 California Administrative Code sections 15550-15595.

ENFORCEMENT: Labor commissioner.

An employer or any supervisor who ignores a stop order is subject to 60 days in jail and $1,000 fine.

EXCEPTIONS: Workers' compensation exceptions.*

**Law Suits** -- If you are injured on the job, and your employer does not have compensation insurance, you can sue in court. And when you do, it is presumed that your injury or illness was caused by your employer's negligence. The employer has the burden of showing the opposite.

And your employer cannot claim that your injury is your own fault (no "contributory negligence"), or is the fault of another worker (no "fellow employee"), or even that you knew about the job's danger (no "assumption of risk").

Even if you signed a contract or agreement giving up these rights, or stating that you are an "independent contractor," that doesn't matter. You still have these rights.

**LAW:** Labor Code sections 3706-3709 and 5001.

**ENFORCEMENT:** Civil action.

**EXCEPTIONS:** Workers' compensation exceptions.*

**Who to Sue** -- Who is your employer, so far as job injuries and illnesses are concerned? The definition of "employer" is very broad. And there is a presumption that you were the employee of anyone for whom you did work or rendered services.

The "employer" has the burden of proving that you really were not an "employee."

On a given job, you can have more than one "employer." For example, if you work for one person, and s/he has you do work for another, both may be your employer. If both of them control your work (tell you what to do and how to do it), then both are liable for your job injury or illness.

If your employer actually hired you to work for someone else, even though you never even heard of that other person, then both your employer and the other person are liable for your job injury or illness.

Be sure to tell your lawyer about everyone connected with your job.

**LAW:** Labor Code sections 3300, 3351, 3553, 3357, 3601, and 5705.

**ENFORCEMENT:** Civil action.

**EXCEPTIONS:** Workers' compensation exceptions.*

Uninsured Employers Fund -- California has an Uninsured Employers Fund. If you choose to proceed under the Workers' Compensation Appeals Board, instead of filing a lawsuit, this Fund will make sure your benefits are paid.

Usually you can get more money in a law suit, but (depending upon your employers) it may be difficult to collect. You need to carefully discuss this issue with your compensation lawyer.

If you use the Uninsured Employers Fund, your employer will be subject to financial and criminal penalties for failing to provide proper coverage.

LAW: Labor Code sections 3710-3732 and 3708-3709.5.

ENFORCEMENT: Labor commissioner; Workers' Compensation Appeals Board.

EXCEPTIONS: Workers' compensation exceptions.*


## YOUR COMPENSATION RIGHTS CANNOT BE WAIVED

You have all these rights to workers' compensation even if your employer has made you sign a "waiver," or a "release," or a "contract," or a "settlement" to the contrary. You have these rights, even if your employer has had you agree that you are an "independent contractor." If you "waived" any rights, or if you paid any amount towards compensation insurance, you may sue your employer for damages.

No waiver or release of your compensation rights is any good, unless and until it has been approved by the Workers' Compensation Appeals Board or a workers' compensation judge.

LAW: Labor Code sections 2801, 2804, 3708, 3751, and 5000-5005.

ENFORCEMENT: Labor commissioner; Workers' Compensation Appeals Board; civil action.

EXCEPTIONS: Workers' compensation exceptions.*

## CHAPTER 7

## BASIC ORGANIZING RIGHTS AND PROTECTIONS

**YOU HAVE THE RIGHT TO ORGANIZE, TO BARGAIN COLLECTIVELY, AND TO TAKE CONCERTED ACTION**

Workers in California and nationwide have certain basic rights and protections which are enforced under a number of different laws and by several different agencies. Every private sector worker is protected by at least **one** basic source of rights; in most cases, this source is the federal National Labor Relations Act. But some private sector workers are not covered by the NLRA. Sometimes workers are excluded from coverage by the federal labor laws themselves. For example, domestic workers employed directly by a family are not protected by the NLRB (but are protected by Labor Code section 923). In other cases, the National Labor Relations Board (the enforcement agency for the NLRA) has declined jurisdiction: i.e., the Board (as the NLRB is called) has refused to extend its protections to certain workers and their employers. (Usually this is because the employer's business is very small and/or it does not involve interstate commerce.)

Workers in certain industries are covered separately. Railroad and airline workers are protected by the Railway Labor Act (RLA). Farm workers, excluded from NLRB coverage, are protected in California by the Agricultural Labor Relations Act (ALRA). Federal, state, public, educational, and local government employees are protected under a variety of public sector bargaining laws.

If you are a private sector worker and not covered by the NLRB, the RLA, or the ALRA, you are protected in California by the statement of basic labor rights included in Labor Code section 923. This law proclaims the official State policy:

*In the interpretation and application of this chapter, the public policy of this State is declared as follows:*

*Negotiation of terms and conditions of labor should result from voluntary agreement between employer and employees. Governmental authority has permitted and encouraged employers to organize in the corporate and other forms of capital control.*

*In dealing with such employers, the individual unorganized worker is helpless to exercise actual liberty of contract and to protect his freedom of labor, and thereby to obtain acceptable terms and conditions of employment.*

*Therefore it is necessary that the individual workman have full freedom of association, self-organization, and designation of representatives of his own choosing, to negotiate the terms and conditions of his employment, and that he shall be free from the interference, restraint, or coercion of employers of labor, or their agents, in the designation of such representatives or in self-organization or in other concerted activities for the purpose of collective bargaining or other mutual aid or protection.*

**ENFORCEMENT**: Enforcement methods vary. If you are covered by the National Labor Relations Board or the Railway Labor Act or the Agricultural Labor Relations Act, then you must protect your fundamental organizational rights using the particular procedures of the federal or state laws under which you are covered. If you are a private sector worker but are not covered by the NLRB, the RLA, or the ALRA, then you can proceed directly under Labor Code section 923. In some cases, the labor commisssioner can act to protect your section 923 rights, but usually you must act on your own. In addition to the usual concerted means of mutual aid and protection available to you (strikes, picketing, and so forth), you can go to court to protect your rights.

EXCEPTIONS: This right to sue in a California court under Section 923 does not apply if you are covered by the National Labor Relations Act or the Railway Labor Act. The reason for this is a legal doctrine called "preemption." This doctrine limits the ability of a state, like California, to regulate an area which the federal government has already regulated. Where the NLRB regulates the basic labor/management relationship, the state is not allowed to intrude. (Just how far this preemption applies is never completely clear. Beyond the core organizing rights, preemption becomes an issue for lawyers to battle over.)

Supervisors in most private sector industries are denied bargaining rights. Who is a "supervisor" under the law is a technical question. Consult your union or lawyer.

## BASIC ORGANIZING RIGHTS UNDER LABOR CODE SECTION 923

Section 923 provides you with certain specific rights, which are outlined below. If you are covered by the NLRA, RLA, ALRA or are a government employee, you have these same rights, but they are enforced by the particular agency that protects you.

(1) Your employer cannot legally discipline or discharge you because of union membership or activities.

(2) Your employer cannot ask you how you feel about unions, strikes, or any related topics.

(3) Your employer cannot legally discipline or discharge you because you and your fellow workers join together in any effort to improve your working conditions or pay or benefits.

(4) Your employer cannot legally solicit union withdrawal. No supervisor can ask for or encourage withdrawal or resignation from a union.

(5) Your employer cannot attend (or send supervisors to) union meetings. S/he cannot watch to see who attends union meetings.

(6) You and your fellow workers have the right to choose your own spokesperson. Your employer cannot legally insist on bargaining only with "her own" or "his own" workers. You can have an outsider (a union official, a lawyer) act as your spokesperson.

LAW: Labor Code section 923.

ENFORCEMENT: Civil action.

EXCEPTIONS: Consult your union or attorney.


**Promises or Commitments to Not Join a Union are Illegal--** Your employer cannot require you (or any employee or job applicant) to promise to not join a union. You cannot be made to promise to leave work if you do join a union. Even if you make a promise like this, it cannot be enforced. If you lose your job, or a promotion, or any other benefit because of this kind of promise (or because you refuse to make such a promise), you can win back your job or other benefit.

LAW: Labor Code sections 920-923.

ENFORCEMENT: Labor commissioner; district attorney; civil action.

Violation is a misdemeanor.

EXCEPTIONS: Consult your union or attorney.


**Company Unions Are Illegal --** An employer or employer association cannot finance or contribute toward a union (or any employee group which fulfills any bargaining or representation function). An employer or employer association may not dominate or in any way interfere with a union or employee group. An employer cannot contribute money or help to candidates for union office.

Any person who organizes a "company union" (one controlled by the employer) can be sued, along with the employer or employer association involved. If a company union keeps out a real union, the workers can sue for the difference between what they are receiving in wages and benefits and what they would receive if a legitimate union were representing them.

**LAW:** Labor Code sections 923 and 1122.

**ENFORCEMENT:** Civil action.

**EXCEPTIONS:** Consult your union or attorney.

**You Have The Right To Exchange Salary Information With Your Co-Workers** -- Sometimes employers tell their workers not to discuss wage and salary information, saying that it is "secret". Sometimes this prohibition extends to vacation or other leave arrangements, or to other information about job conditions. All such restrictions and prohibitions are illegal. Workers can exchange information, discuss what they learn, and organize to improve things. Any action taken against you for exercising these basic rights is illegal.

**LAW:** Labor Code sections 232 and 923.

**ENFORCEMENT:** Labor commissioner; civil action.

**EXCEPTIONS:** Consult your union or attorney.

**No Ordinance May Be Enforced That Interferes With Basic Union Rights** -- The State of California and the federal government have enacted laws protecting the rights of private sector workers and their unions to engage in union activities and peaceful picketing. No local government may enforce an ordinance or rule which interferes with these activities.

No local government may require registration or licensing of union organizers, or representatives, or solicitors.

Cities, counties, and special districts may adopt ordinances regulating the employer-employee relations of their own workers, so long as these regulations do not abridge the rights given them under state law (Meyers-Milias-Brown Act and other laws).

> LAW: U.S. Constitution Article VI, clause 2; California Constitution Article III, section 1, Article IV, sections 1 and 16, Article XI, section 7.

> ENFORCEMENT: Civil action.

> EXCEPTIONS: Consult your union or attorney.


## UNION ACTIVITIES ON PRIVATE OR POSTED PROPERTY ARE PROTECTED BY LAW

Union representatives may not lawfully be arrested for trespass at jobsites, if they are engaged in lawful union activities. For example, they may enter to make safety investigations or for any other legitimate union purpose.

Union representatives should carry written authorization from the union to make safety investigations or otherwise represent the union.

These protections apply to property whether or not it is posted "no trespassing".

> LAW: Penal Code sections 552.1, 555.2, and 602.

> ENFORCEMENT: District attorney; State Attorney General; National Labor Relations Board; Agricultural Labor Relations Board; civil action.

> An NLRB or ALRB complaint should be filed immediately if someone demands that you leave the property or threatens you with arrest or citation.

> EXCEPTIONS: If, during an organizing campaign, you are entering areas not open to the public, check with your attorney for possible exceptions. Also check for special rules concerning picketing and distributing leaflets.

> Special rules apply to government and defense contractor property.

## JOB SEEKERS HAVE A RIGHT TO KNOW IF A LABOR DISPUTE EXISTS

Anyone advertising to fill any job must, plainly and explicitly, mention any labor problem at the workplace. This law applies to any form of advertisement: newspaper, word of mouth, posters, letters, or any other form of communication.

This law applies to any labor dispute, whether existing or pending: a strike, a lockout, a trade dispute, a labor disturbance, a jurisdictional dispute, a picket line.

Anyone advertising, soliciting, or communicating for job applicants before or during a labor dispute must:

(1) plainly state that a strike, or lockout, or other labor dispute exists;

(2) state his/her own name; and

(3) if acting for someone else, give that person's name as well.

LAW: Labor Code sections 970-974.

ENFORCEMENT: Labor commissioner; district attorney; civil action.

Each communication or advertisement that fails to contain the required information subjects the employer to six months in jail and a $500 fine. A worker injured by the violation may sue for double damages.

## EMPLOYMENT AGENCY REFERRALS TO STRIKE/LOCKOUT JOBS

There are two types of employment agencies, and each is covered by different rules regarding referrals to struck or locked-out jobs.

**Employment Agency** -- The first type is known simply as an employment agency. This type of agency takes a fee for referring a worker to a job. Some nurses' registries operate this way. The nurse is referred by the agency to a health facility. The nurse's salary is paid directly by the hospital and the registry receives a referral or placement fee (from either the nurse or the hospital).

In the event of a labor dispute, this type of employment agency (or registry) must give to each applicant a written notice concerning the strike (or lockout or other labor dispute) that exists or is pending at any location to which s/he is referred.

LAW: Business and Professions Code sections 9984(a)(8), 9988 and 9994; Labor Code sections 970-974.

ENFORCEMENT: District attorney; Personnel Services Bureau; civil action.

Violation is a crime punishable by jail and a fine.

**Temporary Employment Service** -- A second type of employment agency is known as a temporary employment service. This type of agency actually employs individuals to be dispatched as "temporary help" or as "leased" workers. The worker receives his/her salary from the temporary employment service or the service sets the rate of pay and controls the worker's schedule. Some nurses' registries operate this way as well. The nurse is employed by the registry and the health care facility pays not the nurse, but the registry, for the nurse's services.

This type of employment service or nurses' registry may not send its workers to any place where a strike, lockout, or other labor dispute exists. Where the struck employer supervises the work or controls how it is done, this law also applies to personnel service companies, labor contractors, labor pools, and job shops.

LAW: Business and Professions Code sections 9902 and 9994; Volume 63 California Attorney General's Opinions page 723; Wage and Hour Division Opinion Letter No. 1403 (WH-350).

ENFORCEMENT: District attorney; Personnel Services Bureau; civil action.

Each referral or dispatch to a struck or locked-out worksite is punishable by 60 days in jail and a $500 fine.

EXCEPTIONS: Farm labor contractors or employers and talent, musician, artist or athletes' agencies are governed by other similar laws.


## YOU HAVE A RIGHT TO YOUR EARNED WAGES, EVEN IF YOU ARE ON STRIKE OR LOCKED OUT

When you go out on strike, your employer must pay you all wages that you have already earned. These wages must be paid no later than the next regular pay day. Your employer cannot make any special deduction from or offset against these wages.

If you request that your accrued vacation benefits be given to you in the form of wages, your employer must include vacation pay in your paycheck. Your employer must also include in the paycheck any deposit, money, or other guarantee which you have given or left with her/him.

If there is a disagreement over how much is due, your employer must include in the paycheck all amounts which s/he admits are due. (See Chapter 4, WAGES, FRINGE BENEFITS AND HOURS OF WORK, for more information about disputed pay.)

LAW: Labor Code sections 200, 206, and 209.

ENFORCEMENT: Labor commissioner; district attorney; civil action.

Any employer who violates these laws is subject to six months in jail and a $500 fine.

EXCEPTIONS: Employees of the state or any county, city, town, or other municipal corporation.

## POLICE OFFICERS CANNOT BE EMPLOYED AS GUARDS DURING A STRIKE

Sometimes police officers are allowed to "moonlight" as security guards. However, no employer may hire a local police officer (directly or through a security services agency) to act as a security guard during a labor dispute.

Police officers cannot act as guards at a strike, lockout, picket line, or demonstration that occurs in the officers' own jurisdiction.

LAW: Labor Code section 1112.

ENFORCEMENT: Labor commissioner; district attorney; the public entity employing the police officer; civil action.


## EMPLOYING PROFESSIONAL STRIKEBREAKERS IS ILLEGAL

A professional strikebreaker is anyone who has replaced a striking or locked-out worker at least three times in the last five years. (The three previous occasions must have involved at least two separate employers.)

It is a crime for an employer to hire a professional strikebreaker to replace a striking or locked-out worker. It is a crime for a professional strikebreaker to offer to replace a locked-out or striking worker.

LAW: Labor Code sections 1130, 1133, 1134, 1134.2, and 1136.

ENFORCEMENT: Labor commissioner; district attorney; civil action.

Any employer who knowingly uses a professional strikebreaker, and any professional strikebreaker who offers to replace a locked-out or striking worker, is subject to 90 days in jail and a fine.

## UNION BUGS, LABELS, CARDS, AND BUTTONS MAY NOT BE USED WITHOUT THE UNION'S PERMISSION

Unions control their labels, trademarks, bugs, cards, signs, and buttons. An employer must have the union's permission to use any of these identification marks. This permission must be in writing (and must not have been revoked by the union).

Only a worker entitled to use a union card by the rules and regulations of that union can legally do so. Only a worker entitled by the rules of her/his union to wear a union button may do so.

LAW: Labor Code sections 1010-1018.

ENFORCEMENT: Labor commissioner; district attorney; civil action.

Anyone who fraudulently uses a union card is guilty of a misdemeanor. Anyone who uses a union bug, label, or sign without permisssion is guilty of a misdemeanor, and can also be sued for damages.


## RULES GOVERNING PRODUCT LABELS AND CLAIMS

Any employer who falsely claims to utilize union labor is guilty of a misdemeanor. Anyone who sells a product or service, and who falsely claims that the product or service was produced by union labor, is also guilty of a misdemeanor. No one who makes or sells any product in California can lawfully misrepresent the kind of labor involved in making the product. Violation is a misdemeanor. Falsely claiming that a product was made in California, or was made in the U.S.A., is a crime.


**Products Made at Home** -- Any article or any material which is made or repaired in someone's home is made by "industrial homework." Any article or material altered, finished, inspected, wrapped, packaged, assembled, or prepared at home is also made by industrial homework.

Any article made by industrial homework must have a label or mark conspicuously attached. This label or mark must have printed, in English, the employer's name and address. If the object or article cannot be individually marked, then its package or container must be marked.

**Convict Labor** -- Any article manufactured **in California** by convict labor can be sold only to a government agency or in markets outside of the United States. The only exceptions are (1) small items of handiwork made by the prisoners, and (2) agricultural and husbandry products; these may be sold under special rules.

Any article wholly or partly made or assembled by prison or convict labor **outside of California** (for sale within this state) must be labeled. These items must be labeled "Convict-made" in bold, clear letters. These items must also be labeled with the name of the prison where they were made or assembled. These items must also be sterilized or disinfected in California, and must be labeled with a sterilization certificate. Anyone selling convict-made goods must post a sign (at least 36 inches by 10 inches) saying: "Convict-made products on sale here." Any ad for these articles must say: "Convict-made."

LAW: Calif. Constitution, Article XIV, section 5; Labor Code sections 1010-1018, 2663, and 2667; Unemployment Insurance Code section 621(c)(1)(c); Penal Code sections 2807, 2812-2815, and 2880-2891; Title 15 U.S. Code sections 68-68b and 70-70b; Title 18 U.S. Code sections 1761 and 1762; Title 41 U.S. Code section 35(d); Title 19 U.S. Code section 1307; Title 16 Code of Federal Regulations sections 300.25a, 300.25b, 303.33 and 303.34; state and federal trademark and unfair competition laws.

ENFORCEMENT: Labor commissioner; district attorney; State Attorney General; Measurement Standards, Chief of Division; civil action.

Any violation is a misdemeanor.

**EXCEPTION:** Federal rules concerning industrial homework are of broader application. Employees or "independent contractors" doing **clerical, or computer-terminal, or phone-calling work at home** are covered by federal "industrial homework" laws and regulations. The employer must keep special records and give special notices to the workers; each worker must keep special records on her/his own; wage and hour laws apply; and federal government contractors may **not** use such homeworkers. (See Title 29 Code of Federal Regulations section 516.31 and Part 530; Title 19 Code of Federal Regulations section 12.42; Title 41 Code of Federal Regulations Part 50-201.)

## USE OF EMERGENCY POWERS IS LIMITED IN LABOR DISPUTES

State laws protect workers against the misuse of emergency powers by officials. Local or state authorities can, under some circumstances, declare a "state of emergency" or a "local emergency." This sort of emergency allows special procedures to be used. However, to make sure that workers' rights are not interfered with, these emergency powers cannot be used in any labor dispute or in any "conditions resulting from a labor controversy."

The power of California courts to restrict picket lines is also limited by state law.

**LAW:** Code of Civil Procedure section 527.3; Government Code section 8558.

**ENFORCEMENT:** Civil action.

## ANTI-LABOR EMPLOYERS CANNOT BE AWARDED STATE CONTRACTS

State agencies will not contract with employers who repeatedly violate National Labor Relations Board orders. If, in the last two years, the employer has more than once been held in contempt for violating NLRB orders, s/he may not contract with the State of California.

LAW: Public Contract Code sections 10232 and 10281.

ENFORCEMENT: State Attorney General; the contracting state agency; civil action.

Violation may be a felony. A contract signed in violation of this law may be cancelled.

EXCEPTION: This law applies to contracts for providing services to the state or for doing work for the state (including contracting out). It does not apply to purchases of goods or supplies. It does apply to construction contracts. (A case is before the U.S. Supreme Court which may invalidate or limit the application of this law.)

# CHAPTER 8

## DISCIPLINE AND DISCHARGE

### WHAT IS A TERMINATION OR DISCHARGE

Whenever reference is made to a termination or a discharge, this means any permanent or long-term break in your employment. It includes a release, a medical release, a medical termination, a firing, a layoff, as well as having your job or position eliminated or reorganized out of existence.

Sometimes a resignation is really a discharge. If you are told to "resign or be fired," that is a discharge, even if you do resign. Sometimes employers say that failure to report to work for a given number of days is a voluntary quit. If you are forced to "quit" after an absence, that is a discharge. If you are out sick, and your employer says s/he will consider you released or resigned if s/he doesn't hear from you, and then you lose your job--that is also a discharge.

If your employment is made so intolerable that a "reasonable" person would leave rather than put up with it, and you do leave--that counts as a termination. (This is called a "constructive discharge" and is often caused by sexual or racial harassment, by serious safety hazards which the employer will not correct, or by extreme invasions of privacy.) If a new and unreasonable condition is imposed, so that you just cannot keep your job, that may also be a discharge.

If you are on layoff and your employer refuses to rehire you, in violation of a rehire policy, that is considered a termination. If your employer refuses to let you return to work after a sick leave, or any other kind of leave, that is also a discharge. If your employer places you on an indefinite suspension, that may also be a discharge.

Having your contract ended or cancelled or not renewed where you are an employee working as if you are an independent contractor may also be a discharge. (See Chapter 1, INTRODUCTION, for definition of an independent contractor.)

## WHAT TO DO IF YOU ARE TERMINATED

More than three million American workers are fired each year. Millions more are "released," "let go" or laid off. If you find yourself fired, you need to take certain actions.

(1) If you have a union, contact your union officials as soon as possible.

(2) Do not sign a "release" or "exit agreement" or any other form in which you promise to make no more claims against the employer.

(3) Look very carefully at any benefits or exit forms you are given to sign. Do not sign anything which you have questions about. Do not rely on the statements of the person giving you the forms to sign.

(4) Take a union officer or friend to any "exit" interview.

(5) Take careful notes of anything said to you at an "exit" interview or any other time concerning your termination. Be careful of what you say during the exit interview. Save all letters and memos. Demand a copy of anything you are asked to sign.

(6) Get the home telephone numbers and addresses of your co-workers, so they can be reached later.

(7) Do not take your contributions or shares out of a pension or profit plan or fund, if you may be contesting the termination, or if you might make a disability claim or disability retirement claim. Consult your union, lawyer, tax and retirement advisors about pension and similar funds.

(8) At the "exit" interview ask what benefits you will receive. Ask how long your medical and dental insurance, disability and other fringe benefits will continue and ask how you can convert them to individual coverage. Ask about all the options in your pension coverage. Ask to see everything in your

personnel files. Make a copy of anything connected to your termination. Ask for a letter of recommendation.

(9) Make your employer be specific about the reason for your termination. Pin the employer down and, if possible, get the reason for the termination in writing. This will inhibit the employer from coming up with "better" reasons later.

(10) If medical reasons are given for your termination, inform your employer that you contest the discharge. Send contrary medical opinions to the employer as you get them (even after your termination). Send the employer a letter asking for reasonable accommodation of your medical condition. If you go or are sent to a company doctor, or an independent doctor, or to your own doctor, a vocational counselor, a rehabilitation counselor, a psychiatrist or therapist, watch what you say. Generally everything you say will be written down and given to your employer. If you are sent to a psychiatrist or psychotherapist, do not go until you have discussed it with an attorney or your union. Even then, watch what you say. Generally, everything you say will be reported to the employer. This also applies at other times, even when you are not terminated.

(11) If you apply for unemployment insurance, and your employer contests your right to receive it, contact your union or an attorney if at all possible. Find out how to put up the best possible fight for your unemployment benefits. If you think that you might have a law suit against the employer, you must get an attorney before the unemployment insurance benefit hearing.

## EMPLOYERS CANNOT DISCHARGE "AT WILL"

Employees covered by a collective bargaining agreement (a union contract) are usually protected by a "just cause"* provision: An independent arbitrator may determine the fairness of any discipline or discharge. Public employees have constitutional and civil service protections. Any discharge must be justified: hearing and appeal rights are provided for almost all government workers.

Private sector workers without union protection also have job security rights, but these are more limited. Nineteenth century court rulings established the policy that employees worked "at the will" of their employers (unless a contract specified otherwise). Workers could be discharged for good reason, bad reason, or no reason at all. In California, this doctrine is expressed in Labor Code section 2922:

> *An employment, having no specified term, may be terminated at the will of either party on notice to the other. Employment for a specified term means an employment for a period greater than one month.*

There is no provision in the law for a "just cause" standard. However, despite section 2922, a private sector employer may no longer discharge "at will."

**You Have the Right to Sue for Wrongful Discharge --** You can sue your employer for a wrongful termination and/or for other kinds of wrongdoing. This is a potentially powerful weapon. You have the right to a jury trial. If the jury agrees with you that your employer (or supervisor, manager, etc.) has violated the law or your employment rights, you may recover compensatory damages (e.g., lost wages and benefits) and be reinstated in your job. In some cases you may also be awarded punitive damages.

It is important to remember that your right to sue may exist even before you are discharged. For example, you may sue for humiliation, harassment, slurs and insults, or invasion of privacy.

Every California employer is held to have promised "good faith and fair dealing." Any act by an employer which is unfair to the worker, or which shows bad faith, or which treats the worker worse than other employees, may be grounds for legal action.

California courts have held that workers can sue the employer for "wrongful discharge" in the following sorts of cases:

(1) Where the worker was fired for refusing to commit an illegal act or to participate in an illegal conspiracy.

(2) Where the worker was fired for reporting an improper act by the employer, for "whistleblowing." (See Chapter 9, WHISTLEBLOWING: REPORTING VIOLATIONS OF THE LAW.)

(3) Where the worker was fired for opposing unsafe or unhealthy working conditions. (See Chapter 5, WORKING CONDITIONS: SAFETY, HEALTH AND SANITATION.)

(4) Where the worker was fired for exercising a right to free speech or another important civil right.

(5) Where the worker was fired for a reason which "violates public policy." (This is the rule that "no citizen can lawfully do that which has a tendency to be injurious to the public or against the public good.")

(6) Where the worker was fired to deprive her/him of the benefits of the employment contract.

(7) Where the worker was fired just before s/he was about to retire or to have her/his pension benefits vest.

(8) Where the worker was fired in violation of a promise of "fairness." This promise may be explicit (actually spelled out) or implicit (implied). It may be a promise not to act "arbitrarily" or a promise to only discharge "for just cause." It is up to the jury to determine whether there was such a promise. They may find that a promise was **implied** by any of the following:

> (a) the existence of a "probation" period (implying "just cause" after you are off probation);
>
> (b) job evaluations or merit increases;
>
> (c) the fact that the worker was employed for a long period of time;
>
> (d) the job announcement, pre-employment interviews, or other expressions by the employer;

(e) employee handbooks, posters, bulletins, training materials, affirmative action plans, or commitments;

(f) the existence of a company complaint or grievance procedure;

(g) the employer's knowledge that the worker gave up a valuable job and/or incurred substantial expense to accept the new position.


**Other Grounds for Lawsuits** -- California courts allow workers (even when not terminated) to sue their employers for various kinds of wrongdoing. The following list is not exhaustive; it supplies selected examples only:

(1) humiliating the worker;

(2) directing slurs and insults at the worker;

(3) treating the worker in a rude and derogatory manner;

(4) denigrating the worker or her union position or her work ability or performance;

(5) defamation, libel, slander; publishing or communicating injurious falsehoods about the worker, about the reason for her discharge, about the quality of her work, etc.;

(6) physically assaulting the worker; battery or assault by a supervisor or co-worker;

(7) rape, attempted rape, other sexual assaults;

(8) wrongful suspension of the worker; demotion; denial of pay increases; punitive transfers; denial of job assignments; etc.;

(9) use of false evidence against the worker;

(10) permitting discharge or suspension proceedings to remain pending without final resolution;

(11) retaliation for protected union activity;

(12) refusing to allow the worker to recover her personal property, tools, or papers in her desk or locker; theft or "conversion" of property;

(13) failing to exercise reasonable care in evaluating the worker;

(14) invading the worker's privacy; spying on private matters;

(15) revealing private information about the worker to others;

(16) issuing truthful statements which give a false impression about the worker;

(17) statutory violations related to privacy (e.g., eavesdropping; misuse of photos or fingerprints; release of medical or psychological information). (See Chapter 3, BLACKLISTING, INVESTIGATIONS, AND POLICE RECORDS);

(18) inducing breach of contract; interference with contractual relations or prospective economic advantage;

(19) wrongfully attempting to cause a termination;

(20) intentional infliction of emotional distress; abusing the employer/employee relationship with the intent to harm the worker (e.g., suspending or terminating the worker when the employer knew she was especially vulnerable, as on sick leave);

(21) inflicting physical or mental injuries as a result of a termination;

(22) fraud or deceit in connection with employment-related matters.

**Specific Statutes** -- Specific statutes impose certain restrictions on employers. Many of these are described in other chapters of this book and are listed briefly below. Other specific statutory protections are outlined in the remaining sections of this chapter. You may sue your employer if you are disciplined or discharged in violation of any of these laws.

**You may not be discharged or disciplined for:**

(1) refusal to invest in a business;

(2) refusal to be sterilized or have an abortion;

(3) refusal to patronize a particular business;

(4) refusal to answer illegal questions;

(5) use of bankruptcy or wage-earner protection plans;

(6) refusal to authorize the release of health-care information;

(7) refusing to take, or not passing an AIDS antibody test;

(8) the possibility you might suffer injury or illness;

(9) being a retiree;

(10) living outside a city, county, or district (public employees only);

(11) traveling to or dealing with a foreign country.

(See Chapter 2, HIRING RIGHTS.)

**You may not be discharged or disciplined for:**

(1) old marijuana convictions;

(2) arrests that did not lead to conviction;

(3) refusing to show your "rap" sheet;

(4) refusing to give your fingerprints or photo to a third party;

(5) refusing to take a lie detector test or voice stress analysis.

(See Chapter 3, BLACKLISTING, INVESTIGATIONS, AND POLICE RECORDS.)

**You may not be discharged or disciplined for:**

(1) refusal to work seven (7) days straight (except where your employer is exempted by law);

(2) taking necessary time off work to vote (after giving proper notice);

(3) garnishment of wages based on one judgment or one debt;

(4) any number of orders (or garnishments or attachments of wages) for child support or family support;

(5) pregnancy or absence due to pregnancy;

(6) appearing as a witness;

(7) jury duty;

(8) bankruptcy.

(See Chapter 4, WAGES, FRINGE BENEFITS, AND HOURS OF WORK.)

**You may not be discharged or disciplined for:**

(1) refusing to perform imminently hazardous work;

(2) exercising any of your health and safety rights.

(See Chapter 5, WORKING CONDITIONS: SAFETY, HEALTH AND SANITATION.)

**You may not be disciplined or discharged for:**

(1) filing a Workers' Compensation claim;

(2) being injured on the job;

(3) receiving any Workers' Compensation rating, award, settlement, benefits, or payment;

(4) absences due to an industrial injury or illness, or due to a condition made worse by job conditions;

(5) refusing to participate in a vocational rehabilitation program under the Workers' Compensation laws;

(6) exercising any of your Workers' Compensation rights.

(See Chapter 6, WORKERS' COMPENSATION.)


**You may not be disciplined or discharged for:**

(1) refusing to join, or promise to join, a company union, or to maintain membership in a company union;

(2) refusing to sign, or violating, a promise not to join a union;

(3) engaging in any union activity, union organizing, exchanging salary or other job information, or holding or expressing union opinions;

(4) naming a union, a lawyer, or another person as your bargaining representative.

(See Chapter 7, BASIC ORGANIZING RIGHTS AND PROTECTIONS.)

**You may not be discharged or disciplined:**

(1) for exercising any rights under a pension plan or employee benefits plan. See Title 29 U.S. Code sections 1140 and 1141;

(2) to prevent you from receiving a pension, or to keep your pension from vesting, or to keep you from enjoying any other employee-benefits plan rights. Title 29 U.S. Code sections 1140 and 1141.

**You may not be discharged or disciplined for:**

(1) appearing before a government body;

(2) reporting suspected violations of the law.

(See Chapter 9, WHISTLEBLOWING: REPORTING VIOLATIONS OF THE LAW.)

**You may not be disciplined or discharged for:**

(1) past military service;

(2) present or future military, reserve, or national guard obligations;

(3) absences due to military service.

(See *Military Obligations and Employment Rights*, pamphlet, Center for Labor Research and Education, Institute of Industrial Relations, U.C. Berkeley.)

**You may not be disciplined or discharged for:**

(1) refusing to assign rights to an invention (see Labor Code section 2871);

(2) exercising constitutionally protected rights;

(3) exercising the special rights of seamen, fishermen, and divers (consult your union or attorney);

(4) exercising the special rights of farm workers and migrant and seasonal workers (consult your union or attorney);

(5) exercising any of your rights under state or federal laws, including complaining (or being about to complain); opposing law violations; assisting others to complain; or providing information to any enforcement agency (Labor Code section 98.6; Government Code section 12,940(f); Title 29 U.S. Code sections 158(a)(4), 623(d), 1140 and 1141; Labor Code sections 6310, 6312, and 6399.7; Title 42 U.S. Code section 2000e-3(a); bargaining rights statutes).

## YOU HAVE SPECIAL RIGHTS WHEN EMPLOYED FOR A SPECIFIED PERIOD OF TIME

If you are employed for a specified period of time (greater than one month), then the law implies a "good cause" standard for any discharge. You are protected against being fired, during the period (the "term") of your employment: you can only be fired or let go for "good cause." This standard is similar to the "just cause"* test usually used in union contracts.

Once your contract expires, your rights are the same as those of any worker, unless you negotiate a new agreement "for a specified term."

**LAW:** Labor Code sections 2922-2925.

**ENFORCEMENT:** Civil action.

**EXCEPTIONS:** This protection depends on the existence of a specific contract (spoken or written) to employ you for a set period of time (for example, for six months). The period must be longer than one month. It is best to have the contract in writing. Simply working for your employer for more than one month does not mean that you have a contract "for a specified term." You must have a contract which spells out the exact period of time: four months; one year; three years.

## YOU HAVE CERTAIN RIGHTS IF YOU ARE DISCIPLINED OR DISCHARGED ON THE BASIS OF AN INVESTIGATION REPORT

**Right to Inspect Investigation Reports** -- Every worker has the right to inspect any investigation report which the employer has used as the basis for discharge or discipline. (This right continues even after you are terminated.) Your employer must make the report available within a reasonable period of time after you ask to see it.

**LAW:** Labor Code sections 1198.5 and 1199; Labor Standards Enforcement Division Memo 76-2.

**ENFORCEMENT:** Labor commissioner; civil action.

Violation is a misdemeanor.

**EXCEPTIONS:** A public sector employer has five working days to make the report available. For state government and school employees, see Chapter 10, EMPLOYEE RECORDS: COLLECTING, STORING, AND ACCESSING INFORMATION.

**Right to Notice of Investigation** -- If your employer has you investigated, s/he must notify you within three (3) days. This notification must be in writing. It must inform you that you can request details about the investigation, and that you can inspect the files of the investigating agency. If you ask (in writing) to be given further details, then your employer must tell you the exact nature and scope of the investigation.

This law applies to private sector and public sector employers; to any investigation in which the investigator interviews or talks with anyone about the worker; and to any investigation of the worker's personal characteristics, honesty or dishonesty, mode of living, drug use, arrest records, or character. This law also applies whether or not the worker is ultimately disciplined or discharged as a result of the investigation.

The three-day notice period begins when the employer requests the investigation (not when it is completed).

LAW: Title 15 U.S. Code sections 1681a, 1681d, 1681n, and 1681o.

ENFORCEMENT: Civil action.

Damages, punitive damages, and attorney's fees may be available.

EXCEPTIONS: This law does not apply to most investigations conducted solely by the employer's "in house" staff.

**Public Employees** -- Public sector (government) workers generally have the right to receive copies of **any** reports relied upon to discipline or discharge them. They have a right to these copies **before** the discipline or discharge is imposed, in most cases. They also usually have rights of hearing and appeal. All workers have the right to the assistance of a union representative at any hearing.

LAW: Federal and state constitutions; bargaining rights statutes.

ENFORCEMENT: Civil action.

There may be short time limits.

## WORKERS IN CERTAIN JOBS HAVE SPECIAL PROTECTIONS WHEN THE EMPLOYER USES AN INVESTIGATOR, DETECTIVE, "SPOTTER," OR "SHOPPER."

**Public Utility Employees** -- Workers for any public utility or public service corporation have special rights. If any detective, special agent, or "spotter" is used to report on the integrity or honesty of a worker, or about any breach of company rules, then this law applies. The company cannot legally discipline or discharge the worker, relying in whole or in part upon that report, unless it provides "due process" rights. If the worker requests specific charges and a hearing, then the company must give the worker (a) specifics of any alleged misconduct, (b) a hearing, and (c) allow the worker to present testimony in her/his defense. All workers have the right to the assistance of a union representative at any hearing.

LAW: Public Utilities Code sections 8251 and 8252; bargaining rights statutes.

ENFORCEMENT: District attorney; civil action.

Violation is a misdemeanor; violators are subject to one year in jail and a $300 fine.

**Commercial, Retail, and Service Employees** -- Workers in any service or retail or commercial establishment have two closely-related rights. (1) If the employer intends to discipline or discharge the worker as a result of the report of a "shopping investigator," then the worker must be given a copy of the report. The worker must be given a copy **before** s/he is disciplined or discharged. (2) If the employer wants to interview the worker, and that interview might result in a discharge for dishonesty, and the interview will be based wholly or partially upon the report of a "shopping investigator," then the worker must be given a copy of the report **before** the end of the interview.

LAW: Labor Code section 2930; bargaining rights statutes; Business and Professions Code sections 7521, 7522 and 7523.

ENFORCEMENT: Civil action.

**EXCEPTIONS:** This law applies only to "shopping investigators."

A shopping investigator is a person who is not employed exclusively by the disciplined worker's own company; s/he is **not**, that is, an "in house" person.

A "shopping investigator" is defined as a person who: *"shops . . . to test integrity of sales, warehouse, stockroom, and service personnel, and evaluates sales techniques and services rendered customers"*; or *"reviews an establishment's policies and standards to ascertain employee performance requirements"*; or *"buys merchandise, orders food, or utilizes services to evaluate sales technique and courtesy of employees, carries merchandise to check stand or sales counter and observes employees during sales transaction to detect irregularities in listing or calling prices, itemizing merchandise, or handling cash"*; or *"delivers purchases to an agency conducting shopping investigation service"* and who writes a report of investigations. Such a person must be licensed as a private investigator, or be employed by a licensed private investigator (in which case only the licensed investigator may report to the employer).

## YOU HAVE THE RIGHT TO KNOW WHY YOU WERE FIRED

You have the right to inspect and copy any reports or other papers which your employer used to fire you (or to discipline you in any other way). This right continues even after you have been terminated. Your employer must make these reports and papers (and the rest of your personnel file) available to you within a reasonable period of time after you ask to see them.

If you are fired as a result of an investigation conducted by an outside agency, then your employer must promptly tell you that this is the reason for your discharge. Your employer must tell you that the investigation report was a basis for your discharge whether you ask or not. The employer must also give you the name and address of the investigating agency. (See Chapter 4, BLACKLISTING, INVESTIGATIONS AND POLICE

RECORDS for information on how to inspect that agency's files about you.)

> LAW: Labor Code sections 1198.5 and 1199; Labor Standards Enforcement Division Memo 76-2; Title 15 U.S. Code sections 1681m, 1681n, and 1681o.

> ENFORCEMENT: Labor commissioner; civil action.

> EXCEPTIONS: A public sector employer has five working days to make your files available. For state government and school employees, see Chapter 10, EMPLOYEE RECORDS: COLLECTING, STORING, AND ACCESSING INFORMATION.

## DISCRIMINATORY DISCHARGE OR DISCIPLINE IS ILLEGAL

Both state and federal laws restrict your employer's right to terminate or discipline you because of discriminatory motives or in ways which discriminate (regardless of motive). None of the following may be used as a basis for discharge or discipline:

(1) gender (being male or female);

(2) sexual orientation: homosexuality, bisexuality; being or acting openly gay or lesbian;

(3) marital status: being married, single, divorced, separated, widowed; being married to another employee or manager of the same employer;

(4) living with a partner to whom you are not married;

(5) pregnancy; fertility; being fertile or of childbearing years or capacity or intention; being sterile; refusing to be sterilized; having an abortion; refusing to have an abortion;

(6) race; color; ethnicity;

(7) ancestry; national origin; native tongue; citizenship (for most jobs);

(8) religion; creed; religious activities or beliefs; lack of religion; atheism;

(9) age (over 40); reaching a "mandatory" retirement age, provided you give the employer a written statement that you wish to continue working (Government Code section 12942 and Title 29 Code of Federal Regulations section 1625.9);

(10) "medical condition" (meaning controlled cancer);

(11) having a physical handicap or disability, or being thought to have one, or having a history of having had one;

(12) having a cosmetic disfigurement (e.g., extreme obesity);

(13) being at a possible higher risk due to a physical condition or disability; causing higher insurance or medical costs because of a physical condition or disability; having a risk of future disability (unless the risk or hazard is immediate and substantial). Protections extend to high blood pressure, low back conditions, AIDS, smoking, obesity, etc.

It is also illegal for your employer to discharge or discriminate against you for associating with people disfavored because of any of the above characteristics. Your employer is also prohibited from discriminating against you for taking reasonable steps to oppose discrimination based on any of the above characteristics.

Your employer may not utilize a "neutral" policy or practice (or test, program, selection device, or disciplinary standard) which has a significantly heavier adverse impact (a "disparate impact") upon those workers who possess any of the above characteristics. For example, a program which discharges a high percentage of Black workers (or women workers, or older workers), as compared to other workers, may be illegal. To justify such a disparate impact, the employer must show a substantial "business necessity" for the program or policy or practice.

LAW, ENFORCEMENT, EXCEPTIONS: See Chapter 2, HIRING RIGHTS.

## HARASSMENT BASED ON PERSONAL CHARACTERISTICS IS ILLEGAL

It is against the law for your employer to harass you, or to allow other employees, supervisors, customers, clients, or patients to harass you because of your age, sex, race, marital status, physical handicap, etc. (See previous section.). Sexual harassment is illegal. Harassment of gays is illegal. Embarassing or making life difficult for a worker with a handicap or a particular religion is illegal. Title 2 California Administrative Code provides:

*Harassment includes but is not limited to:*

*(A) Verbal harassment, e.g., epithets, derogatory comments or slurs. . .;*

*(B) Physical harassment, e.g., assault, impeding or blocking any movement, or any physical interference with normal work or movement. . .;*

*(C) Visual forms of harassment, e.g., derogatory posters, cartoons, or drawings. . .*

*(D) Sexual favors, e.g., unwanted sexual advances which condition an employment benefit upon an exchange of sexual favors.*

Your employer must take action to prevent harassment by anyone.

LAW: Government Code section 12,940(i, j); Title 2 California Administrative Code section 7287.6(b); Title 29 Code of Federal Regulations sections 1604.11 and 1606.8; Title 22 California Administrative Code section 98244.

ENFORCEMENT: Fair Employment and Housing Dept. (DFE&H); civil action.

EXCEPTIONS: Religious nonprofit corporations. All other employers are covered, even those with fewer than five employees. Harassment at a religious nonprofit employer may be dealt with by a civil action under different laws.

## YOUR EMPLOYER MUST TRY TO ACCOMMODATE YOUR PHYSICAL DISABILITY AND/OR RELIGIOUS BELIEFS

You cannot be discharged or disciminated against for religious beliefs or physical handicap if you can do the job with "reasonable accommodation."

Reasonable accommodation is defined to include a wide range of actions by your employer. Title 2 of the California Administrative Code provides:

> *Reasonable accommodation may include, but is not limited to, job re-structuring, job reassignment, modification of work practices, or allowing time off in an amount equal to the amount of non-regularly scheduled time the employee has worked in order to avoid a conflict with his or her religious observations.*

> *Reasonable accommodation includes, but is not limited to, the following specific employment policies or practices:*

> *(1) Interview and examination times. Scheduled times for interviews, examination, and other functions related to employment opportunities shall reasonably accommodate religious practices.*

> *(2) Dress standards. Dress standards or requirements for personal appearance shall be flexible enough to take into account religious practices.*

*Reasonable accommodation may, but does not necessarily include, nor is it limited to, such measures as:*

*(1) Accessibility. Making facilities used by employees readily assessible to and usable by handicapped individuals; and*

*(2) Job restructuring. Job restructuring, reassignment or transfer, part-time or modified work schedules, acquisition or modification of equipment or devices, the provision of readers or interpreters, and other similar action.*

Your employer has the duty to gather sufficient information, from you and from qualified experts as needed, to determine what accommodations are necessary to enable you to perform the job safely.

LAW: Government Code sections 12926 and 12940; Title 2 California Administrative Code sections 7293.3 and 7293.9; Title 29 Code of Federal Regulations section 1605.2 and Appendix; Title 41 Code of Federal Regulations section 60-50.3; Title 28 Code of Federal Regulations Part 41; Title 22 California Administrative Code sections 98221 and 98255.

ENFORCEMENT: Fair Employment and Housing Dept. (DFE&H); civil action.

EXCEPTIONS: Employers with fewer than five employees, and religious nonprofit corporations, are only covered if they have a state or federal contract, or receive state or federal grants or funds, including receipt of Medi-Cal or Medicare funds.

## YOUR EMPLOYER MUST TRY TO ACCOMMODATE YOUR ALCOHOLIC REHABILITATION PROGRAM

If you voluntarily enter an alcoholic rehabilitation program, your employer must make an effort to accommodate your participation in that program. Unless it poses an "undue hardship" on the employer, s/he must give you the necessary time off. If you have paid sick leave available, you must be allowed to use it for the rehabilitation program. The employer must safeguard your privacy concerning the program.

**LAW:** Labor Code sections 1025-1028.

**ENFORCEMENT:** Labor commissioner; civil action.

**EXCEPTIONS:** This specific law applies only to private-sector employers with 25 or more regular workers. It does not prevent you from being disciplined or discharged for "current use of alcohol" which makes you unable to safely perform your job duties.

Similar "reasonable accommodation" rules apply to any other employer who receives state or federal grants or contracts (including the receipt of Medicare or Medi-Cal funds).

## YOUR EMPLOYER CANNOT DISCHARGE OR HARASS YOU FOR POLITICAL REASONS

No employee may be threatened, disciplined, or discharged for political reasons. This protection extends to:

(1) voting

(2) not voting

(3) how you vote

(4) registering to vote

(5) not registering to vote

(6) signing or not signing petitions

(7) party membership or other affiliation

(8) membership in political or interest group

(9) political opinions

(10) political activities.

Your employer is responsible for the acts of supervisors, managers, officers, and agents. No one may ask about (or keep records about) your opinions or activities. No political materials may be attached to any pay envelopes or pay checks. Any worker subjected to political pressure may sue for damages and other relief.

LAW: Labor Code sections 1101-1105; Elections Code sections 29,612 and 29,620-29,631; Government Code sections 3302 and 19,703; Education Code sections 7050-7057; California Constitution, Article I, section 3; Article II, sections 1 and 7; and Article VII, section 8(b).

ENFORCEMENT: State Attorney General; district attorney; State Personnel Board; civil action.

Violation of these laws is a crime. Violators are subject to at least one year in jail and a fine. In some cases, violation is a felony.

EXCEPTIONS: Police and other public safety officers may not engage in political activity while on duty or in uniform.

## HEALTH CARE WORKERS CANNOT BE PENALIZED FOR PARTICIPATING OR REFUSING TO PARTICIPATE IN THE PERFORMANCE OF ABORTIONS

Abortion-related rights of an R.N., an L.V.N., a physician, or any employee of a hospital, facility, or clinic are fully protected.

You cannot be required to participate in the induction or the performance of an abortion, if you file in advance a written statement with the employer or facility. This statement need only indicate that you have an ethical, moral, or religious basis for your refusal to participate in abortions. You cannot be penalized in any way for filing this statement or for refusing to participate in abortions. But these rights do **not** apply (1) to medical emergency situations; (2) to jobs where your **normal** assignment is to work in those parts of the facility where abortion patients are cared for.

If you work at a hospital, facility, or clinic which does **not** perform abortions, you are also protected. You cannot be penalized in any way because you participate in abortions performed elsewhere.

**LAW:** Health and Safety Code section 25,955.

**ENFORCEMENT:** Civil action; district attorney.

Violation is a misdemeanor.


## RUNNING FOR AND HOLDING OFFICE

No employer can discriminate against employees who run for public office or hold public office. A company rule against this kind of political activity is unlawful. No worker can be harassed, disciplined, suspended, or discharged for seeking or holding public office.

**LAW:** Labor Code sections 1101-1105; California Constitution, Article I, section 3, and Article II, section 1.

**ENFORCEMENT:** Civil action; district attorney; State Attorney General.

Violation is a crime.

**EXCEPTIONS:** This protection does not necessarily mean that you can get time off from work to run for or hold office. But the employer cannot refuse to grant leave for political activities, if leave is granted for educational or other personal activities.

State and local government employees who are involved in activities funded by federal monies may not be candidates for election to a partisan public office. But they can be candidates for any California local or county or judicial office (since all California non-statewide offices are nonpartisan). They can be candidates for any position on a political party central committee or as a convention delegate or other party office. No restrictions apply to any school, college, county superintendent of schools, university, or research institution employee. Such employees can run for any office.

Title 5 U.S. Code sections 1501-1508; Title 5 Code of Federal Regualations sections 151.101-151.122; Education Code sections 7050-7057.


## SERVING AS ELECTION OFFICER

No employee can be discriminated against because s/he serves as an election officer on election day. S/he cannot be disciplined or suspended or discharged for absence from work to fulfill this civic duty. Be sure to give the employer advance notice that you will be absent and serving as an election officer.

**LAW:** Elections Code sections 1655 and 29612.

**ENFORCEMENT:** State Attorney General; district attorney; civil action.

In some cases, violation is a felony.


## YOU HAVE THE RIGHT TO RECEIVE YOUR WAGES IMMEDIATELY UPON DISCHARGE

If you are fired or laid off (or suspended "indefinitely" or "pending investigation"), your wages are due and payable immediately. When you quit, giving at least 72 hours notice, your wages are due and payable at the end of your last shift. If you quit giving no notice, your wages are due and payable within 72 hours (unless you had a written contract promising to work for a definite period). Your employer must pay your wages when due; if s/he fails to do so, your wages will continue to accrue until they are paid. Wages will not, however, accrue for more than 30 days (or during any time you are refusing or avoiding payment of your wages).

The "wages" which (1) must be paid immediately, and which (2) accrue for up to 30 days, are **all forms of compensation.** See the next section and the first section in Chapter 4, WAGES, FRINGE BENEFITS, AND HOURS OF WORK. If your employer fails to immediately pay even a small part of the "wages" due you, the employer may have to pay you an additional month's full "wages."

You must be paid at the place you are discharged. (If you quit, you must be paid in the county where you worked.)

**LAW:** Labor Code sections 201-203 and 208.

**ENFORCEMENT:** Labor commissioner. Ask for "Section 203 waiting time pay."

**EXCEPTIONS:** Public employees.

For discharged motion picture or oil drilling employees, payment must be made (or postmarked) within 24 hours of termination (excluding Saturdays, Sundays, and holidays). For fruit, vegetable, or fish processing workers, laid off at the end of the season, payment must be made (or postmarked) within 72 hours.

## YOU HAVE A RIGHT TO YOUR ACCRUED PAID VACATION TIME UPON DISCHARGE

Employers are not required by law to provide paid vacation time. However, if your employer agrees to provide paid vacation time by promise, policy, or collective bargaining agreement, s/he must make good on that agreement. Paid vacation time is considered wages and, if not used, is due and payable as wages **(at your final rate of pay)** when you terminate your employment. This is true whether you quit, are laid off, or are fired. An employer cannot lawfully establish a policy which forces you to give up your right to vacation pay when you leave your employment.

LAW: Labor Code section 227.3.

ENFORCEMENT: Labor commissioner; civil action.

EXCEPTIONS: Vacation plans covered by collective bargaining agreements.

## WORKFARE JOB PROTECTIONS

The term "Workfare" refers to any employment, pre-employment preparation, on-the-job training, transitional employment, supported work, grant diversion, training program positions, or other job or training established or conducted for welfare recipients.

You cannot lose your job as a result of your employer providing any Workfare job or training. You cannot be displaced by any Workfare participant. You cannot be denied currently available overtime opportunities because your employer hires a Workfare participant. Your employer cannot use Workfare participants in any positions to which current employees might be promoted.

Your employer cannot fill a position by Workfare until s/he has complied with all provisions of your union contract or merit system.

No work can be done by any Workfare participant if that work is available as a result of any strike or other labor dispute. No Workfare is legal which results in a strike or other labor dispute.

All Workfare and on-the-job training must be paid at comparable wage rates. No age, race, disability, physical or mental handicap, sex, religion, or national origin discrimination is allowed.

No Workfare participant can fill any position which was created by any termination or layoff or reduction in the workforce, where the employer intended to obtain Workfare participants as replacements.

No Workfare participant can be penalized in any way for refusing to accept any employment or training assignment which:

(1) violates any of these rules;

(2) involves more than the daily or weekly hours of work customary to the occupation;

(3) involves conditions that are in violation of applicable health and safety standards;

(4) involves employment not covered by workers' compensation insurance;

(5) would cause a violation of the terms of the participant's union membership.

There are numerous other grounds for nonparticipation.

All Workfare participants are "employees" and are covered by all the rights described in this book.

**Additional Protections** -- The Workfare program establishes "Preemployment Preparation Positions" which involve short-term work (maximum one year), limited hours (maximum 32 hours per week), and are limited to public employers and nonprofit agencies.

No Preemployment Preparation Position is allowed which involves doing any work:

(1) which had been done by an employee who was terminated or laid off or whose position was eliminated by any reduction in workforce. (The intent of the employer is irrelevant.)

(2) customarily performed by a worker in a job classification within a recognized bargaining unit.

(3) in a bargaining unit in which funded positions are vacant.

(4) in a bargaining unit in which any employee is on layoff.

**LAW:** Welfare and Institutions Code sections 11320.38, 11320.35, 11320.3(d), and 11320.7.

**ENFORCEMENT:** State Dept. of Social Services; county welfare department; civil action.

# CHAPTER 9

## WHISTLEBLOWING: REPORTING VIOLATIONS OF THE LAW

### YOU HAVE THE RIGHT TO REPORT VIOLATIONS OF THE LAW

You have the right, and the duty, to report possible violations of law. This is a "fundamental right" protected by the First Amendment of the U.S. Constitution and by Article I, sections 2 and 3, of the California Constitution.

Reporting suspected violations of a state or federal law or regulation is called whistleblowing. It is illegal for your employer to adopt any policy prohibiting whistleblowing. Your employer may not put pressure on you to keep you from reporting suspected violations of the law to the appropriate law enforcement or governmental authorities. It is a crime for your employer to fire you (or otherwise punish you) for reporting a suspected law violation. (See also Chapter 8, DISCIPLINE AND DISCHARGE, for more information about illegal terminations.) If you have to remain silent about violations of the law in order to keep your job, then your employer is committing a crime.

> **LAW:** Labor Code sections 1102.5-1105; Penal Code sections 136, 136.1, and 137; Title 18 U.S. Code sections 1505 and 1512-1515.

> **ENFORCEMENT:** Labor commissioner; district attorney; U.S. Attorney for your area; civil action.

> Anyone who violates these laws is subject to a maximum of 10 years in prison and a $250,000 fine. (Violators of state Labor Code may receive one year in prison and a $5000 fine.)

> **EXCEPTIONS:** Whistleblowers may not reveal confidential lawyer-client or physician-patient information or trade secrets.

## YOU HAVE THE RIGHT TO APPEAR BEFORE A LEGISLATIVE COMMITTEE

Every employee has the right to testify as a witness before any committee (or subcommittee) of the State Legislature. It is a crime to coerce anyone to not appear before a legislative committee. It is a crime to suspend or discharge anyone because s/he appears before a committee. It is a crime to even ask an employer to prevent an employee from testifying. This protection extends to communications which may lead to appearance before a committee.

LAW: Government Code sections 9400, 9414, and 19251.5.

ENFORCEMENT: District attorney; State Attorney General; State Personnel Board; the legislative committee; civil action.

Similar protections extend to your appearance before any U.S. House or Senate committee or subcommittee. Violators are subject to fines up to $250,000 and prison up to 10 years. Title 18 U.S. Code sections 1505 and 1512-1515.

## ALL STATE EMPLOYEES HAVE WHISTLEBLOWING RIGHTS

Every state employee has the right to report possible violations of the law to the State Attorney General, or to the Joint Legislative Audit Committee or to the Auditor General, or to any other appropriate authority. All facts or information related to the suspected violation may be reported. This applies to any actual or suspected violation of state or federal law occurring on the job or directly related to the job. This also applies to governmental activities which are economically wasteful or involve gross misconduct, incompetency or inefficiency.

It is unlawful for anyone to pressure a state worker to not report possible violations of the law. It is unlawful to discharge, discipline, discriminate against, or coerce any worker who reports or intends to report violations of the law.

LAW: Government Code sections 10540-10548 and 19683.

ENFORCEMENT: State Personnel Board; civil action.


## IN CERTAIN CIRCUMSTANCES YOU ARE OBLIGED TO REPORT VIOLATIONS OF THE LAW

**State Contracts** -- You have special whistleblowing obligations if your employer has a construction or service contract with the state government. These obligations apply whether your employer is a contractor or a subcontractor.

If you learn of any work being done in violation of the contract, then you must report the violation.

**LAW:** Public Contract Code sections 10281-10282.

**ENFORCEMENT:** You must immediately notify the contracting department of the State government (or the project inspector or resident engineer). Failure to do so is a felony; in addition, you might also have to pay to the State twice as much money as it loses due to the violation.


**Reporting to Government Agencies** -- It is a crime for you or your employer to:

(1) give false information to a government agency;

(2) use threats (or misleading conduct or offers of advantage) to cause anyone to withhold information from a government investigation;

(3) use threats (or misleading conduct or offers of advantage) to cause anyone to give misleading information to a government agency;

(4) destroy or conceal records needed or requested by a government agency;

(5) alter records needed or requested by a government agency;

(6) give false records to a government agency;

(7) ask or pressure anyone to do any of the above.

If your employer pressures you to do any of the above-listed acts, then the employer is guilty of a serious crime. If you submit and do any of the above, then you are guilty of a serious crime.

LAW: Penal Code sections 7(3), 7(6), 118, 126-137, and 153; Title 18 U.S. Code sections 1505 and 1512-1515.

ENFORCEMENT: District attorney; U.S. Attorney for your area. Penalties up to 10 years in prison and $250,000 fine; civil action.

**School Employees are Obliged to Report Menace by Students** -- School employees have the right to report menace or attack by students. In fact, both the menaced employee and her/his supervisor have a legal duty to report it. The report must be made to the appropriate law enforcement authorities of the county or city where the assault or menace occurred. This applies to all employees of school districts and community college districts, as well as those working for the county superintendent of schools.

It is a crime for any other district employee (or official or governing board member) to inhibit or attempt to inhibit an employee from making such a report. It is a crime to harass, discipline, suspend or discharge anyone for making a report.

LAW: Education Code sections 44,014 and 87,014; Labor Code sections 1102.5-1105.

ENFORCEMENT: District attorney; civil action.

## SCHOOL EMPLOYEES HAVE A RIGHT TO APPEAR BEFORE BOARDS, COMMISSIONS, AND COUNCILS

Special protections apply to any employee of any school district, community college district, or county superintendent of schools office. It is a crime for anyone to discipline, or attempt to discipline, a school or community college worker for appearing before a government body. This protection covers appearances before the district's governing board, a board of education, a legislative committee, or any other government board, commission, or council.

LAW: Education Code sections 44040 and 87039.

ENFORCEMENT: District attorney; State Attorney General; civil action.

## YOU HAVE THE RIGHT TO REPORT PHYSICAL OR PSYCHOLOGICAL ABUSE

Everyone has the right to report the illegal abuse of themselves or of another person. As an employee you are specifically protected by law from harassment, discipline, or discharge for reporting to a protective agency the abuse (or suspected abuse) of children, senior citizens, or dependent adults.

Child Abuse -- A "child" is anyone under the age of 18 years. "Child abuse" includes any nonaccidental physical injury, sexual assault (including engaging a child in sexual activity or pornography), cruelty, unreasonable punishment, or neglect. Neglect includes the failure to provide adequate food, clothing, or health care.

The protective agencies for reporting child abuse are: the police or sheriff, county probation department, and county welfare department.

LAW: Penal Code sections 11,165-11,174; Labor Code sections 1102.5-1105.

**ENFORCEMENT:** District attorney; civil action.

**Elder Abuse** -- An "elder" is anyone 65 years of age or older. "Elder abuse" includes physical abuse, such as punishment, injury, sexual assault, unreasonable physical constraint, deprivation of food and water; and neglect, such as failure to help with personal hygiene, or failure to provide food, clothing, medical care, or mental health needs. Elder abuse also includes: abandonment by those responsible for care; "fiduciary abuse" (such as stealing, hiding, or taking the elder's money or property); and failure to protect from health and safety hazards.

The protective agencies for reporting elder abuse are: the Community Care Licensing Division, State Department of Social Services, the county probation department, the county welfare department, the police or sheriff, and the nursing home ombudsman.

**LAW:** Welfare and Institutions Code sections 9380-9386; Labor Code sections 1102.5-1105.

**ENFORCEMENT:** Labor commissioner; district attorney; civil action.

**Abuse of Dependent Adults** -- A "dependent adult" is a person between 18 and 65 years of age who has limitations which restrict his/her ability to live an independent life. These limitations may be physical, mental, or financial. "Abuse" includes injury, intimidation, cruel punishment, physical harm, pain, threats, harassment, or mental suffering. The institution or individuals responsible for the care of a dependent adult must provide the goods and services necessary for the physical and mental well-being of that person, including: adequate medical care, assistance in personal hygiene, adequate clothing, adequately heated and ventilated shelter, protection from health and safety hazards, and the transportation and assistance needed to secure any of these goods and services.

The protective agency for reporting abuse of a dependent adult is your county welfare department.

LAW: Welfare and Institutions Code sections 15600-15640; Labor Code sections 1102.5-1105.

ENFORCEMENT: Labor commissioner; district attorney; civil action.

## HOSPITAL WORKERS HAVE THE RIGHT TO REPORT PATIENT OR CLIENT ABUSE

For reporting child abuse, elder abuse, and dependent adult abuse, hospital workers have the same rights and protections described above. A special law, however, protects reports about patients or clients transferred into a hospital. This law applies to any physican, surgeon, nurse, LVN, clinical social worker, and anyone in charge of any ward or part of a hospital.

If someone is transferred into the hospital who appears to have suffered neglect or abuse, a report must be made (to both the police and the county health department) stating the extent and nature of the injury or condition. No employee can be harassed, disciplined, suspended, or discharged for making this report.

LAW: Penal Code sections 11,161.8 and 11,162; Government Code section 12,940(a); Labor Code sections 1102.5-1105.

ENFORCEMENT: Fair Employment and Housing Dept.; labor commissioner; district attorney; civil action.

Any supervisor or employer who violates this law is subject to six months in jail and a fine.

EXCEPTION: This law applies to patients transferred from a "health facility" or a "community care facility." "Health facilities" include hospitals, intermediate care facilities, and skilled nursing facilities. "Community care facilities" include foster homes, day care centers, "small family homes" for handicapped children, homefinding agencies, care facilities for the elderly, and residential facilities providing 24-hour nonmedical care.

## WORKERS IN CHILD DAY CARE CENTERS HAVE SPECIAL RIGHTS

You are protected by a special state whistleblowing rule if you work at a child day care facility.

You are protected against retaliation if you report a violation (or possible violation) of the day care licensing laws or regulations. You are also protected if you refuse to perform work in violation of a licensing law or regulation. (You must notify your employer of the violation before you refuse to do the work.)

You are also protected if you report a possible violation of other laws, including those concerning staff-child ratios, transportation of children, and child abuse. You are protected if you testify (or are about to testify) at hearings, or assist others in complaining, or provide information to enforcement agencies.

Your employer cannot discharge, demote, or suspend you. You cannot be threatened, disciplined, or in any way discriminated against.

**LAW:** Health and Safety Code sections 1596.881, 1596.882, and 1596.70-1597.65.

**ENFORCEMENT:** Labor commissioner.

If your rights under this law have been violated, you must file a claim with your employer within 30 days, and with the labor commissioner within 60 days. If you miss these time limits, or if you want to file a law suit, you must use the other laws discussed in this chapter.

**EXCEPTIONS:** This law does not apply to clinics; health care facilities; state-licensed community care facilities (providing 24-hour nonmedical residential care); public recreation programs; cooperative child care where no payment is involved; family day care homes where the operator cares only for her/his own children and those of one other family.

## WORKERS IN LONG-TERM HEALTH CARE AND COMMUNITY CARE FACILITIES HAVE SPECIAL WHISTLEBLOWING RIGHTS

You are protected by a special State whistleblowing rule if you work at one of the following institutions:

a nursing home;
a residential care facility;
a skilled nursing facility;
an adult day care facility;
an extended care facility;
a home-finding agency;
an intermediate care facility;
a foster family home;
a social rehabilitation facility;
any other long term health care or residential facility.

You are protected against retaliation if you report a violation (or possible violation) of the rights of the patients or residents in these facilities (e.g., the right to privacy and dignity, the right to leave the facility, etc.) or ask for an inspection.

You are also protected if you help a patient or resident or another employee to report violations, or if you provide information or testimony to an investigating agency. Your employer cannot discharge or discipline you, or in any way retaliate against or harass you. And the employer cannot expel or in any way retaliate against a patient or resident who lodges a complaint or cooperates with an investigation.

LAW: Health and Safety Code sections 1432, 1430, 1417-1439, 1502, 1538, 1539 and 1599; Labor Code sections 1102.5-1105; Welfare and Institutions Code sections 9701 and 9715; Title 22 California Administrative Code sections 70707, 70819, 71507, 71545, 71619, 72527, 72615, 73523, 74743, 76525-76535, 76918, 76941, 78437, 79313, 79315, 85072, 86072, 87072, 87072.1, 87144, 101223, 101323.1, and 102423.

ENFORCEMENT: Complaint to Licensing and Certification Division, State Dept. of Health Services; Office of the

State Longterm Care Ombudsman; district attorney; labor commissioner; civil action.

Violation may be a misdemeanor and attorney's fees may be available. Civil penalties, up to $10,000 for each violation. Any discipline or termination within 120 days of complaining raises a presumption of unlawful retaliation.

## YOU HAVE THE RIGHT TO PROTECT PATIENTS, PRISONERS, AND OTHER INSTITUTIONALIZED CLIENTS

You can report any suspected violations of the rights of institutionalized people. This includes all prisoners, resident juveniles, patients, retarded or handicapped clients, and all recipients of custodial or residential care. You cannot be discharged, disciplined, threatened, harassed, blacklisted, or discriminated against for making a report. You can report, to the proper authorities, any denial of the following rights to these clients or prisoners.

(1) The right to privacy and dignity.

(2) The right to private meetings with physicians, lawyers, advisors, visitors, and advocates.

(3) The right to keep information confidential.

(4) The right to speak freely.

(5) The right to complain to whomever one chooses, and not to be threatened or punished for complaining.

(6) The right to private calls.

(7) The right to send and receive unopened mail, and to have access to letterwriting materials and stamps.

(8) The right to visitors.

(9) The right to social interaction.

(10) The right to leave (does not apply to prisons).

(11) The right to physical exercise and recreational opportunities.

(12) The right to religious practice and worship.

(13) The right to adequate treatment.

(14) The right to prompt medical care.

(15) The right to decline treatment.

(16) The right to a clean, safe, and adequately staffed facility.

(17) The right to be free of physical or drug restraints.

(18) The right not to be experimented on.

(19) The right to be free from physical, mental, or sexual abuse or threats.

(20) The right to control one's own money.

(21) The right to not work for the facility.

(22) The right to participate in appropriate educational opportunities.

(23) The right to resist guardianships or conservatorships.

(24) The right to contraception.

(25) The right to be free from racial or other discrimination.

(26) The right to not be sterilized.

(27) The right to information about one's condition, about plans for one's future, about costs and charges, about ownership and control of the facility, and about reports concerning the facility.

(28) The right to be informed, in language and manner one can understand, of one's rights.

A very few of these rights may be restricted for medical or legal reasons. In each case, the restriction must be recorded in the patient's or client's records, along with an explanation and the name of the person ordering the restriction. Some of these rights do not apply to a jail, prison, or detention facility.

A client may not be evicted, transferred, or discriminated against because s/he pays by Medi-Cal or Medicare.

> LAW: Title 42 U.S. Code sections 1997d, 1997-1997j, and 9501; Health and Safety Code sections 1424(e) and 1599.1; Labor Code sections 1102.5-1105; Welfare and Institutions Code sections 5325, 5325.1, 14124.7 and 14124.10; Penal Code sections 2600, 2601, 2650-2680, 3400-3409, 3500-3524, 4011, 4019.5-4023.6, and 4027-4030; Title 28 Code of Federal Regulations Part 40; Title 9 California Administrative Code sections 835-868 and 10,569; Title 15 California Administrative Code sections 3279-3282 and 3287.

> ENFORCEMENT: To ensure you are protected, send a copy of your complaint or report to the Justice Department, Office of Civil Rights, and to the appropriate state enforcement agency; labor commissioner; civil action.

> See also previous section.

> EXCEPTIONS: The special federal protection is limited to any facility which is run by a state or local government agency, or which provides services to or for any state or local government agency, or which receives funding (other than or in addition to Medi-Cal, Medicare, and SSI) from any state or local government agency.

## YOU HAVE THE RIGHT TO REPORT ENVIRONMENTAL, ASBESTOS, AND NUCLEAR SAFETY VIOLATIONS

Federal laws protect you if you report possible violations of environmental protection or nuclear safety laws. It is illegal for your employer to discharge or discipline you, to harass or blacklist you, or to discriminate or retaliate against you in any way. You are protected if you report (or are about to report) any violation, or if you provide (or are about to provide) any information or testimony to any investigating agency. These protections apply to any problems you report concerning:

air pollution;
safe drinking water;
water pollution;
thermal discharges into waters;
toxic substances;
waste oil disposal;
hazardous wastes;
emission standards;
nuclear safety;
marine sanitation;
radiation safety;
waste disposal or management;
related environmental issues.

LAW: Title 29 Code of Federal Regulations sections 24.1-24.9; Title 15 U.S. Code section 2622; Title 33 U.S. Code section 1367; Title 42 U.S. Code sections 300j-9(i), 5851, 6971, 7622, and 9610; Labor Code sections 1102.5-1105.

ENFORCEMENT: You must file a written complaint within 30 days with the U.S. Dept. of Labor, Wage and Hour Division; keep a copy of your complaint.

Labor commissioner; district attorney; civil action.

Under state law, concealing, altering, or destroying records about, or lying about hazardous materials may be punishable by fines up to $50,000 per day and two years in prison (Health and Safety Code section 25191).

## YOU HAVE THE RIGHT TO REPORT STRIP MINING VIOLATIONS

Federal law protects you if you report possible violation of the strip mining, surface mining, and land reclamation laws. It is illegal for your employer to discharge or discipline you, to harass or blacklist you, or to retaliate or discriminate against you in any way. You are protected if you report (or are about to report) any violation, or if you provide (or are about to provide) any information or testimony to an investigating agency.

LAW: Title 30 U.S. Code section 1293; Labor Code sections 1102.5-1105.

ENFORCEMENT: You must file a written complaint **within 30 days** with the Interior Secretary, U.S. Dept. of the Interior. You must send a copy of your complaint to your employer. Send another copy to the U.S. Dept. of Labor, Wage and Hour Division. Keep a copy. Labor commissioner; district attorney; civil action.


## ASBESTOS VIOLATIONS IN SCHOOLS

You have special protection in connection with asbestos violations in schools.

You have the right to notify the public about any asbestos problem in school buildings. No state or local educational agency receiving federal funds can retaliate against you in any way.

LAW: Title 20 U.S. Code section 3608.

ENFORCEMENT: Civil action.


## YOU HAVE SPECIAL RIGHTS IF YOU ARE AT SEA

If you go to sea, you have a very complex and unique set of protections. Your rights to complain about unseaworthy vessels, unfit food or quarters, or unsafe conditions are provided for in a number of ways. Consult your union. Enforcement agencies include the U.S. District Court, the Coast Guard shipping commissioner, U.S. consular officials, Customs Service officials, and the commanding officers of U.S. Navy vessels

## YOU CANNOT BE DISCHARGED OR DISCIPLINED FOR REPORTING UNSAFE BOATING CONDITIONS OR ENFORCING BOAT SAFETY

It is a crime for your employer to retaliate against you for enforcing boat safety rules. This applies to charter or "for hire" boats, including "whale watching" boats. It is illegal to threaten any loss of work or charter earnings for enforcement of boat safety rules. Safety rules include life preserver requirements, bad-weather cancellations, and Coast Guard licensing. You cannot be discharged or disciplined for reporting unsafe boating conditions.

**LAW:** Harbors and Navigation Code sections 773-774.4; Labor Code sections 1102.5-1105.

**ENFORCEMENT:** District attorney; civil action.

Violators are subject to one year in jail and a $50,000 fine.

## YOU CANNOT BE DISCHARGED OR DISCIPLINED FOR REPORTING MARINE ACCIDENTS OR INJURIES

Your rights to report and testify about "marine casualties" are protected. A "marine casualty" is any of the following events, if it happens at sea or on board a maritime vessel:

(1) the death of a person;

(2) any serious injury to a person;

(3) the material loss of property; or

(4) material damage affecting the seaworthiness or efficiency of the vessel.

It is a crime for anyone to threaten, discharge, harass, discipline, blacklist, discriminate against you, or in any way try to coerce you, in order to:

(1) prevent you from reporting or testifying;

(2) make you give a false report or testimony;

(3) get you to leave the country; or

(4) get you to change your report or testimony.

These protections apply to any reports or testimony about a marine casualty.

LAW: Title 46 U.S. Code sections 6306 and 6101; Labor Code sections 1102.5-1105.

ENFORCEMENT: U.S. Secretary of Transportation; U.S. Attorney for your area; civil action.

Anyone who violates these laws is subject to one year in jail and a $5,000 fine.

## YOU CANNOT BE DISCHARGED OR DISCIPLINED FOR REPORTING UNSAFE CARGO

"Containers" are those cargo containers which can be carried by ship, train, and truck, and transferred from one to another without the need to unload and reload the contents. Federal law requires that these containers be designed, built, labeled, periodically inspected, and maintained in a safe manner. A "safe" container will not break or spill cargo, can safely be hoisted, can support other containers stacked on top, and is properly labeled and inspected.

You cannot be discharged, disciplined, or discriminated against in any way for reporting an unsafe container (or reporting any related violation). To be sure of protection, send a copy of your report to the U.S. Secretary of Transportation (keep a copy for yourself, as well). The complaint must be submitted within 60 days.

LAW: Title 46 U.S. Code sections 1506 and 1501-1505; Volume 29 U.S. Treaties, pages 3707-3730; Labor Code sections 1102.5-1105.

ENFORCEMENT: U.S. Dept. of Labor; civil action.

EXCEPTIONS: Special container safety rules protect longshoremen and related harbor workers (see Title 29

Code of Federal Regulations sections 1918.85 and 1918.86; and Title 8 California Administrative Code sections 3466 and 3460).

## YOU CANNOT BE DISCHARGED OR DISCIPLINED FOR REPORTING RAILROAD ACCIDENTS, INJURIES, OR UNSAFE CONDITIONS

Your rights to report, complain, and testify about railroad accidents or unsafe railroad conditions and violations of railroad safety laws are protected by federal law.

Your employer cannot discipline or discharge you, or in any way discriminate against you, for any safety-related report, complaint, or testimony. Your employer cannot keep you, or try to keep you, from voluntarily telling people what you have witnessed in connection with any job-related injury or death.

**LAW:** Title 45 U.S. Code sections 60 and 441.

**ENFORCEMENT:** U.S. Attorney for your area; civil action.

Some violations are crimes; violators are subject to imprisonment and fines.

## YOU CANNOT BE DISCHARGED OR DISCIPLINED FOR REPORTING UNSAFE CONDITIONS IN COMMERCIAL MOTOR VEHICLES

Your rights to report, complain, and testify about unsafe commercial motor vehicles are fully protected.

Your employer cannot discipline or discharge you, or in any way discriminate against you, for complaining about any possible violation of a commercial motor vehicle safety rule or regulation. These protections extend to independent contractor drivers.

For this federal law to apply, a "commercial motor vehicle" is any of the following:

(1) a truck or truck-trailer vehicle with a gross vehicle weight rating of 10,000 or more pounds;

(2) a vehicle designed to transport more than 10 people (counting the driver); or

(3) a vehicle used to haul hazardous substances.

LAW: Title 49 Appendix U.S. Code sections 2301-2305; Title 29 Code of Federal Regulations Parts 1977 and 1978; Labor Code sections 1102.5-1105, 6310 and 6312.

ENFORCEMENT: Federal OSHA, Regional Offices (file a written complaint [citing "Section 405 of the Surface Transportation or Truck Safety Act"] within 180 days); labor commissioner; district attorney; civil action.

# CHAPTER 10

## EMPLOYEE RECORDS: COLLECTING, STORING, AND ACCESSING INFORMATION

### YOU HAVE THE RIGHT TO SEE YOUR PERSONNEL FILE

All records about you kept by your employer are your "personnel files." Your personnel file is defined by law as any files, papers, or computer records which are used (or have been used) to make an employment decision about you. These include decisions to hire, promote, discipline, fire, transfer, or set or raise salary or benefits.

You have the right to see these records whether they are kept in one file or many files. It is important to check your files to make sure they do not contain false or restricted information (e.g., arrest records). (See Chapters 2, 3, and 8.) Your employer must make your records available for your inspection at your work location during normal business hours, and "within a reasonable period of time" after you have asked to see your files. If you are a public employee, you have the right to inspect your files during normal working hours (at the location at which they are stored) with no loss of pay.

Upon your request, you must be given a copy of any document that you sign.

Your legal access to employee records continues even after you have left the job. You have at least three years to inspect all of your files (and at least 30 years for health and safety files).

LAW: Labor Code sections 432, 1198.5, and 1199; Title 8 Calif. Administrative Code section 3204; Industrial Welfare Commission Orders 1-14, Section 7; Labor Standards Enforcement Division Memo 76-2.

ENFORCEMENT: Labor commissioner; district attorney; civil action.

Any employer who violates this law is subject to six months in prison and a $500 fine.

EXCEPTIONS: The only records which are not covered by this law are (1) records "relating to the investigation of a possible criminal offense" and (2) letters of reference. However, you may see these records if they are used to discipline or to discharge you. You can see records of investigation under other laws. (See Chapter 8, DISCIPLINE AND DISCHARGE.) State government employees and school employees are not covered by this law, but other laws apply; see below. All other local government and special district employees are covered by the rules listed above. Public safety officers are also protected by Government Code sections 3301, 3305, and 3306.

## WHAT INFORMATION YOUR EMPLOYER CAN ENTER INTO OR RELEASE FROM YOUR PERSONNEL FILE IS RESTRICTED

Your "privacy" rights restrict what can be put into, or released from, your personnel files. Your employer can only collect and keep information about you which is relevant to your job. You can sue anyone (including a supervisor) who places false and defamatory statements about you in your personnel file.

Your employer can only release information about you if there is a valid business reason. Every employer has the duty to take reasonable steps to protect the confidentiality of personal information. The employer must limit access to personal information, and limit what is done with that information. (See also Chapter 3, BLACKLISTING, INVESTIGATIONS, AND POLICE RECORDS.)

LAW: California Constitution, Article I, section I; Labor Code sections 1050-1056; Civil Code section 56.20(a).

ENFORCEMENT: Labor commissioner; civil action.

## YOUR EMPLOYER MUST COLLECT AND KEEP CERTAIN RECORDS

Your employer must keep the information listed below in sufficient detail to calculate correctly the wages and benefits owed to you. You have the right to inspect and copy these records. If your employer does not keep or has not kept adequate records, you will likely win any reasonable claim you make.

Even when your employer has gone out of business, you may be able to get health and exposure records from the U.S. National Institute of Occupational Safety and Health or another agency. Contact your union or attorney.

(A) For at least the previous two years, your employer must keep records of:

(1) job and promotion applications;

(2) job referral records;

(3) job descriptions and classifications;

(4) records of every promotion, demotion, transfer, layoff, or training selection decision;

(5) records of every failure or refusal to hire or promote;

(6) all test papers;

(7) all job notices, ads, and announcements of jobs and of overtime opportunities;

(8) all disciplinary and discharge records;

(9) a written record of every term and condition of employment;

(10) written justifications for all wage differentials between workers of different sexes (including seniority, merit, and evaluation records).

(B) For at least the previous three years, your employer must keep records of:

(1) your sex and date of birth;

(2) your occupation or job assignments;

(3) the basis of your pay rate (e.g., hourly);

(4) your total daily or weekly straight-time earnings;

(5) your total overtime earnings each week;

(6) the date, amount, and nature of each addition to or deduction from your total wages;

(7) total wages paid and the date paid;

(8) the period covered by each payment;

(9) all retroactive wage payments and periods covered;

(10) the value of all board, lodging, and any other non-cash compensation furnished to you, and whether or not you acually received it;

(11) all piece rates; explanations of all incentive plans; and accurate production records when used in any incentive plan;

(12) all tips and gratuities received for you by your employer (e.g., credit card slips);

(13) all hours you worked in tipped jobs and all hours you worked in non-tipped jobs, plus the amounts paid to you for each kind of job;

(14) a written memo summarizing each unwritten employment understanding or agreement that has an effect on your wages or hours;

(15) a copy of each collective bargaining agreement, trust agreement, benefit plan, or individual employment contract affecting your job;

(16) if you are in a white-collar* exempt occupation, the basis for all wages and benefits you receive;

(17) if you are not in a white-collar* exempt occupation:

> (a) the time of day and day of the week on which your workweek begins;

> (b) your regular hourly rate of pay;

> (c) the nature and amount of every payment which was excluded from your "regular rate of pay";

> (d) time records showing when you began and ended each work period;

> (e) time records showing each meal period, split shift interval and total daily hours worked;

> (f) hours worked each day; and

> (g) hours worked each week.

(C) For at least the previous four years, your employer must keep records of:

(1) your name and Social Security number;

(2) your home address (not a P.O. Box number);

(3) the dates you were hired, rehired, recalled, and terminated;

(4) your place(s) of work;

(5) all remuneraton and compensation paid to you;

(6) all special payments, gifts, bonuses, prizes, etc., given to you, and the periods of service for which the special payments were made;

(7) the cash value of all non-cash remuneration given to you;

(8) the net and gross wages paid to you in each period and the period covered;

(9) all of your W-2, W-3, and W-4 forms;

(10) the amount and date(s) of state and federal income taxes withheld;

(11) the amount of all Unemployment Insurance taxes paid because of you, and the periods of work covered;

(12) copies of all tax returns, schedules, and statements concerning income tax and FICA deductions and Unemployment Insurance taxes;

(13) every report concerning tips and gratuities you gave to your employer.

(D) For at least the previous five years, your employer must keep records of:

(1) the Log and Summary of Occupational Injuries and Illnesses for your workplace (see Chapter 5, WORKING CONDITIONS: SAFETY, HEALTH AND SANITATION);

(2) if your employer is self-insured under the Workers' Compensation system: a case file for each work-injury or illness case or claim (including all those which were denied) for at least five years after the last date of treatment; each case file must contain:

(a) the Employer's Report of Occupational Injury and Illness;

(b) all medical reports;

(c) all Workers' Compensation Appeals Board orders and reports;

(d) a copy of every letter of denial or notice of termination of benefits sent to you;

(e) every report to the Division of Industrial Accidents;

(f) a record of all benefits paid to you and the periods covered;

(g) an estimate of future liability.

(E) For at least the previous six years, your employer must keep records of:

(1) all records used in administering any pension or employee benefit plan, including all vouchers, worksheets, and receipts;

(2) statements indicating what payments have been made to any benefit funds on your behalf, and for what periods.

(F) For at least the entire period of your employment, plus at least thirty years after you leave the job, your employer must keep records of:

(1) all your medical records, including medical and employment questionnaires; medical histories; results of medical exams; all reports of lab tests; x-rays; medical opinions; medical diagnoses, progress notes, and recommendations; descriptions of medical treatments and prescriptions; employee medical complaints; and doctors' reports concerning industrial injuries;

(2) the employer's report of every occupational injury or illness where you had medical treatment beyond first aid or where you lost time from work after the date of injury;

(3) all exposure records concerning exposure to any toxic substance (chemical or biological) or exposure to any harmful physical agent or stress (e.g., heat, noise, vibration), including records of your own

personal exposure and all biological and environmental monitoring; records of the exposure in your workplace; plus records of the exposure in the workplace to which you are being assigned or transferred; records of the exposure of other employees with past or present job duties or working conditions related to or similar to yours; the MSDS (Material Safety Data Sheet) or equivalent information for each and every hazardous substance in your workplace (see Chapter 5, WORKING CONDITIONS: SAFETY, HEALTH AND SANITATION);

(4) any study and any compilation of data (whether performed by your employer or by an outsider) which was based in whole or in part on the exposure records, medical records, or insurance claim records pertaining to you, your fellow workers, or your workplace.

LAW: Business and Professions Code section 140; Labor Code sections 226, 226.2, 227.5, 353, 354, 1174, 1175, 1197.5, 1199, 6360-6399.9 and 6408-6410; Health and Safety Code sections 25,150 and 25180; Government Code sections 12946 and 12976; Unemployment Insurance Code sections 986, 1085, 1088, 1093, and 13050-13055; Title 18 U.S. Code section 1001; Title 29 U.S. Code sections 1027, 1821, 1831, 1851, and 1854; Title 26 U.S. Code sections 3101-3126, 3301-3311, 3402, and 6001; Title 2 California Administrative Code section 7287.0; Title 8 California Administrative Code sections 3204, 5194(c), 14000-14007, 14301-14315, and 15400-15400.3; Title 22 California Administrative Code sections 1085-2, 1085-3, 4350-1, and 4353-1; Title 26 Code of Federal Regulations sections 31.6001-1 to 31.6001-5, and 31.6051-1 to 31.6051-3; Title 29 Code of Federal Regulations sections 516.2-516.7, 516.28 and 516.29, Part 1602, sections 1627.3, 1627.6, and 2520.104b-1; Industrial Welfare Commission Orders 1-15, section 7; Labor Standards Enforcement Division Memos 77-2 and 84-5.

Special record-keeping rules on the health care, community care and child care industries are found at Title 22 California Administrative Code sections 70725, 71525, 72533, 73527, 74723, 75052, 76541, 76920, 78429, 79333, 87520, and 101217.

**ENFORCEMENT**: Complaint to enforcement agencies; civil action

Any employer who violates these laws is subject to five years in jail and fines up to $50,000 per day, depending upon the violation.

## COUNTY EMPLOYEES HAVE SPECIAL RIGHTS OF ACCESS

The California Labor Code (section 1198.5) extends to county employees all of the protections outlined in the previous sections. In addition, if you are a county employee, you have the right to see any records relating to any grievance concerning yourself.

You also have the right to respond to any information in your file about which you disagree. This response may be in writing or in a personal interview. Your written responses become a permanent part of your personnel record.

**LAW**: Government Code section 31,011.

**ENFORCEMENT**: Civil action.

**EXCEPTIONS**: County employees do not have the right to see letters of reference or records relating to a pending investigation of a possible criminal offense. See Chapter 8, DISCIPLINE AND DISCHARGE.

## SCHOOL DISTRICT AND COMMUNITY COLLEGE EMPLOYEES HAVE SPECIAL RIGHTS OF ACCESS

If you are a school district or community college employee, you have the right to see all materials in your files. You also have the right to be given notice of any derogatory material before it is entered in your files. You have the right to review and comment on the derogatory material; your comments must be attached to the material in the files. You have the right to be released from duty, without salary reduction, to review and comment on derogatory materials. (The employer cannot use derogatory materials in any employment decision, unless you have been given these rights.)

A certified employee has the right to a copy of her/his evaluation. This must be given to the employee at least 30 days prior to the end of the school year. The employee has the right to attach a written response to the evaluation; both must be placed in the personnel file.

**LAW:** Education Code sections 44031, 44663, 44934-44938, 87031, 87733, and 87734.

**ENFORCEMENT:** Public Employment Relations Board (PERB); civil action.

**EXCEPTIONS:** School district and community college employees may not see pre-employment letters of reference and certain promotional exam materials prepared by identifiable committee members.

## STATE UNIVERSITY AND COLLEGE EMPLOYEES HAVE SPECIAL RIGHTS OF ACCESS

If you are a state university or state college employee, you have the right to see your own personnel file.

This includes the right to see any reports, documents, correspondence, or other materials which pertain to you. You have the right to have a union representative or any other person accompany you when the file is inspected. The employer must, within 10 calendar days of a written request, provide you with an exact copy of the entire file, or of the specific portion that you request. (You may be required to pay the cost of duplicating file material.)

You may request (in writing) correction of file material which you believe to be inaccurate, irrelevant, untimely, or incomplete. You may also submit a written statement of the reasons for the corrections. That statement becomes part of your personnel file.

The president of the State University or College must respond to the request to correct the personnel file within 21 calendar days. If the president refuses to make the corrections, s/he must state the reasons for the refusal in writing. That statement also becomes part of the employee's personnel file.

The employer is required to base decisions regarding promotions, retention, termination, and other personnel actions primarily on information contained in the employee's personnel file. If a personnel decision or recommendation is based on reasons not contained in the file, those reasons must be put in writing and placed in the personnel file so that the employee has access to them.

**LAW**: Education Code section 89546.

**ENFORCEMENT**: Civil action.

**EXCEPTIONS**: A union agreement may modify these rules. Employees do **not** have access, using the above-specified procedure, to pre-employment materials in their files, unless those materials are considered in any post-hiring personnel action. However university and college employees **can** get pre-employment materials by using the general procedures for access to State government files (see below).

## YOU HAVE THE RIGHT TO SEE ALL STATE GOVERNMENT FILES KEPT ABOUT YOU

This right applies whether or not you are a state employee. Upon request, every state agency must allow you to examine (and copy) all records kept about you. Your files must be made available at a location near your residence (or must be mailed to you). You have the right to have a person of your choosing help you to inspect the files. The agency has 30 days to make all of the files available. (For inactive records in central storage, the agency has 60 days.)

All state files about you must "to the maximum extent possible" be accurate, relevant, timely, and complete. You can ask (in writing) that any item be eliminated or corrected. (Keep a copy of each request you make to examine and to correct files.) If the agency refuses your request, it must tell you why and also how you can appeal the refusal. After you appeal, if the correction is not made, you have the right to insert in the file a statement of your disagreement and your reasons.

If you work for the state, you must be given a performance appraisal or report. You have the right to receive a copy of this (and to discuss it) before it is placed in your file.

If you are a state employee, you have other rights. If you receive notice of an "adverse action" (a dismissal, demotion, suspension, or other discipline), you (or your representative) have a right to inspect all documents relevant to the adverse action. You (or your representative) also have the right to interview all employees who might have information about the acts (or omissions) upon which the adverse action is based.

As a state employee, you also have the right to have stale letters of reprimand removed from your files. Letters of reprimand must be removed and destroyed not later than three years from the date the letters were issued.

LAW: Civil Code sections 1798-1798.76; Government Code sections 19172-19173, 19570, 19574, 19574.1-19574.2, 19589, and 19992-19992.13; Title 2 California Administrative Code sections 599.795 and 599.798.

**ENFORCEMENT**: State Personnel Board, Office of Information Practices and Hearing Office; civil action (attorney's fees and damages available).

**EXCEPTIONS**: (1) These rules do **not** apply to the State Legislature or to the courts. (Note that some courtroom personnel are county employees, while others are court employees.) These rules do **not** apply to non-employee files at the State Compensation Insurance Fund; these rules **do** apply to State Compensation Insurance Fund employee files. If you are a University of California employee, consult your union or lawyer about current rules for your files.

(2) If the state agency is a law enforcement agency, then it does not have to reveal information used for identifying offenders or for criminal investigations or prosecutions. Consult an attorney for access to these records.

(3) These rules do not apply to civil service exam materials. Consult your union or lawyer if you need these materials.

(4) The state agency does not have to reveal certain investigatory materials. Information being used solely to investigate a specific grievance, complaint, or law violation does **not** have to be disclosed, during the actual investigation. (As soon as any material is used to support an adverse action, you can see all materials relevant to the charges.)

(5) The state agency can withhold the identity of the source of information, **if** it obtained the information with a promise of confidentiality. But this does **not** apply to any information from one of your supervisors; the identity of a supervisory source must always be revealed. (For this specific purpose, an academic department chairman in an institution of higher education is not a "supervisor.")

But even where the identity of the source is withheld, the state agency **must** give you access to **all** information which might be detrimental to you in any way.

(6) For inspecting and correcting your arrest and conviction records, see Penal Code sections 11,120-11,127.

## YOU HAVE THE RIGHT TO INSPECT AND COPY LOCAL GOVERNMENT FILES ABOUT YOU

Local government agencies are governed by the California Public Records Act; everyone has the right to see the files kept about themselves. (If you are an employee of local government, you are also protected by personnel file access laws. See previous entries in this chapter.)

Decide what identifiable information you want. Then give a written request (keep a copy) to the local government agency. Within 10 working days, the agency must make the information available to you or tell you why it is not available. (In certain cases, the answer may be delayed for a total of 20 working days.)

**LAW**: California Constitution, Article I, section 1; Government Code sections 6250-6259.

**ENFORCEMENT**: Civil action (attorney's fees available).

**EXCEPTIONS**: (1) Agencies do not have to reveal certain records concerning pending claims or law suits; certain records concerning licensing, employment, or academic exams; and certain law enforcement records. There are a few other technical exceptions; consult your attorney.

(2) For access to federal government records, see Title 5 U.S. Code sections 551-552a (attorney's fees available).

(3) For inspection and correction of your local arrest and conviction records, see Penal Code sections 13300-13305 and 13320-13326.

(4) For inspection and correction of student records (yours or your children's: primary, secondary, community college, university, or college), see Education Code sections 49060-49078 and 67100-67147.5; Title 20 U.S. Code section 1232g; Title 34 Code of Federal Regulations sections 99.1-99.67 (attorney's fees available).

## YOUR UNION MAY OBTAIN FILE INFORMATION FOR YOU

Besides your rights to see your personnel files, you have a right to get other information through your union. The union has the right to all information relevant to its bargaining duties. This means **both** information needed to negotiate a contract **and** information needed to handle your grievance or disciplinary action.

This is very important. Often your success in a grievance or disciplinary hearing depends upon comparing how the employer treated you with the treatment given other workers. Your union has an enforceable right to obtain this comparative information. It can also obtain any other information relevant to the grievance or discipline.

**LAW:** Bargaining rights statutes.

**ENFORCEMENT:** Complaint to the National Labor Relations Board or other enforcement agency; civil action if the employer is a local government agency or is under Labor Code section 923.


## YOU HAVE THE RIGHT TO SEE INSURANCE FILES KEPT ABOUT YOU

You have the right to see (and copy) any records about you which are held by an insurance company, broker, agent, or claims service. This applies **whether or not** the insurance files are work-related (e.g., disability, illness, occupational injury, sick leave, medical care, workers' compensation).

Once you submit a written request (keep a copy), the insurance institution has 30 days to allow you to see and copy all information about yourself. If you choose, you have the right to be mailed a copy of the information. If any of the information is in coded form, the insurance institution must give you a "plain language" translation in writing. The institution must also tell you the name(s) of anyone who has received any of the information within the previous two years.

The insurance institution must also tell you how you can have the files corrected. If you submit a written request that information be eliminated or corrected, the institution has 30 business days to respond. If it does not do what you ask, it must give you an explanation. You then have the right to submit a statement to be inserted in your file, giving your version of the facts.

LAW: Insurance Code sections 791-791.26.

ENFORCEMENT: Civil action (attorney's fees and damages available).

EXCEPTIONS: The insurance institution has the option to send mental health record information to a medical professional you name, instead of directly to you. In that case, be sure to name someone other than the health care provider who submitted the information in the first place. This option applies **only** to mental health record information. You have the right to see all other information, including the notes in the file saying what the insurer was doing about your claim(s) and why.

## YOU HAVE THE RIGHT TO INSPECT YOUR HEALTH CARE RECORDS

You have the right to inspect your health care records and receive copies of your medical records from your health care provider (i.e., from your physician, psychiatrist, dentist, optometrist, osteopath, chiropractor, podiatrist, clinic, or hospital). Within five working days from making a written request, you must be permitted to inspect your records. You may be accompanied by one other person of your choosing.

You are entitled to copies of all or any specific portion of your medical records. You may be required to pay reasonable clerical costs incurred in locating your records, making them available, and copying them. The copies must be provided within fifteen days of a written request.

LAW: Health and Safety Code sections 25250-25258; Evidence Code section 1158.

ENFORCEMENT: Complaint to the appropriate state licensing board; district attorney; civil action (attorney's fees are available).

EXCEPTIONS: (1) Your health care provider may choose to prepare a summary of your record rather than allow access. In most cases, s/he is required to provide this summary within ten working days (and in no case more than 30 working days).

(2) Your health care provider may choose to deny you direct access to mental health records, or alcohol abuse or drug abuse records. If so, the provider must make an entry in your records about the refusal, including a description of the specific adverse or detrimental consequences s/he fears if you see the records. The provider must also, at the time of refusal, inform you of your right to have copies of all of your mental health (and drug or alcohol abuse records) given to any physician, psychiatrist, licensed psychologist, or licensed clinical social worker you name.

(3) Your health care provider may choose to deny you direct access to x-rays, EKGs, EEGs, and electromyography tracings. If so, these records must be given to any health care provider you name (within 15 days of your written request).

(4) You can get a complete set of medical records (no summary allowed) by having an attorney give the health care provider a written authorization signed by you. The health care provider must make all records available for copying within five days. (A provider who resists must pay all costs required to enforce this right, including attorney's fees.) The most you can be charged for this copying is (a) actual copying costs, not to exceed ten cents per page, and (b) actual clerical costs incurred in locating the records and making them available.

## HEALTH CARE PROVIDERS CANNOT GIVE DETAILED INFORMATION ABOUT YOU TO YOUR EMPLOYER

For your employer to gain access to your medical records, you must sign and receive a copy of an "authorization for release of medical information."

You cannot be discharged, disciplined, or discriminated against in any way for refusing to sign (or for cancelling) an authorization.

Sometimes you will need to give certain information to your employer (e.g., to support a disability claim). If you do sign an authorization, you should limit what medical information can be disclosed, and to whom, for what purpose, and for how long.

This law applies to all doctors, dentists, osteopaths, chiropractors, podiatrists, psychologists, psychiatrists, clinics, hospitals, group health care plans, and other health care providers.

**LAW:** Civil Code sections 56-56.37.

**ENFORCEMENT:** Complaint to the appropriate licensing boards; district attorney; civil action.

Violation is a crime; attorney's fees and actual and punitive damages may be available

**EXCEPTIONS:** (1) A health care provider can release certain information without an authorization. You must give the provider a specific written request to the contrary if you do **not** want the following released:

(a) your name, address, and sex;

(b) a general description of the reason for treatment (e.g., an injury, a burn, poisoning, etc.);

c) the general nature of the injury, burn, poisoning, or other condition; and

(d) your general condition.

(2) If your employer has paid for employment-related health services, and has requested (in advance) that s/he be notified of the results, then the health care provider **can** tell the employer any functional limitations which may entitle you to leave from work for medical reasons or which limit your fitness to perform your present employment. But, without an authorization from you, the provider **cannot** give the employer any statement of the medical cause for the limitations.

(3) If your employer has paid for employment-related health care services, and has requested (in advance) that s/he be notified of the results; **and** if you have raised an issue concerning your own medical history, mental or physical condition, or treatment (in a law suit, arbitration, or grievance proceeding), then the employer-paid health care provider can disclose other medical information to your employer (but only for use in the proceeding where **you** have made it an issue).

(4) Where the employer is paying for medical treatment for occupational injuries or illness (workers' compensation), then the employer-paid health care provider can and will give information to the employer. You have a right to a copy of all these reports.

(5) Even without an authorization, a health-care provider can disclose enough information to an insurer, employer, or employee benefit plan to allow responsibility for payment to be determined.

(6) A health care provider can disclose information required by a search warrant or subpena.

## YOUR EMPLOYER IS REQUIRED TO PROTECT THE CONFIDENTIALITY OF YOUR MEDICAL RECORDS

Your employer cannot release any medical information about you (this includes any facts about your medical history, mental or physical condition, or treatment) without your permission. This permission can be granted only in the form of an "authorization for release of medical information".

Your employer's authority to use medical information to terminate or discipline you, or to deny you job opportunities, is very limited. (See previous section and Chapter 2, HIRING RIGHTS, for details.)

LAW: Civil Code sections 56-56.37; Labor Code section 1026.

ENFORCEMENT: District attorney; civil action (damages and attorney's fees may be available).

Violation is a crime.

EXCEPTIONS: (1) Your employer can provide required occupational injury and illness information without an authorization.

(2) An employer which is a health care provider (or an insurance institution) is controlled by the health care provider rules (or the insurance institution rules) when it is disclosing information obtained as a health care provider (or as an insurer). When it is dealing with information obtained as an employer, however, then any employer (private or public) is bound by these employer rules.

(3) Your employer may give medical information to your treating doctor or hospital when you are unconscious or otherwise unable to sign an authorization.

(4) Your employer can release medical information as required by a search warrant or subpena.

(5) Your employer can use properly obtained medical information to determine eligibility for paid and unpaid leave from work for medical reasons.

6) Your employer can use properly obtained medical information in administering employee benefit plans (including health care plans, disability income plans, and workers' compensation plans).

(7) When you raise an issue concerning your own medical history, mental or physical condition, or treatment (in a law suit, arbitration, or grievance proceeding), then your employer can use properly obtained medical information in answering that issue.

## LIMITS ON YOUR EMPLOYER'S ACCESS TO PSYCHIATRIC, MENTAL OR DEVELOPMENTAL DISABILITY, GENETIC DISEASE, DRUG ABUSE, AND ALCOHOL ABUSE RECORDS

These rules apply to any provider of psychiatric care, treatment for a developmental disability or genetic disease, drug abuse or alcohol abuse care, halfway house, crisis line, free clinic, mental disability service, suicide prevention service, detoxification clinic, methadone program, drug screening lab or clinic, counseling center, rehabilitation or other program. Even if you sign an authorization for release of this information, there are limits on what can be released to your employer.

Any information of this sort is likely to be used to deny you employment opportunities. You should **not** sign any authorization for its release without first consulting your union or lawyer. If you have already signed an authorization, you can cancel it. Immediately give a written note (cancelling any authorization for release of information) to the doctor or clinic or hospital or other health care provider. (Keep a copy of the cancellation.) As soon as the health care provider receives the cancellation, no information can be given out.

LAW: Health and Safety Code sections 150-155, 11879 and 11970.5-11978; Welfare and Institutions Code sections 4514 and 5328-5330; Title 21 U.S. Code section 1103; Title 42

U.S. Code sections 290dd-3, 290ee-3 and 9501(1)(H); Title 42 Code of Federal Regulations sections 2 through 2.67-1, especially 2.38; Title 29 U.S. Code sections 706(7), 793, and 794; Government Code sections 11135-11139.5.

**ENFORCEMENT:** U.S. Attorney; U.S. Dept. of Labor, Office of Federal Contract Compliance Programs; district attorney; civil action.

Violation is a crime; violators are subject to fines up to $5,000. In most cases, treble damages are available in a civil action.

**EXCEPTIONS:** Employers who are federal or state contractors, or federal or state grant recipients, cannot discriminate against you for any physical or psychiatric disability, or drug abuse or alcohol abuse history, **unless** it currently keeps you from doing the job or presents a current safety hazard.

# APPENDIX

## STATE AND FEDERAL AGENCIES

**Agricultural Labor Relations Board (ALRB)**

Sacramento (95814)
915 Capitol Mall
916/322-4612

Delano (93215)
627 Main St.
805/725-5770

El Centro (92243)
319 Waterman Ave.
714/353-2130

Oxnard (93030)
528 South A St.
805/486-4475

Salinas (93907)
112 Boronda Rd.
408/443-3160

**Apprenticeship Standards Division**

San Francisco (94101)
525 Golden Gate Ave.
415/557-1700

## Cal OSHA -- District Offices

Bakersfield (93309)
4800 Stockdale Hwy
Suite 212
805/395-2718

Berkeley (94709)
1625 Shattuck Ave. Room 305
415/540-3030

Chico (95926)
555 Rio Lindo Ave. Suite A
916/345-7131

Concord (94520)
1070 Concord Ave. Room 270
415/676-5333

El Monte (91731)
3415 Fletcher Ave.
Suite 204
213/575-6960

Eureka (95501)
619 Second St. Room 109
707/442-6232

Fresno (93721)
2550 Mariposa St. Room 4000
209/445-5302

Long Beach (90802)
245 W. Broadway, Suite 245
213/590-5035

Los Angeles (90010)
3460 Wilshire Blvd.
Room 310
213/736-3041

Modesto (95355)
1800 Coffee Road
Bldg. J, Suite 55
209/576-6260

Sacramento (95825)
2422 Arden Way Suite 55
916/920-6123

Salinas (93906)
21 W. Laurel Dr. Suite 45
408/443-3050

San Bernardino (92401)
303 W. Third St. Room 2
714/383-4321

San Diego (92111)
7870 Convey Ct. Suite 140
714/237-7325

San Francisco (94102)
455 Golden Gate Ave.
Room 1193
415/557-1677

San Jose (95113)
100 Paseo de San Antonio
Room 101
408/277-1260

Santa Ana (92701)
28 Civic Center Plaza
Room 552
714/558-4141

Santa Barbara (93105)
3704 State St. Suite 307
805/682-2578

Santa Fe Springs (90607)
14111 E. Freeway Dr.
Suite 203
213/802-1711

Santa Rosa (95404)
50 D St. Room 430
707/542-8802

Stockton (95202)
31 E. Channel St. Room 418
209/948-7762

Ukiah (95482)
776 S. State St.
Suite 204
707/462-8850

Ventura (93003)
5720 Ralston St. Suite 303
805/654-4581


**Cal OSHA Standards Board**

Sacramento (95841)
1006 Fourth Street, Third Floor
916/322-3641


**Cal OSHA Appeals Board**

Sacramento (95814)
1006 Fourth Street, Fourth Floor
916/322-5080

Los Angeles (90012)
107 S. Broadway Room 7112
213/620-5264

## Collection and Investigative Services Bureau

Department of Consumer Affairs
Sacramento (95814)
1920 20th Street
916/620-5901

San Francisco
415/557-0966

## Community Care Licensing Division, State Department of Social Service

Dept. of Social Service
Sacramento (95814)
744 P Street
916/445-4500

Public Inquiry and Response
916/322-2400
213/620-4730

Deputy Director: 916/322-8538
Chico: 916/895-5033
Emeryville: 415/464-1319
Fresno: 209/445-5691
Los Angeles: 213/620-4375
Riverside: 714/781-4200
Sacramento: 916/920-6855
San Diego: 714/237-7381
San Jose: 408/277-1286
Santa Ana: 714/558-4563
Santa Barbara: 805/966-7107
Santa Rosa: 707/576-2210

## Corporations Commissioner

Department of Corporations
Sacramento (95814)
1107 Ninth Street Room 800
915/324-9011

Los Angeles (90005)
600 Commonwealth
213/736-3481

San Francisco (94102)
1390 Market Street
415/557-8575


## Employment Development Department

Sacramento (95814)
800 Capitol Mall
916/445-8008

Bakersfield (93301)
1529 F St.
805/395-2728

Fresno (93706)
1963 E St.
209/445-5373

Los Angeles County (90012)
322 W. First St
213/620-3100

Oakland (94607)
1111 Jackson St. Room 5040
415/464-4095

San Bernardino (92401)
303 W. Third St. Suite 150
714/383-4711

San Diego (92101)
110 W. C St. Suite 1702
714/237-7405

San Francisco (92101)
30 W. Van Ness Ave. Third floor
415/557-2005

San Jose (95112)
888 N. First St., Suite 316 (95112)
408/227-1264

Santa Ana (92707)
28 Civil Center Plaza, Suite 538
714/558-4159

Ventura (93003)
5720 Ralston St. Suite 302
805/654-4513


**Equal Employment Opportunity Commission**

Fresno Area (93721)
1313 P St. Suite 103
209/487-5793

Los Angeles District (90010)
3255 Wilshire Blvd. 9th floor
213/894-3400

Oakland Area (94612)
1515 Clay St. Room 640
415/273-7588

San Diego (92188)
880 Front St. Room 4521
619/293-6288

San Francisco District (94102)
10 United Nations Plaza 4th floor
415/556-0260

San Jose Area (95113)
280 So. First St. Suite 4150
408/291-7352


## Fair Employment and Housing--District Offices

Bakersfield (93301)
1529 F. St.
805/395-2725

Fresno (93706)
1963 E St.
209/445-5373

Los Angeles Central (90012)
322 W. First St.
213/620-2610

Los Angeles County (90012)
322 W. First St.
213/620-3100

Oakland (94607)
1111 Jackson St. Room 5040
415/464-4095


Sacramento (95814)
1202 I St. Suite 214
916/445-9918

San Bernardino (92401)
303 W. Third St. Suite 150
714/383-4711

San Diego (92101)
110 W. C St. Suite 1702
714/237-7405

San Francisco (94102)
30 Van Ness Ave. Third Floor
415/557-2005

San Jose (95112)
888 N. First St. Suite 316
408/227-1264

Santa Ana (92701)
28 Civic Center Plaza Suite 538
714/558-4159

Ventura (93003)
5720 Ralston St. Suite 302
805/654-4513


**Federal OSHA**

Berkeley Area (94704)
1960 Addison St. Room 290
415/485-3410

Long Beach Area (90802)
400 Oceangate, Room 530
213/432-3434

San Francisco Regional (94102)
450 Golden Gate Ave.
415/556-7260

**Federal Trade Commission**

Los Angeles Regional Office (90024)
11000 Wilshire Blvd. Room 13209
213/209-7575

San Francisco Regional Office (94102)
450 Golden Gate Avenue, Room 12470
415/556-1270

**Health Services Department**

Sacramento (95814)
714/744 P Street
916/445-4171

**Industrial Relations, Dept. Director**

San Francisco (94101)
525 Golden Gate Avenue
P.O. Box 603
415/557-3356

**Industrial Welfare Commission (I.W.C.)**

San Francisco (94101)
525 Golden Gate Avenue
PO Box 603
415/557-2590

Los Angeles
213/620-4036

**Insurance Commissioner**

Department of Insurance
San Francisco (94103)
100 Van Ness Avenue, 17th Floor
415/557-3245

Los Angeles (90005)
600 Commonwealth Avenue, 14th Floor
213/736-2551

**Interior Secretary,**
**U.S. Department of the Interior**

San Francisco (94102)
450 Golden Gate Avenue
415/556-8206

**Justice Department, Office of Civil Rights**

San Francisco (94103)
1275 Market, 18th Floor
415/556-8586

**Labor Commissioner, Division of**
**Labor Standards Enforcement**

Bakersfield (93309)
5555 California Ave.
Suite 200
805/395-2710

Burlingame (94010)
1290 Howard Ave. Room 325
415/572-9453

El Centro (92243)
380 N. Eighth St. Suite 2
619/353-0585

Eureka (95501)
619 Second St. Room 109
707/442-5748

Fresno (93706)
1987 E Street
209/445-5144

Hollywood (90028)
6430 Sunset Blvd. Suite 301
213/464-8268

Inglewood (90301)
One Manchester Blvd.
Suite 604
213/412-6380

Long Beach (90802)
245 W. Broadway, 4th Floor
213/590-5044

Los Angeles (90012)
107 S. Broadway, Room 5015
213/620-5877

Marysville (95901)
922 G Street
916/743-1161

Napa (94558)
3273 Claremont Way, 2nd Fl.
707/257-0060

Oakland (94607)
1111 Jackson St. Room 3023
415/464-1353

Panorama City (91402)
8155 Van Nuys Blvd.
Room 950
213/782-3733

Pomona (91769)
300 S. Park Ave. Room 830
714/622-4236

Redding (96001)
2115 Akard Ave. Room 17
916/246-6406

Sacramento (95825)
2422 Arden Way, Suite 50
916/920-6116

Salinas (93906)
21 W. Laurel Dr. Suite 61
408/443-3040

San Bernardino (92401)
303 W. Third St. Room 140
714/383-4333

San Diego (92123)
8765 Aero Dr. Suite 120
714/237-7334

San Francisco (94101)
525 Golden Gate Ave.
1st Floor
415/557-0860

San Jose (95113)
100 Paseo de San Antonio
Room 120
408/277-1265

Santa Ana (92701)
28 Civic Center Plaza
Room 429
714/558-4111

Santa Barbara (93101)
411 E. Canon Perdido Room 3
805/963-1438

Santa Rosa (95404)
50 D St. Suite 360
707/576-2390

Stockton (95202)
31 E. Channel St. Room 328
209/948-7770

Ventura (93003)
3319 Telegraph Road.
Suite 212
805/644-6886

Whittier (90602)
13215 E. Penn Suite 300
213/698-2278


**Labor Standards Enforcement Division**

Department of Industrial Relations
San Francisco (94101)
525 Golden Gate Avenue
PO Box 603
415/557-3827

**Licensing and Certification Division,
State Department of Health Services**

Dept. of Health Services
Sacramento (95814)
714/744 P Street
916/445-4171

District Offices:

Berkeley (94709)
1625 Shattuck Avenue
415/540-2417

Fresno (93704)
666 West Shaw Avenue
209/445-5168

Redding (96002)
331 Hemsted Drive
916/246-6241

Sacramento (95825)
2422 Arden Way
916/920-6851

San Diego (92120)
6150 Mission Gorge Road
714/237-7781

San Francisco (94103)
939 Market Street
415/557-1711

San Jose (95113)
100 Paseo de San Antonio
408/277-1784

**Measurement Standards, Chief of Division**

Department of Food and Agriculture
Sacramento (95826)
8500 Fruitridge Road
916/366-5119

**National Labor Relations Board (NLRB)**

Los Angeles Region 21 (90014)
2890 North Main St. Suite 101
213/894-5254

West Los Angeles Region 32 (90024)
11000 Wilshire Blvd. Room 12100
213/209-7351

Oakland Region 32 (94612)
2201 Broadway 2nd floor
415/273-7200

San Diego Resident Office (92189)
940 Front St. Room 2N20
619/293-6184

San Francisco Region 20 (94102)
450 Golden Gate Room 13018
415/556-3197

**Office of the State Long-Term Care
Ombudsman**

Department of Aging
Sacramento (95814)
1020 19th Street
916/323-6681

**Personnel Services Bureau**

Department of Consumer Affairs
Sacramento (95825)
1426 Howe Avenue
916/920-6311

Los Angeles
213/620-5272

**Polygraph Examiners Board**

Department of Consumer Affairs
Sacramento (95814)
1021 Ost, Room A-608
916/324-3966

**Public Employment Relations Board (PERB)**

Sacramento (95814)
1031 18th St.
916/322-3088

San Francisco (94108)
177 Post St. 9th Floor
415/557-1350

Los Angeles (90010)
3470 Wilshire Blvd. Suite 1001
213/736-3127

## Social Security Administration

San Francisco Regional Office (94102)
100 Van Ness
415/956-3000

## State Attorney General

Sacramento (95814
1515 K St. Suite 511
916/324-5437

Los Angeles (90010)
3580 Wilshire Blvd. Suite 800
213/736-2273

## State Bar of California

San Francisco (94102)
555 Franklin Street
415/561-8200

Los Angeles (90017)
230 W. Third Street
213/482-8220

## State Department of Social Services

Sacramento (95814)
744 P Street
916/445-4500

**State Personnel Board,**
**Office of Information Practices**

Sacramento (95814)
801 Capitol Mall
916/322-7468

Sacramento (95814)
1201 I Street, Suite 214
916/445-9918

San Bernardino (92401)
303 W. Third Street, Suite 150
714/558-4159

San Diego (92101)
110 W. C Street, Suite 1702
714/237-7405

San Francisco (94102)
30 Van Ness Avenue, Third Floor
415/557-2005

San Jose
888 N. First Street, Suite 316
408/227-1264

Santa Ana (92701)
28 Civic Center Plaza Suite 538
714/558-4159

Hearing Office, Appeals Division
Sacramento (95814
801 Capitol Mall
916/445-7398

## U.S. Attorney

Central District--Los Angeles (90012)
312 N. Spring St.
213/894-2400

Eastern District, Sacramento (95814)
650 Capitol Mall
916/551-2695

Fresno (93721)
1130 O St. Room 4304
209/487-5172

No. District San Francisco (94102)
450 Golden Gate Ave.
415/556-1126

San Jose Branch Office (90012)
280 S. 1st St. Room 371
408/466-7221

So. District, San Diego (92189)
940 Front St. Room LLB71
619/293-6620


## U.S. Department of Labor

Regional Representative
San Francisco (94102)
450 Golden Gate Ave. Room 11001
415/556-9326

**U.S. Dept. of Labor, Office of
Federal Contract Compliance Programs**

San Francisco Region (94102)
450 Golden Gate Ave. Room 11435
415/556-6060

Los Angeles Area (90010)
3660 Wilshire Blvd. Suite 603
213/894-4961

Oakland Area (94612)
1330 Broadway, Suite 550
415/273-4055

San Diego Field Station (92188)
880 Front Room 2517
714/293-6489

San Francisco Area (94105)
211 Main St. Room 328
415/974-8750

San Jose Area (95113)
280 So. First St. Suite 390
408/291-7384

Santa Ana Field Station (92712)
34 Civic Center Room 703
714/836-2784

Van Nuys Area (91408)
6230 Van Nuys Blvd. Room 1S1
818/904-6285

**U.S. Dept. of Labor,
Wage and Hour Division**

Fresno Field Station (93721)
2202 Monterey
209/487-5317

Laguna Niguel Field Office (92677)
24000 Avila Road
714/643-4180

Los Angeles Area
115 N. Central
Glendale 91203

Los Angeles Field Station (90010)
3660 Wilshire Blvd.
213/894-4958

Oakland Field Station (94612)
1330 Broadway
415/273-7146

Sacramento Area (95821)
2981 Fulton
916/978-4233

Salinas Field Station (93901)
344 Salinas
408/443-2052

San Bernardino Field Station (92401)
255 N. D Street
714/383-5731

San Diego Field Station (92188)
880 Front Room 2517
619/293-5606

San Francisco Region (94102)
450 Golden Gate Ave. Room 10447
415/556-3592

San Francisco Area Office (94105)
211 Main Street
415/974-0535

San Jose Field Station (95113)
280 S. First St. Room 392
408/291-7730

Santa Ana Area Office (92712)
34 Civic Center
714/836-2156

## U.S. Secretary of Transportation

Department of Transportation
San Francisco (94105)
211 Main Street, Room 1005
415/974-8464

## Workers Compensation Appeals Board

San Francisco (94102)
455 Golden Gate Avenue
415/557-2250

# CALIFORNIA AFL-CIO LABOR COUNCILS

Alameda County CLC
7992 Capwell Dr.
Oakland CA 94621
415/632-4242

Butte & Glenn Co. CLC
PO Box 3729
Chico, CA 95927
916/343-9474

Contra Costa County CLC
917 Alhambra Ave., Suite B
Martinez CA 94553
415/228-0161

Five Counties CLC
(Modoc, Siskiyu, Shasta, Tehama, Trinity)
900 Locust St., Room 7
Redding CA 96001
916/241-0319

Fresno & Madera Co. CLC
4831 E. Shields
Fresno CA 93726
209/252-1815

Humboldt & Del Norte Counties CLC
9th & E Streets
Labor Temple
Eureka, CA 95501
707/445-1245

Kern, Inyo & Mono Co. CLC
200 W. Jeffrey St.
Bakersfield, CA 93305
805/324-6451

Los Angeles County Federation of Labor
2130 W. Ninth St.
PO Box 20630
Los Angeles CA 90006
213/381-5611

Marin County CLC
701 Mission Ave.
San Rafael CA 94901
415/454-2593

Marysville CLC
PO Box 206
Marysville CA 95901
916/743-7321

Merced-Mariposa Co. CLC
557 W. Main, Suite 206
Merced CA 95340
209/723-8858

Monterey County CLC
1145 N. Main St.
Salinas CA 93906
408/757-3094

Napa-Solano Co. CLC
441 Nebraska St.
Vallejo CA 94590
707/557-5036

Orange County CLC
2521 N. Grand, Suite B
Santa Ana CA 92701
714/771-3640

Sacramento CLC
2625 J St.t
PO Box 162038
Sacramento CA 95816
916/448-3252

San Bernardino & Riverside
Counties CLC
1074 La Cedena Dr., Suite 7
Riverside CA
714/825-7871

San Diego-Imperial Co. CLC
3945 Idaho St.
San Diego, CA 92104
619/291-4692

San Francisco CLC
510 Harrison St.
San Francisco CA 94105
415/543-2699

San Joaquin-Calaveras
Counties CLC
121 E. Vine St.
Stockton CA 95202
209/948-5526

San Mateo County CLC
300 Eighth Ave., Room 1
San Mateo CA 94401
415/340-0418

Santa Clara County CLC
2102 Almaden Road, Room 102
San Jose CA 95125
408/266-3790

Santa Cruz County CLC
c/o SEIU Local 415
10094 Soquel Dr.
Aptos CA 95503
408/662-3633

Sonoma, Mendocino & Lake
Counties CLC
PO Box 3587
Santa Rosa CA 95402
707/576-1677

Stanislaus & Tuolumne
Counties CLC
1340 Lone Palm
Modesto CA 95351-1537
209/523-8079

Tri-Counties CLC
c/o UFCW Local 899
7190 Hollister Ave.
Goleta CA 93117
805/685-0125

Tulare-Kings Co. CLC
4831 E. Shields, Room 33
Fresno CA 93726
209/252-1815

**California Labor Federation, AFL-CIO**
San Francisco (94103)
995 Market Street, Suite 310
415/986-3585

**AFL-CIO Region VI**
995 Market Street Suite 1404
San Francisco CA 94103
415/543-0165

**AFL-CIO Region VI**
3556 Lexington Ave., 2d Floor
El Monte, CA 91731
818/401-0111

## INTERNATIONAL BROTHERHOOD OF TEAMSTERS
## CALIFORNIA JOINT COUNCILS

IBT Joint Council 7
150 Executive Park #2900
San Francisco, CA 94134
415/467-7768

IBT Joint Council 38
1130 12th Street, Suite 8B
Modesto, CA 95354
209/577-0500

IBT Joint Council 42
1616 West 9th Street, Room 500
Los Angeles, CA 90015
213/388-3144

# GLOSSARY

## ATTENDANTS, BABYSITTERS AND COMPANIONS

### Federal Law

Attendants, babysitters, and companions are covered by the federal minimum wage ($3.35 per hour) and overtime rules (one and one-half times your regular rate of pay for all time over 40 hours/week), unless you fall under one of the following exceptions:

**Companions:** You are not covered if you are a companion for the aged or infirm, unless you are trained personnel (e.g., an R.N. or L.V.N.), or you provide services to a person who is not aged or disabled, or you do general household work more than 20% of the total time worked in one week.

**Live-ins:** If you are a live-in babysitter or other live-in domestic worker, you are covered by the federal minimum wage. You are not covered by the federal overtime rules if you reside permanently (not temporarily) in one family's household and work only for that family. (You must be paid for all time when you have duties and for all time when you are not free to leave the home. Contact the Wage and Hour Division, U.S. Department of Labor, to learn the rules governing your paid work time.)

**Casual Babysitters:** You are not covered if you are a casual babysitter. To be a casual babysitter, you must babysit only irregularly or intermittently You are covered if you babysit as a vocation; or you are employed by a service or referral agency (not by the family); or you are trained personnel (e.g., an R.N. or L.V.N.); or you work more than 20 hours per week (for all your employers added together); or you accompany an employer family on their vacation; or you spend more than 20% of your total worktime (on any given assignment) doing work other than just babysitting.

**Babysitters:** You are not covered if you babysit children in your own home. You are not covered by the federal rules if you are the only employee of someone who takes other people's children into their home to babysit (and your only duties are babysitting). You will usually be covered if there are at least two employees (counting yourself) of someone who babysits children.

**Casual Workers:** You are not covered if you work no more than eight hours in your busiest week (adding together all hours worked for all employers) and you earn less than $50.00 in the whole calendar quarter (three months).

### State Law--In a Private Home

**Babysitters:** If you are a babysitter, employed directly by a private household, to care for the children of that household in that household, then you are not covered by the state wage and hour protections (state minimum wage; state overtime pay rules; reporting pay; split shift pay; rest breaks and meal periods; certain uniform and meal rules). But this exemption applies only if you do no significant amount of other work. If you do a significant amount of other work, e.g., wash the dishes or clean the house, then you are covered by these state protections.

**Attendants:** The same test applies if you are a **companion or attendant** caring for a person (who by reason of advanced age or physical or mental disability needs supervision). If you are employed directly by the household, to supervise, feed, or dress a disabled person within that household, then you are not covered by the state protections if you do no significant amount of other work.

**Domestics:** If you do not fit one of the above babysitter or attendant state exemptions, then you are protected by all the state wage and hour laws. If you are a domestic worker employed directly by a private household, but do not live in that household, then the following rules apply to you:

> (1) You must be paid at least one-and-one-half times your regular rate of pay for all time over eight hours per day and for all time over 40 hours per week.

(2) You must be paid at least one-and-one-half times your regular rate of pay for the first eight hours worked on the seventh day of you workweek (even if the total does not exceed 40 hours for the week).

(3) You must be paid at least two-times your regular rate of pay for all time worked after the first eight hours on the seventh day of your week (even if not over 40 or 48 hours).

**Live-ins:** If you do not fit one of the above state babysitter or attendant exemptions, but you are a **domestic worker** directly employed by a private household and you live in the employer's household, then the following rules apply to you:

(1) Your total work hours each day cannot exceed twelve.

(2) You must be given at least 12 consecutive hours off each day.

(3) During your work day (maximum 12 hours), you must be given at least three hours of free time. These three free hours during your work day do not have to be consecutive. They must be scheduled by mutual agreement.

(4) During your 12 (or more) consecutive hours off, and during your three free hours (during the work day), you must be completely free of all duties, and completely free to leave the home.

(5) If you are required or allowed to work during your three free hours or during your 12 consecutive hours off, then you must be paid at least one-and-one-half times your regular rate of pay.

(6) Any time you work on the sixth day of your workweek, you must be paid at least one-and-one-half times your regular rate of pay for the first eight hours, and at least two-times your regular rate of pay for all time over eight hours (no matter how many hours you worked during the first five days).

(7) Any time you work on the seventh day of your week, you must be paid at least two-times your regular rate of

pay, no matter how many hours you worked earlier in the week.

(8) After five work days, you must be given at least 24 consecutive hours off, unless there is a bona fide emergency. This means an unpredictable or unavoidable occurrence happening at unscheduled intervals, which requires immediate action.

If you work for someone who takes other people's children into their home, or who cares for the aged or infirm as a business, then the "Outside a Private Home" rules apply.

### State Law--Outside a Private Home

If you are a babysitter, a childcare worker, a domestic worker, or if you care for an aged or disabled person, and you work outside of your employer's private home, then the state wage and hour laws apply to you. If you work for someone who takes care of other people's children, or of the aged or infirm, as a business, in their own home, then the state laws apply to you. You are protected by the state minimum wage rules, uniform and meal rules, and rules on reporting pay, split shift pay, rest breaks and meal periods. The state overtime and work-on-a-seventh- day rules (in Chapter 4, WAGES, FRINGE BENEFITS, AND HOURS OF WORK) apply to you, unless you fall into one of the following categories:

(1) resident managers of homes for the aged which have fewer than eight beds;

(2) organized camp counselors;

(3) employees with direct responsibility for children under 18 who are receiving 24-hour care;

(4) personal attendants who care for a child, or for an aged or disabled person who needs supervision; and who do no significant amount of other work; and who are employed by a nonprofit organization.

If you do fit into one of these four categories, then the following overtime and work-on-seventh-day rules apply:

(a) You must be paid one-and-one-half times your regular rate of pay for all time worked over 54 hours per week.

(b) You must be paid one-and-one-half times your regular rate of pay for all hours worked on a seventh day per week (even if not over 54 hours).

(c) You cannot be required to work more than 54 hours per week, nor more than six days per week, unless there is a bona fide emergency. This means an unpredictable or unavoidable occurrence, happening at unscheduled intervals, requiring immediate action.

## BFOQ (BONA FIDE OCCUPATIONAL QUALIFICATION)

In certain rare situations, an employer may exclude entire groups of people from a job. For example, the sex or age of actors or models may be restricted to ensure authenticity ("woman over 65," "young boy.") If the employer can prove that the restriction is necessary to essential functions of the job, then the restriction is a Bona Fide Occupational Qualification.

Customer preference or tradition does **not** justify a restriction. For example, hiring only male waiters for a specialty dining room is unlawful.

## CAL-OSHA EXCEPTIONS

Cal-OSHA is responsible for protecting the health and safety of workers in every workplace in California except where another state or federal agency actively exercises jurisdiction. In some areas the question of which agency is unsettled and must be determined on a case by case basis. If you are unsure which agency is responsible for protecting your workplace, make your complaint to Cal-OSHA and if they do not have jurisdiction they will refer you to the appropriate agency.

The following workplaces, agencies, and/or work classifications are not covered by Cal-OSHA:

(1) federal government agencies;

(2) mining establishments;

(3) offshore maritime workers;

(4) domestic service workers in private households;

(5) ship loading and unloading workers (where the safety problem is aboard the ship, rather than on the dock);

(6) ships beyond the three mile limit;

(7) pesticide application (and field reentry incidents);

(8) the National Guard;

(9) employer-provided housing; and

(10) for safety violations, employees on the rolling stock of railroads (although health issues for these workers are covered under Cal-OSHA).

## I.W.C. EXCEPTIONS

(1) public employees;

(2) any individual who is the parent, spouse, child, or legally adopted child of the employer;

(3) white collar exemptions (see below);

(4) outside salespersons (see below);

(5) on-site construction workers;

(6) on-site drilling, mining and logging employees;

(7) drivers whose hours of service are governed by the regulations issued by the United States Department of Transportation or by Title 13 of the California

Administrative Code (exempt from "Hours and Days of Work" provisions only);

(8) taxicab drivers (exempt from overtime provisions);

(9) student nurses (R.N., L.V.N., and Psych. Techs) in an accredited school;

(10) employees covered by a collective bargaining agreement under the Railway Labor Act (exempt from all provisions except minimum wage, meal and lodging credits, meal and rest periods, inspections, penalties, and posting);

(11) full-time traveling carnival ride operators who assemble, disassemble and move ride equipment (exempt from minimum wage and overtime provisions);

(12) employees of ski establishments (exempt from hours provisions;

(13) professional (full-time) actors;

(14) employees of organized camps (exempt from wage and hour rules);

(15) sheepherders;

(16) attendants, babysitters, and companions (see above);

(17) employers who have fewer than five employees are exempted from the reporting time pay provisions only;

(18) some fishermen (see below).

The I.W.C. Orders are at Title 8 California Administrative Code sections 11,000-11,150.


## FISHERMEN

**Commerical Fishermen:** Workers wholly engaged in commercial fishing as crewmen are not covered by the state I.W.C. minimum wage and overtime rules or other I.W.C. protections (split shift pay; reporting time pay; rest breaks and meal periods; certain uniform and meal rules). Workers who are crewmen but also do other work (e.g., boat maintenance at dockside) may be covered and should contact the labor commissioner. Workers who do 100% commercial fishing are not covered by the federal minimum wage and overtime rules. If 20% or more of a worker's time (in a week) is spent on other activities, s/he is covered by the federal minimum wage and overtime rules (one-and-one-half times the regular rate of pay for all time over 40 in one week). If a worker performs both commercial fishing work and other duties, but no detailed records are kept, then s/he is also covered by the federal protections and should contact the Wage and Hour Division, U.S. Department of Labor.

**Sport Fishermen:** Workers on sport fishing boats are covered by all the wage and hour protections listed in Chapter 4, WAGES, FRINGE BENEFITS, AND WORKING CONDITIONS. They are covered by the state I.W.C. Orders. The federal wage and hour (minimum wage and overtime) rules protect workers on a sport fishing (or other) vessel if: (a) they are employees of a concessionaire; or (b) 20% or more of their work is not seaman's work (i.e., is not part of the navigation of the vessel); or (c) they do both seaman's work and other work, but no detailed records are kept. Crewmen on a U.S. flag vessel are always covered by the federal minimum wage protections.

## JUST CAUSE

There is no hard and fast definition of "just cause." However, Arbitrator Carroll Daugherty outlined a series of questions to use as "tests" of the principle of "just cause." These tests are generally accepted as guidelines for determining whether or not to uphold a termination or other discipline:

> (1) Did the employer give the worker forewarning of the possible disciplinary consequences of the worker's conduct?

> (2) Was the employer's rule or order reasonably related to the orderly, efficient, and safe operation of the company's business?

(3) Before administering discipline to an employee, did the company make an effort to discover whether the employee did in fact violate or disobey a rule or order of management?

(4) Did the employer conduct a fair and objective investigation of the alleged offense?

(5) Did the investigation produce substantial evidence or proof that the employee committed the offense?

(6) Has the employer applied its rules, orders, and penalties even-handedly and without discrimination?

(7) Was the degree of discipline imposed reasonably related to the seriousness of the offense and the record of the worker's previous service?

## LEARNERS

Learners are sometimes employed in semi-skilled work requiring short periods of training. Certain learners may be exempted from the minimum wage provisions of state and federal law for specified periods of time.

### Federal Exemptions

In some cases the federal Wage and Hour Division will grant employers exemptions to the minimum wage for learners. Employers can pay a subminimum wage only if first granted a learner's certificate from the Wage and Hour Division. The Wage and Hour Division will grant these certificates only if (a) the occupation requires a learning period; (b) no labor skilled in that occupation is available in the vicinity; (c) the exemption is in compliance with state law and any applicable union contract; (d) the exempt employee has not finished a training period in a similar occupation. The employer must post the certificate of exemption where it can be viewed by employees.

The Wage and Hour Division will **not** grant learner certificates for the following work:

(1) office or clerical jobs;

(2) maintenance jobs, such as watchmen or porters;

(3) industrial homework;

(4) temporary or sporadic operations;

(5) manufacture of rainwear;

(6) manufacture of robes and dressing gowns (in most cases);

(7) manufacture of women's dresses wholesaling above $6.75 each;

(8) manufacture of women's blouses and shirts wholesaling above $3.00 each;

(9) final inspection of assembled garments (in most cases);

(10) operation of machines other than sewing and pressing (in most cases);

(11) floor girls and bundle boys.

The amount of the reduced wage and the number of hours allowed as the training period are set by the Wage and Hour Division for each job.

### State Exemptions

State law allows employers to pay a subminimum wage to learners under the following circumstances:

(1) the employee must be over 18;

(2) the wage must be not less than 85% of the minimum wage;

(3) the period during which the subminimum is paid cannot exceed 160 hours; and

(4) the employee must not have had similar or related work experience.

## Federal and State Exemptions

Certain minors (under 18 years of age) employed in retail or service establishments, who are also full time students may be paid a subminimum wage ($2.85) under exemptions in both state and federal law if:

(1) their employer received an exemption certificate from the federal Wage and Hour Division;

(2) the student minor is not employed more than 20 hours a week (40 during vacation time) at the reduced rate;

(3) no more than 25% (except during vacations) of the persons regularly employed by the establishment are paid a subminimum wage (however, an employer with fewer than 10 employees may employ three student minors at the subminimum wage).

Certain messengers may be exempt from the federal minimum wage. But all messengers are covered by the state minimum wage and hour law.

## OUTSIDE SALESPERSONS

Outside salespersons are not protected by state Industrial Welfare Commission Orders or by the overtime and minimum wage provisions of the federal Fair Labor Standards Act (FLSA). An outside salesperson is a person who "customarily and regularly" works away from the employer's place of business, selling or obtaining orders or contracts. Trainees preparing to become outside salespersons, inside salespeople, telephone solicitors, and people working at any fixed site are not outside salespersons. The test used to determine if you are an outside salesperson is different under state and federal law. You should keep very detailed records of how much time you spend at each kind of work.

## Outside Salespersons--State Law

Under state law, you are an outside salesperson if you spend more than 50% of your working time selling or obtaining orders away from your employer's place of business. This 50% test is applied to each work week. If you meet the test, you are not protected by the I.W.C. Orders but may still be covered by the FLSA. Every week in which you work less than 50% of the time at outside sales, the I.W.C. Order protections cover you for all hours, including those spent in outside sales.

## Outside Salespersons--Federal Law

Under federal law, the test is how much time you spend doing nonexempt work each week. Add up all the working time during which you are not doing outside sales work. If you meet the federal law standards for an executive, administrative, or professional exemption (see White Collar employees in the GLOSSARY), you can subtract any hours spent doing exempt white collar work. The total non-outside-sales time cannot exceed 20% of the average hours worked that week by other employees doing the same kind of non-outside-sales work. For example, if you do clerical work, look at your employer's clerical workers. If they average 36 hours a week, then 20% of that is 7.2 hours. If you spend more than 7.2 hours in a given week doing clerical work, then you are not an outside salesperson under federal law and the minimum wage and overtime protections apply to all your hours that week. If there are no other workers doing the same kind of non-outside-sales work, then your limit is eight (8) hours per week.

## WHITE COLLAR EXCEPTIONS

Certain executive, administrative, and professional occupations are exempt from coverage under wage and hour laws. However, the state law and the federal law (FLSA) have differing definitions of these exempt classes. Therefore it is possible for an individual to be exempt from the state's wage and hour laws but covered by the federal protections, or vice versa. For example a registered nurse (R.N.) is exempt from coverage as a professional under the federal law, but covered under the state law. However, since public employees are covered only by the federal law (FLSA), a registered nurse employed by a county hospital, for example, would have no protection. Listed below are white collar exceptions to both the federal law and the state law. It is important to check both because the standards are different. (A trainee preparing for an executive, adminstrative or professional position is **not** exempt.)

### White-collar Exceptions -- State Law

**Executive and adminstrative exemptions:** To be exempt, the employee must be engaged at least 50% of the time in work which is intellectual, managerial, or creative. The work must require the exercise of discretion and independent judgment **and** the individual must be paid a salary or wage of at least $900 per month. First line supervisors are generally included in this definition.

**Professional exemptions:** To be exempt, the employee must be licensed or certified by the State of California and engaged in the practice of law, medicine, dentistry, pharmacy, optometry, architecture, engineering, teaching, or accounting. Registered nurses are **not** exempt by this definition. (By special rule teachers working in the motion picture and television film and video tape industry are not exempt.)

### White-collar Exceptions -- Federal Law

**Executive exemptions:** To be exempt the employee's primary duty must consist of the management of the entire enterprise or at least of a recognizable departmental subdivision, **and** must include the "customary and regular" supervision of two (fulltime equivalent) or more employees. To be exempt the employee must be paid a salary* of at least $250 per week. An employee paid less than $250 per week (but not less than $155 per week) may also be exempt if these **additional** requirements are met: The employee must have the authority to hire, fire, transfer, promote, etc, or effectively recommend such actions. The employee must regularly

---

*Federal white collar exemptions apply only to an employee paid on a "salary basis." If you are paid on an hourly basis, or if your pay can be reduced for an absence or tardiness of less than one full day, then you are not exempt.

exercise discretionary powers. The employee must spend at least 60% to 80% (depending on the industry) of his/her time on the duties described above; or be in total charge of an independent establishment; or own at least 20% of the business.

**Administrative exemptions:** To be exempt the employee's primary duties must require the exercise of discretion and independent judgment. The employee's primary duty must also consist either of the performance of office work directly related to management policies, or of functions in the administration of a school or school system in work directly related to the academic instruction or training conducted there. The employee must earn a salary* or fee of at least $250 per week. An employee earning less than $250 per week (but not less than $155 a week) may also be exempt if these **additional** requirements are met: The employee must regularly and directly assist a proprietor or an executive or administrator; or perform specialized or technical work requiring special training, experience, or knowledge, under only general supervision; or execute, under minimal supervision, special assignments and tasks. The employee must spend at least 60% to 80% (depending on the industry ) of his/her time on the duties descibed above.

**Professional exemptions:** To be exempt the employee's primary duty must include work requiring the consistent exercise of discretion and judgment. The work must either (a) require knowledge of an advanced type (acquired by a prolonged course of specialized intellectual instruction) in a field of science or learning; or (b) be teaching in an educational institution; or (c) be original and creative requiring talent in a recognized field of artistic endeavor such as music, writing, theater, or plastic and graphic arts, and distinguished from work that can be produced by a person with general training. In any case, the employee must be paid at least $250 a week on a salary* or fee basis. An employee who is paid less than $250 a week, but at least $170 a week may also be exempt if these **additional** requirements are met: The work must be predominately intellectual and varied and somewhat unquantifiable; and the employee must devote at least 80% of his/her time to the duties described above. Employees licensed and practicing law or medicine (as well as interns and residents) and teachers in an educational institution are exempt from the salary and fee requirements.

## WORKERS' COMPENSATION EXCEPTIONS

The following workers and volunteers are exempted from coverage under the California Workers' Compensation program:

(1) Any person employed by a parent, spouse, or child.

(2) A domestic worker who was employed for less than 52 hours (or earned less than $100 in wages from the employer) during the 90 days peceding the date of a specific injury or exposure to an occupational disease.

(3) Any person (other than a regular employee) participating in sports or athletics, who receives no compensation except transportation, travel, meals, lodging or other incidental expenses.

(4) Any person (other than a regular employee) officiating at an amateur sporting event sponsored by a public agency or a public or nonprofit school, who receives compensation no greater than the per diem authorized for state employees.

(5) Any student athlete participating in amateur sports sponsored by a public agency or public or private nonprofit school who receives no compensation except travel, meals, lodging, or other incidental expenses or scholarships.

(6) Any person performing services in return for aid or sustenance only, from any religious, charitable, or relief organization. (This exclusion applies to private relief agencies only, not government "workfare" programs. Participants in government programs are covered by workers' compensation.)

(7) Any person performing voluntary services for a public agency, or a private nonprofit organization, who receives no compensation other than meals, transportation, lodging or incidental expenses. (Except that a public agency **may** chose to cover such volunteers.)

(8) Any person performing voluntary services at or for a recreational camp operated by a nonprofit organization of which s/he or a relative is a member, and who receives no compensation except meals, lodging or transportation.

(9) Any person acting as a voluntary ski patrolperson who receives no compensation except meals or lodging or the use of ski tow and lift facilities.

(10) Any person appointed for his/her own convenience as deputy clerk, deputy sheriff, or deputy constable and who receives no compensation from the county or municipal corporation or citizens for service.

(11) Federal employees. (Covered by Federal Employees' Compensation Act.)

(12) Civilian employees on military bases and military exchange posts. (Covered by federal Longshoremen's and Harbor Workers' Compensation Act.)

(13) Employees (other than crew members) working beyond the three-mile limit in off-shore development of natural resources. (Covered by Longshoremen's and Harbor Workers' Compensation Act.)

(14) Any person employed as a master, officer, or crew member of any pleasure or commercial vessel, including the special craft used for oil drilling (even though resting on the ocean floor). (Covered by Jones Act.)

(15) Employees (other than crew members) who work on navigable waters, including any adjoining pier, wharf, dry dock, terminal, building way, marine railway or other adjoining area customarily used by an employer in loading, unloading, repairing or building a vessel. (Covered by Longshoremen's and Harbor Workers' Compensation Act.)

(16) Certain employees of railroads and associated industries. (Covered by Federal Employers' Liability Act.)